D1453511

Parenting

Parenting

Contemporary Clinical Perspectives

Edited by Steven Tuber

ROWMAN & LITTLEFIELD
Lanham • Boulder • New York • London

Published by Rowman & Littlefield
A wholly owned subsidiary of The Rowman & Littlefield Publishing Group, Inc.
4501 Forbes Boulevard, Suite 200, Lanham, Maryland 20706
www.rowman.com

Unit A, Whitacre Mews, 26-34 Stannary Street, London SE11 4AB

British Library Cataloguing in Publication Information Available

Library of Congress Cataloging-in-Publication Data

Names: Tuber, Steven, 1954– editor.
Title: Parenting : contemporary clinical perspectives / edited by Steven Tuber.
Description: Lanham : Rowman & Littlefield, [2016] | Includes index.
Identifiers: LCCN 2016011450 | LCCN 2016018196 (ebook) | ISBN 9781442254817 (cloth : alk.
    paper) | ISBN 9781442254824 (electronic)
Subjects: LCSH: Parent and child. | Parenting—Psychological aspects.
Classification: LCC BF723.P25 P3185 2016 (print) | LCC BF723.P25 (ebook) | DDC 306.874—dc23
LC record available at https://lccn.loc.gov/2016011450

∞ ™ The paper used in this publication meets the minimum requirements of American
National Standard for Information Sciences Permanence of Paper for Printed Library
Materials, ANSI/NISO Z39.48-1992.

Printed in the United States of America

To our parents, our grandparents,
our children, and (hopefully) our
grandchildren, with the utmost, love,
respect, and appreciation.

Contents

Acknowledgments

In one sense, a book on the vicissitudes of how parents become parents is a book about heroes: the heroic, yet "good enough," behaviors of parents that permit a child to develop into a healthy, loving person. On a much less dramatic level, acknowledging the inspiration, advocacy, and guidance of those who support the publication of any book is also an affirmation of heroism, a moment to pay tribute to those without whom this work would not be possible. At the top of this list of heroes and heroines for this book is my wife, Jodie Meyer, PhD, whose enthusiasm for the project and expert editing made both the content and the process of creating this volume fundamentally better. I also thank the wonderful contributors to this volume, whose clinical acumen and dedication to the project were utterly inspiring and professional. Thanks to Molly White, Alison Pavan, and Julie Kirsch at Rowman & Littlefield for their unflagging support of both this book and the two that preceded it. I also want to thank several heroes of my personal and professional life: Professionally, Robert W. White, Sybille Escalona, Jeremy Holmes, Arietta Slade, and Sebastiano Santostefano have all been vibrant sources of inspiration to me in different but valued ways. Personally, a major hero for me over the past twenty years has been Edward Schecter, and I take great pleasure in acknowledging his special presence in my life.

Introduction

There have been seemingly countless numbers of books written on the "hows" and "whys" of parenting. Nearly all have had their focus on the impact of parenting on child development, whether in its healthy or pathological aspects. There have been far fewer books on parenting as a state in its own right. The contributors to this volume chose to address this deficit, through a combination of clinical and personal musings on their experience of parenting.

This book has, as its core paradigm, an intrinsic paradox: while we *must* become essential to our children as early as possible in their lives in order to help them create an internalized experience of being valued, we must simultaneously give up this exclusive essentialness over time if we want them to develop a sense of autonomy and individuality. As we give up some, if not most, of our centrality, moreover, how can we maintain a sense of grace, humor, and perspective? Each of the contributors is both a parent and a clinician. Given this complex amalgam of experience, they address three basic questions: How is this grace possible, and what makes it go awry in both ourselves and our patients? And how can our work in one domain inform and ameliorate our work in the other? These questions have powerful implications for clinicians within every mental health discipline, whether they have been a parent or expect to be. This book provides thirteen chapters by exceptional clinicians who come at their work from different, yet overlapping, phases of the parenting process. Each takes some measure of their own personal experience and integrates it with their clinical experience of treating parents and their children. Some of the clinicians describe their work in the context of parenting adult children; others while wrestling with what it means to be both a parent and a grandparent; still others speak to raising adolescents or toddlers or school-aged children, and its impact on their clinical work; and some grapple with their own experience as a parent in light of their own parents/grandparents. Some of the chapters deal with parents for whom positions of privilege are endemic across generations; others describe personal and professional experiences in which aspects of race, immigration, ethnicity, and social class play powerful roles. We hope you find the writing useful.

Part I

Theorizing on the Process of Parenting

ONE

Parenting Across the Lifespan

Some Personal and Conceptual Musings

Steven Tuber

*This book begins with a chapter by **Steven Tuber**, providing an overview of parenting across the lifespan. It describes a number of parental phases as one's child develops from infancy through adulthood. Each of these phases provides its own special challenges, challenges that the remainder of the authors address both as parents and as clinicians. It begins with a focus on the need to be utterly essential to the infant, moves to a shift toward the potential to be essential and moves again to a position of relevance as the child moves toward adulthood. The ability to make these necessary changes with a sense of grace is highlighted.*

Our life is a dance to a song we cannot hear.

—Anonymous

When I was seventeen and my father was seventy-one, I had the single most memorable experience of my life. It was the day I danced with my father. My father was always a most alive, passionate person, a larger-than-life presence even though he was barely 5'3". But the sheer abandon and spontaneity he displayed at that moment was something I had never seen in him before, nor in the twenty-six years following, through to his death in 1997 at age ninety-six. I loved that moment fully at the time; indeed, I giggled with delight all through it. But in the years since his death, I have enjoyed it more fully than ever.

Telling the story, even to myself, always brings tears to my eyes, tears of the warmth and the sweet/bitter/sadness of loss and connection and reunion. I briefly described the moment at my father's funeral and at my elder son's bar mitzvah. I've portrayed the event other times to friends and colleagues and recently had a version of it published in a small journal. It has always been the most compelling snapshot of some of the best aspects of my father and of our tie to each other, our culture, and our shared heritage.

In the terminology of this chapter, this memory, over time, became the conscious core of my experiencing my dad as essential to me. It obviously wasn't the dawn of this experience. Actually, the moment was the harbinger of my taking leave of him, as I never lived full-time in his home again once I left for college a few months later. Clearly the fact that he was moved to dance by my achievement (not his) told me that I was essential to him. It is also certainly true that one does not become essential after one moment, no matter how vital that moment may be. But the spontaneous intensity of his joy altered me irrevocably. If he could feel this depth of pleasure through me, I must be a vital part of him. If I was that vital to him, then a part of me lived in him, and I was no longer as existentially alone as a seventeen-year-old can often feel.

When my father was seventy-one, he also seemed unfathomably ancient to me, the way elders do to adolescents. Now I'm sixty-one. My wife and most of my dearest friends are a bit older, making seventy-one an oh-so-recognizable reality in the not-too-distant future. Despite the crazy dialectic wherein we still believe we're immortal although we know so powerfully that our days are numbered, I know that I, too, if lucky, will become ancient all too soon. In this context, I would like to return to my dance with my "popskuchel" (my term of endearment for him) and reconsider it in the context of three particular tasks of parenthood, now more from the perspective of being my dad's "peer" rather than simply his child. While I will begin the next section discussing the first task of parenthood in the context of being a parent of a young child, the focus will shift in the subsequent sections to being a parent of an adolescent and lastly to that of an adult child. I should also note from the start that although most children are born to two parents, and thus the aim and process of parenting often exists within a duality, for the purposes of this chapter, I will speak of a parent as an individual, not as part of a parental unit.

BECOMING ESSENTIAL

Winnicott (1960), in his inimitable way, and Bowlby (1983), albeit less poetically, both stressed how the parent's "preoccupation" with their infant, in some amalgam of nature and nurture, provides the holding environment for the child's psychological and physiological development. Indeed, it is a hallmark of most developmental and object relational theories (Greenberg and Mitchell, 1983) to posit that the almost total dependence of the infant on its caretaker for survival places a premium on this relationship as the cornerstone of developing into a humane human being. From the infant's perspective, the "good-enough" parent repeatedly and predictably stays well attuned enough to her infant to provide a holding environment. This environment tolerates the infant's ruthlessness well enough, without undue retaliation, until the child responds with increasing gratitude to develop an enduring and secure attachment to her caretaker and from this paradigm to the attachment to others throughout the lifespan. In this chapter's terminology, others have become essential to the baby/child, who derives her identity and meaning over time via the prism of her connection to them. Through processes of assimilation and accommodation, moreover, the child expands her capacity to relate to others, evoking both old (transferential) and new paradigms in her interaction with the wider interpersonal world.

But what does it mean to *the parent* to become essential to the baby? Certainly this is also not a static process. In the course of parenting, often on a daily (if not hourly) basis, a parent can be moved to peals of laughter or tears of distress and disruption, or burdened to the point of fury or numbness by the behavior of their young child. Does this emotional roller coaster foster a primary sense of responsibility that is more enlivening or more burdensome? Does it enable the parent to become fully realized or hopelessly unmoored? I remember vividly the early evening when my wife and I were first going to see whether our elder son would accept a bottle from me. He had been exclusively breast-fed up to that point, and with his mom about to return to work, it was necessary that he learn to drink from a bottle. Cradling him in my arms, I remember holding my breath while I placed the bottle to his lips. He sucked away smoothly and avidly, and I felt a true sense of triumph! I was now able to be essential to him; I could literally help provide his sustenance. It was a magical moment. It deepened my sense of being useful and, in hindsight, accelerated a process of feeling like I was necessary to his being, a true antidote to the inevitability of aging and death. In its own much more limited way, although I did not make the connection at the time, it was reminiscent of my father's dance with me, sixteen years earlier.

Becoming psychologically essential is a much longer, more complex process than any single behavioral event, no matter how memorable. It is a dialectical experience, composed in varying measure of psychological enhancement and burden. It is forged in the everydayness of being, in the countless responses to the gaze or reach or smile or touch or sounds of the baby. Each of these responses produces its psychological/behavioral correlates: the more we do for and with the baby, the more we feel part of her life. At points along the way, if we are fortunate, this sense of being part of evolves into becoming known by your baby, of being seen as differentiated from other objects and even from other people. As I have written elsewhere (Tuber, 2008), we are thus transformed by the baby from a series of interactions as a milk provider, warmth giver, tenderness supplier, excitement maker, and so on into a noun—a mama or papa.

It is also critical to note that a vibrant part of becoming essential is the feeling of efficacy it generates. Is there anything more satisfying than feeling the contentment of your nursing baby? Or knowing that a piggyback halfway through a long walk can bring deep pleasure to your three-year-old? Or seeing the supreme look of satisfaction on the face of your ten-year-old when you agree to have a football catch? As White (1959) posited, there is a deep and intrinsic motivation in feeling competent, and being essential to our child fosters this competence to a mighty degree. (Of course, being unable to soothe or satisfy your infant/child can evoke incompetence or even despair, but these vicissitudes are beyond the scope of this chapter.) Becoming essential is thus inherently rewarding, as the parent's effectiveness promotes a positive feedback loop between efficacy and essentialness.

This essential-making process changes us. By becoming essential to our children we see the world differently, we feel its vitality differently, we become inseparably linked with the welfare of another being and we cannot avoid its consequences. A wise friend, with children a few years older than mine, once responded to my asking him how he was feeling with this tried-and-true comment: "I'm only as good as my least worrisome child and only as bad as my most worrisome child."

Our children's life journey becomes a prime factor, maybe even *the* prime factor, in how we evaluate our wellbeing. We vacillate, rapidly at first, but then in hopefully more graceful pendulum swings, between feelings of a deepening of purpose as our essentialness takes hold in our psyche and feelings of concern about the fragility and vulnerability of our children. If we are solely responsible for their welfare, do we feel a deeper sense of purpose and meaning in our lives? If we are all they have, conversely, do we chafe under this burden and resent its totality? Who is there for us while we are there for them? Can we sit with this resentment and not retaliate?

In Winnicott's (1971) language, can we allow ourselves to be *used* by the infant before she develops the ability to relate to us? I would argue here that the emerging feeling of being essential is what allows us to forestall our anger at our baby, that as they have become a part of us, we cannot abandon them without feeling that we would be abandoning the most fragile parts of ourselves.

Crucially, this most fragile part of ourselves often can simultaneously be the most hopeful part of us. Being essential carries with it the deepest hopes of new beginnings, that we are ourselves starting from scratch through our newborn and thus we can avoid our own shortcomings and frailties as we help build this new tiny person. How could we then retaliate for her ruthlessness? Doing so would mean that her demands are unjustified, and thus we are placing a limit on what she has the right to own or experience. This, in turn, through our identification with her, would place a limit on our demands and needs. Winnicott's (1960) truism that you cannot spoil an infant thus has the rather surprising corollary that by not spoiling the infant through our devoted attunement with her, we create the illusion that we ourselves also cannot be spoiled, that our needs are vicariously fully warranted and should be met as well.

Our feeling essential to our baby has another important wrinkle as well. It creates, in the first few months of her life, the necessary platform of being taken for granted by her, that she feels that you, her parent, can be counted on with impunity, in perpetuity. From the baby's point of view, our being essential thus creates a paradox: the more essential we are to our child, the more invisible we become to them as distinct external beings, especially in the first months of life. How do we manage emotionally under the pressure of this paradox?

From the parent's perspective, another way to frame this process is to see our role in it as a yardstick of our ability to be generous. In our relationships with other adults, we likely see acts of kindness or support as exemplars of our emotional or financial generosity. When we have become essential to our baby or, more accurately, when we feel like we have become essential to our baby, we no longer see our interrupted sleep or vomited-on dress shirts as acts of generosity. We simply see them as the currency of the realm, tolerating experiences we simply couldn't fathom tolerating with any other person. What does this tolerance say about us? How does it change us?

ESSENTIAL OR NARCISSISTIC?

Is this tolerance primarily selflessness or is it more likely a form of narcissism? Let me go back in time and place my father's dance with me in historical context as one way to address this question. Born to abject poverty and malnourishment in Lithuania, my father grew up knowing of his father's twenty years of exile in Siberia for failing to renounce his Judaism as required by an edict from Czar Nicholas I in the 1860s. At age fourteen, in 1914, on twenty-four hours' notice, my father and his parents were told of a new edict by Nicholas II that all Jews in the region must evacuate their homes or else face the Cossacks. My grandfather had a stroke and died in the wagon pulling their meager belongings away from their shtetl, leaving my teenage father and his mother to fend for themselves. Three years of homelessness followed before my father and grandmother found relatives who would sponsor their trip to America.

This story of ethnic oppression, so endemic to humanity and its history, left its paranoid, traumatized core in my father: from his point of view, you must always assume that a pogrom will rear its malignant head eventually. The trick became how to live in enough denial to (a) avoid its malignancy, (b) appreciate each day of freedom that miraculously occurs, and (c) advance yourself and your family through education to develop an illusion that you can be exempt from the persecution when it, inevitably, recurs. My father eventually settled in New York City and worked for forty years as a house painter, trying his best to support his wife and their family of five children, of whom I was the youngest. Although I have memories of his laughter and more indelible memories of his anger and rigidity, his core feeling that the world was an unsafe place never fully left him and was all too easily absorbed by each of his children in their own way. I grew up largely with him as an "old" man, a man more mellowed and less angry than he had been with my older siblings in their formative years but still gripped by the idea of the world as an often unsafe place.

I'd now like to tell you about my father's dance. It took place on April 15, 1971. We had recently "moved on up" to the projects in Coney Island. The house where we had lived "down the side street" from the projects for fourteen years (in my memory, it was the only house still standing on the block after nearly a half-decade of arson and poverty decimated the neighborhood) had been condemned to build a public school. For the first time in the six years since my father's retirement in 1965, both of my parents were not home when I came home from school that day. They had gone to downtown Brooklyn to sign the official papers turning over their house to the city. April 15 was also the day I heard from the colleges I had applied to, and, much to my astonishment, I had received a scholarship to Yale. Knowing the almost mythical importance my parents placed on education and knowing the fantasy my father held of how an Ivy League education was simultaneously impossible and yet could (hopefully!) provide ample cover during the next pogrom, I knew he'd be delighted at my achievement. Being given the money to attend such a school, moreover, was simply beyond his or my capacity to believe in the generosity of the "oppressors."

So, while I waited impatiently for their return home, I expected shock or even wary disbelief to be his first response. When he and my mom came in the door, I rushed to them with my news of both the acceptance and the scholarship that accompanied it. Instantly, my father took my hand with one hand and my mother's hand in the other. Singing an unrecognized chant in Yiddish, he literally bounded around and around the room for what seemed like hours but was probably only a brief minute or two. The whimsical, excited look on his face, the way the room whirled about, the delight in my mother's eyes . . . well, it doesn't get any better than that! It was, up to that moment, the high point of my life, and maybe his. Suffice it to say, this delight of my father's has warmed me many times over.

I am forever indebted to my father for showing me this part of him, this joyful moment in an often painful, tortured life. It has provided me with a profoundly meaningful integration of theory and reality, a confirmation of the remarkable "messiness" of personality and a sense of wonder and hope that has kept me in good stead in my life as a clinician and a professor, not to mention as a parent.

Central to this chapter, I felt, along with the depth of his delight, that there was something beyond my achievement that was in the air at that moment, although I didn't have the language or perspective to name it or understand it at the time.

What I did get, in 1999 when I first wrote about this "dance," were the following questions: Where did my father find this seemingly newborn capacity for delight? How had this never-before-seen paroxysm of joy been protected, preserved despite pogroms, malnutrition, violence, and other forms of trauma? Was it a kernel of "good-enough" mothering that endured untainted, waiting for the proper, even if once in a lifetime, moment to be expressed? Or was it created far later from the hopes and dreams we harbor for and in our children despite or even because of our defects and limitations?

In the context of the present chapter, I would state that these hopes and dreams emanate from feeling essential to our baby, the competence it evokes in both parent and child, and the resulting overlap of their being and ours.

Certainly as a father now, I can see in ways I could never have imagined when I was a participant in that dance, how much hopefulness played a role in his delight. He was living through me in that instant: my achievement was an amalgam of his achievement by proxy and simultaneously my stretching out beyond him raised the possibility that my life would be "better" than his. Much like the way in which his caretaking of me as an infant wouldn't be described as generous, his happiness for me was not so much an expression of generosity as one of pride, that by being essential to him, my accomplishment was a part of him as well.

So, if I was a part of him, could his delighted dance be not just an expression of pride but also somehow narcissistic? I am arguing here that it is inextricably and inexorably both. Here I am, now ten years younger than my father was at that moment, and I'd like to think that my sons' triumphs, large and small, have been deeply gratifying not only because they are a reflection on me but also because they are a reflection on them and thus an expression of pride.

What, then, is the nature of parental pride? I am proposing here that this form of pride is at its core a dynamic combination of self-congratulation and an appreciation of the other. To the degree that we have internalized a sense of self that has become amended by being a parent, we assess ourselves through the emotional well-being and "success" of our children. It may be useful in this context to consider how the "self-as-parent" is one part of a multiple set of selves that compose the fullness of one's identity. The depth and meaning of the self-as-parent as compared with ourselves as worker, colleague, friend, spouse, and so on are different for everyone and, in the context of feeling essential, change dynamically over time across the lifespan.

It is crucial for me to reemphasize the dynamic nature of this balance between our self-as-parent and our other self-states. It is not simply an additive process, whereby one linearly loses or adds something from our other selves as we evolve in the process of being a parent. Indeed, that couldn't be more simplistic. Being a parent is being in an inherently dialectic, shifting process in which each and every experience impacts us behaviorally and intrapsychically. We constantly receive feedback that causes us to question where we stand in relation to our baby/child throughout the lifespan. This questioning, moreover, occurs both consciously and unconsciously, so that we constantly reverberate intra- and interpersonally with our children for as long as we live.

To reframe my father's dance in this context, perhaps I was so wonderfully surprised by his response to my success because I hadn't believed up to that point that my success would have mattered so much to him, that his self-as-parent was much larger than I had believed it was. And perhaps from his point of view, my success ignited a deeply buried, but not vanished, sense of optimism, an experience of optimism that came rushing to the foreground to my never-ending delight. In that moment, his experience of both self-congratulation (he was the father of an Ivy League student) and pride (I had accomplished something that he was proud of) was reciprocally enhancing to him, such that these emotions combined to empower his parental sense of self and produce this dance of elation for both of us.

THE WEANING FROM FEELING ESSENTIAL

So far I have only discussed the development and growth of feeling essential, to the baby and to the parent. But this is a most inaccurate calibration of the process of parenting, one that only exists in full form, if it ever does, in the very few first months of infancy. Perhaps as early as the second six months of life, but surely in the second year, the very paradoxical nature of the child's taking the good-enough parent for granted has within it the profoundly consequential seeds of her independence and autonomy. The processes behind feeling fully essential at the near onset of life thus take on a push-pull quality, whereby the young child increasingly stakes her claim to consider herself the only truly essential being she needs.

This weaning process begins in tiny droplets of childhood initiative: the desire to drop one's meal off the highchair when the parent wants you to eat; the refusal to put on a winter coat when it's five below outside; the emergence of a universal "no" to any and every request, and so on. Each of these moments of mischief tells the parent that their essentiality is being challenged and that they had better get used to it.

When Erikson (1993) brilliantly delineated the second year of life through the dichotomy of autonomy versus doubt, he was speaking of the developmental process solely through the eyes of the child. From the parent's perspective, this emerging autonomy begins to subtract from the parent's experience of essentialness, for at the heart of the toddler's quest for autonomy is the momentary negation of the need for their parent.

A BRIEF MENTION OF THE ROLE OF ATTACHMENT STATUS

From an attachment perspective, this quest for autonomy raises interesting questions about the nature of the security of attachment. For a securely attached child, the push for autonomy negates the parent only for the moment, with little (if any) apparent distress to either parent or child. The child's securely internalized representation of the parent allows her to cherish her autonomy, knowing full well that the parent can be conjured up either literally or figuratively when the wish to be alone is no longer extant. For an insecurely attached child, the child's experience of the parent is that they are *overly* essential, making them either preoccupied with the always-possible loss of the parent or dismissive of the parent as a form of self-defense against an impending abandonment that would be destabilizing.

From the parent's perspective, the insecurely attached child stirs up feelings of essentialness that likely overburden the parent, compelling them to flee from engagement. This in turn evokes a horribly vicious cycle of dismissal and clinginess in either or both the parent and the child, injecting feelings of being essential with fear (Slade, 2014). These fearful interchanges may forever alter and disrupt what it means to be essential and are thus beyond the scope of this chapter. For the remainder of this chapter, I will therefore assume we are speaking about parents who are reasonably securely attached to their children, and vice versa.

DISAPPOINTMENT AND THE WEANING FROM ESSENTIALITY

Even in the securely connected parent and child, however, there is a process evoked whereby being essential must be tempered with allowing the child to experience life on their own terms. I have labeled this as the weaning from being essential, because it is indeed a process that occurs in fits and starts.

Part of the process has to do with disappointment. What is the role of disappointment in the process of weaning from being essential? I think there are two types of disappointment that must be distinguished from one another. The most obvious one is the degree to which our children's achievements don't mesh with our expectations/needs for specialness. Is our child the fastest runner, the quickest reader, the most feared, the strongest leader, and, if not, can we handle her "failing" to live up to our wishes? This is especially relevant in adolescence, as the teen's choices and our reactions to them may be experienced by the teen as our disappointment in them, pushing them away from us as they experiment with not being like us. This is especially true if their preadolescent life was heretofore one largely of receiving our approbation.

But the more subtle (and, for this chapter, more important) aspect of parental disappointment has to do with the process of losing one's essentialness. Can we tolerate the process of feeling that we are no longer at the center of our child's universe? With each passing developmental milestone, we indeed become less central to her. Her ability to walk without holding our hand may be one of the most glaringly obvious aspects of this process, but there are hundreds more. From the child's learning to read on his own and desire to get lost in a book without you to the greater fun they have with a playmate than with you, to the vital importance of "chums" as their preferred grouping, the first ten or so years of life become increasingly years of parental marginality. How can the parent ride with the ebb and flow of being essential? What allows the parent to do this gracefully?

Once again I believe it is useful to look at the balance between "self-as-parent" and the rest of our self-states. As the experience of being an essential parent declines as a function of the child's emerging autonomy, what can take its place to prevent our overall identity from becoming diminished?

The solution lies in part in the degree to which we redefine parenting such that being essential is modified and amalgamated with being proud. This redefinition permits the parent to see the child's emerging self as proof of parental expertise and not parental diminishment. The self-as-parent thus retains its overall vibrancy, it just shifts its nature as a function of a shifting perspective by the parent in the face of the reality of the child's emerging self.

One can easily see how this paradigm can usefully orient us to better understand those parents who enter our consulting room with feelings of despair at their loss of meaning and identity as their children outgrow their essential need for them. Unless the self-as-parent is bolstered through a reframing of their child's autonomous behavior as an indication of good parenting and/or a broadening of this self-state to include other aspects of adult functioning, they remain at significant risk for heightened depression and anomie. The shift to increased work responsibilities on the part of the parent as children mature can be seen as a common and often necessary response to bolster the parental self, using advances in self-as-worker or self-as-colleague to balance out the loss of essentialness in their definition of self-as-parent.

ADOLESCENCE AND THE SHIFT IN FEELING ESSENTIAL

Adolescence surely puts extreme pressure on a parent's ability to transform their parental self such that feeling essential would not be the sole means of self-validation (see both the Donahue and the Levy-Warren chapters in this volume). The advent of adolescence from the child's perspective often advances the peer group as the centerpiece of their self-esteem, with the values and behaviors of the parents often portrayed, consciously at least, as objects to identify away from rather than toward.

The adolescent's emerging capacity for abstraction places their future within cognitive reach but without the means to actualize it for many years. This gap between vision and actualization can be painful, even dysphoric at times. If we as parents are extremely fortunate, our children may seek comfort or clarity from us during these moments of confusion or discouragement. But it is certainly true that even in the closest of parent-adolescent relationships, there are long periods when the alienation felt by the teenager is left unsaid and/or expressed through behaviors that further alienate parent from child. It is extremely difficult at these moments for parental pride to kick in as a means of balancing out the loss of feeling essential. Indeed, it is at these moments when feeling pride is the very last feeling the parent may have. At best, concern may be the prime affect that replaces pride at these distressful moments in the parenting process. This concern keeps the parent intensely connected to the child, but often to the detriment of the child's feeling of autonomy and vitality. The adolescent often experiences parental concern at these moments as burdensome and constricting. This, in turn, often pushes the child further away from the parents, either toward isolation or to a peer or peers for comfort. If the parent cannot see this movement away by the teenager as viable, a previously secure attachment may turn preoccupied or dismissive, at least in the behavior of the child toward his parent(s). A vicious cycle can easily emerge whereby parental concern is experienced as an impingement upon the adolescent, pushing her to further reject the parent, leading to further impingement.

From the perspective of the parent, the diminution of parental pride coupled with the increase in parental concern may wreak havoc on the parent's sense of self. Although it is present throughout the parenting experience, perhaps here, more than at any other time, it would be most useful to add to our conception of the parenting process the role of parental psychological-mindedness and empathy. Keeping the child's needs and experience of self in mind, even in the context of losing the feeling of being essential, is critical to the parent's balancing narcissistic injury (a lessening of their experience of self-as-parent) with their appreciation of their child's struggle to become fully human. If the parent is self-assured enough to not see their child's posturing as lethal to their sense of self-as-parent, then their child's behavior becomes something to understand rather than squash. The difficulties the child is experiencing, while not a source of pride at the moment, nevertheless keep the parent connected through a sense of concern that is not felt by the child solely as impinging on the emergence of her identity. Indeed, empathy in this context can readily be experienced by the parent as augmenting their sense of self-as-parent if the adolescent feels "held" by the parent's concern. The role and utility of parental empathy cannot be overstated in this context. It is completely necessary as the vital ingredient in the parent's survival from their loss of essentialness vis-à-vis their child.

Perhaps another way to look at these tense moments in the adolescent-parent relationship from the parent's point of view is that these moments represent a shift from actually being essential (as in infancy) to maintaining the potential for being essential. Those rare but treasured moments when the adolescent initiates a conversation that shares their vulnerability with the parent, even if few and far between, can be seen by the parent as an oasis, a place that reaffirms their importance to the child. The psychological health (especially their capacity for empathy and psychological-mindedness) of the parent becomes the crucial variable as to how long they may last in the "desert" between oases. Certainly the degree to which parents can use one another (or extended family and friends) for comfort during these long stretches of endless sand plays a major role in maintaining this potential for essentialness.

This dynamic balance among parental pride, concern, and empathy as the child develops can be summarized in the following manner: the greater the ability of the parent to maintain aspects of their identity outside of parenting (the balance of their other selves with their sense of self-as-parent), coupled with their ability to transform feelings of essentialness to potential essentialness within the realm of self-as-parent, the more likely their relationship to their teen can remain unbroken. From the point of view of the parent, their use of empathy as a catalyst toward maintaining a healthy sense of self-as-parent allows them to shift the nature of their unbroken relationship with their child from being essential to staying potentially essential.

WHEN POTENTIAL ESSENTIALNESS IS NO LONGER VIABLE TO THE ADULT CHILD

As adolescence fades and early adulthood begins, the young man or woman has often had years of living apart from their parents. Their movement into the workforce or college provides repeated experiences where their parents are distant, if not absent, from their minds and daily activities. From the parental point of view, the reliance on what I have called potential essentialness becomes inexorably attenuated. To push our "desert" metaphor one more time, the distance between oases is simply too large for the role of potential essentialness to maintain the viability of self-as-parent in perpetuity.

I posit here that something must again shift in the parent in order for their relationship to their now young adult child to remain vital to both parent and child. The parent can no longer simply rely on feeling essential or even being potentially essential to the child in most circumstances. What needs to occur is for the parents to wean themselves from essentialness and to replace that feeling with the notion of being relevant.

THE NOTION OF RELEVANCE AS
A REPLACEMENT FOR ESSENTIALNESS

What does it mean to be relevant to your child but no longer essential? I would define relevance from the young adult's point of view as their ability to keep their parent in mind but not as their primary option in times of stress, whether negative or positive. I would define relevance from the parent's point of view as the capacity to know that they would be called upon if needed by the child but that, even if not needed, they are not entirely forgotten. A friend of mine recently asked about whether my younger son (aged twenty-three at the time) was involved in any serious relationship. I described to him my son's comment when I had asked him that question several months before. My son told me, "Dad, when it's serious, you and Mom will be the first to know, but until then, there's no need for you to know." I find this remark a lovely example of being internalized as relevant but not necessary to my son's emerging relationships from his point of view.

The key question about this comment from the parent's point of view is whether that demarcation of clear boundaries between parent and child can be tolerated. In a certain sense, what my son described is a fundamental shift in the experience of time in his relationship to his parents. If we need not be told about girlfriends who are seen as transient in his life, it is another way of him saying that his day-to-day needs in this area are well contained, and therefore his sense of self does not need our validation or explication to proceed. If a person became important enough over time to warrant his inclusion of her in his permanent life, then our relevance to him as an ongoing, internalized (but not minute-to-minute) relationship would, in his mind, warrant our getting to know her as well.

In this example, as well as countless others from parents of adult children, the question from the parental side of things has to do with whether we see the shifts from being essential to being potentially essential to being relevant as an accelerating drop in status, a narcissistic blow that at worst trivializes and at best diminishes us. What factors are at play that can minimize this loss of self-as-parent?

THE EMPTY NEST

It is useful to discuss the role of the "empty nest" in this context. The phrase itself is telling. A nest is a very small place, a place where children take up a huge proportion of the space, a place where mother and/or father provide for their child's needs. These parental nourishments are vital and necessary at first, essential ingredients to the child's well-being. There is no way the child could survive without a caregiver at this point in time, so a parent's feeling of being essential is easily engendered. Parents quite naturally are profoundly affected by this essential caregiving and come to count on it as a major part of their feeling a sense of purpose and meaning in their lives. But the child will, inevitably and inexorably, as the song "Summertime" in the musical *Porgy and Bess* so beautifully states, "one of these mornings . . . rise up singing, then [she'll] spread [her] wings and take to the sky." At that moment, the empty nest looms large as a major obstacle to the parent's ongoing sense of value and meaning. The "empty nest" is most emphatically empty of that immediate feedback that characterized life with children in the nest and had a major, moment-to-moment, impact on the viability of parental identity.

This empty nest yields two dilemmas for the parent that must each be addressed. The first is the more literal: What to do with all that time and space in the now cavernous nest? This dilemma has its solution in the context of developing or burnishing the parts of the adult self that do not involve self-as-parent. It can be argued that we attempt, all throughout our adult lives, to make our parental self-states coexist with our other experiences of self so that our total sense of self feels vital, purposeful, and intact. The diminution of the self-as-parent by the "loss" of the child can to a certain extent be ameliorated by gains in other parts of the self as was discussed previously. New jobs, new hobbies, greater travel, more involvement in one's community or in spiritual activities have long been used by "empty nesters" to help fill the void and enliven the silence of a house without children. I don't believe that many parents who have felt essential or potentially essential always feel that these additions to the other aspects of their adult self ever really balance out the loss of the feeling of being essential to their child, but is it "good enough"?

The answer to this question lies, I believe, in the taking on of the second dilemma within the empty nest experience. This dilemma goes back to the question of whether being relevant can really be an adequate substitute for being essential or even potentially essential. If the enrichment of other self-states in the parent is not sufficient in and of itself to mitigate the loss of being essential to one's child, then something within the self-as-parent must shift.

It is here that the usefulness of the paradigm of changing from being essential to staying relevant is most apparent. An internal shift must occur within the self-as-parent, a shift that ideally has been occurring in small doses from the earliest evidence of the child's emerging autonomous self. This shift has at its very core the experience of the child not as a "selfobject" in Kohut's (1971) sense, but as an entity that deserves and should be cherished exactly because she is, and deserves to be, her own person. The easier it is for the self-as-parent to know in an affect-laden way that their child needs to develop her own identity, the more likely it will be that staying relevant to that child has its own plentiful rewards that may compensate quite fully for the loss of being essential.

I would also add a third component to the tasks of adjusting to relevance vis-à-vis your now adult child. Part of being essential, as I discussed much earlier in the chapter, is linked with the experience of being competent due to our ability to provide a level of complete, if momentary, satisfaction in our child. One of the major adjustments a parent has to make with their adolescent and (even more so) with their adult child is to realize that many, if not most, of their child's problems can no longer be resolved by them, nor should they be. Being relevant thus also means giving up the "magical" qualities inherent in being the parent of a young child and the intractability of adult children's difficulties may thus serve as yet another narcissistic injury to the parent's experience of self (this is above and beyond any feelings of guilt we may retain for "causing" certain maladaptive and now lifelong patterns of behavior in our child).

The potentially significant blow to parental narcissism of becoming "only" relevant is another way of stating that being relevant is *not* the same as being essential. Indeed, I am saying that the two states of being are dramatically different, for both parent and child. But the fact that they are not equivalent is not the same as saying that one is always less than the other. Again, the level of empathy and psychological-mindedness of the parent is a critical factor in this weaning process from being essential to being relevant. Being able to maintain the ability to read the adult child's states of mind even while we are grieving the loss of "our" little boy or girl (and the loss of our "magically competent" parental self) is crucial to recognizing the validity of their need to make their own decisions and to develop their own values and sense of purpose.

Not surprisingly, much as a secure early attachment is correlated with a host of positive outcomes for the child in later life (Sroufe et al., 2005), the more easily and less ambivalently a parent becomes essential to their child, the more readily they can tolerate the shifts over time to becoming potentially essential and eventually to staying relevant. In a parallel manner, the more easily the child fully embraces their parent as essential from his earliest days, the more easily he can turn to them when the potential arises for their being essential once again. If potential essentialness is embraced repeatedly by one's parents, moreover, the more likely it is that they will stay relevant in their child's psychological and everyday life.

STAYING RELEVANT AS WE AGE

What has so far been glaringly omitted in this discussion of the transition to staying relevant from the parent's perspective is the role of aging. The shifts in self-as-parent do not occur in a vacuum. Rather, they most pointedly occur in the context of getting older, with all of the attendant strains on feeling essential and relevant across all the adult self-states that cohere into an identity. Depending on one's actual age, physical health, occupation and cultural rituals for treating the elderly, the transition from essentialness to relevance as a parent can be paralleled by equivalent shifts across many, if not all, of one's other self-states. While for some, an increase in job status and/or the development of the role of a wise "elder" may more than compensate for the loss of feeling essential as a parent, for most older folk this is not the case. For many parents, the shift in parental status to relevance (at best) is matched by impending or actual retirement, a decline in physical well-being or the loss of close friends and family members (especially one's own parents). When these losses occur across multiple self-states, the vulnerability of the parent's identity is markedly heightened. These multiple assaults on the viability of the parental self places the entire identity at risk, as the ravages of aging may reduce the possibility that other self-states can compensate for the loss of feeling essential in the self-as-parent state of being.

What is especially worrisome in this regard is the generally insidious role that ageism plays in our culture. Perhaps this will change as the large "baby boomer" generation moves from beginning old age (sixty to seventy) to middle and late old age (seventy to a hundred), providing a large population to whom marketers will still want to cater. But our culture's infatuation with youthfulness and glamour will hardly disappear overnight and thus the aging process will not be friendly to the need to maintain a sense of relevance, much less being essential or potentially essential, as one ages. Certainly the ability to stay mentally and physically healthy will play an increasingly enormous role in this process. The more fit we stay across both physical and mental dimensions, the greater the chance of desiring and having the opportunity for experiences of generativity (Erikson, 1993), of mentoring and modeling for those younger than ourselves. In a sense, this capacity to mentor carries with it the chance to parent others. We may find it possible to increasingly apply what we learned and internalized as parents to those outside our family circle. Indeed, the self-as-mentor may be close enough psychologically to the self-as-parent to allow for a transition to the former that is relatively seamless, or at least eases the sense of grieving that we struggle with as our children become increasingly independent.

This notion of generativity can usefully be seen as a psychological bridge between those aspects of self-as-parent that need to change as our children become adults and those aspects of self-as-non-parent that need to be enhanced to compensate for the loss of parental experience. Becoming generative to others may be close enough to being a parent as to enhance that aspect of self, while simultaneously keeping our working or "volunteer" selves vital and purposeful.

BECOMING A GRANDPARENT—A SECOND CHANCE AT BECOMING ESSENTIAL?

There is another possibility in the life cycle that may dramatically affect the parenting process and its impact on our feeling of value. That is the process of becoming a grandparent (see Meyer in this volume), especially if our grandchildren are physically and/or emotionally proximate.

There are two profound ways in which becoming a grandparent can dramatically alter the equation of what it means to feel essential over time. The first way is the degree to which we may become essential to our grandchildren. Having the chance to revisit infancy and the essentialness it requires without the 24/7 burdens of being a parent may prove to be the ultimate tonic for a revitalized essentialness over time. The ease with which one is permitted access to one's grandchildren is the prime variable in this process. Having consistent access to the grandchild allows him to internalize you as a part of his core circle of meaningful caretakers. The experience of bearing witness to a grandchild's developmental achievements can be the elixir in mitigating advancing age to a grandparent, especially as it is often drunk without the anxieties that attended being a parent the first time around. If one is fortunate enough to be physically and psychologically empowered through a long stretch of the grandchild's upbringing, one can have the deliciously intoxicating reexperience of what it is like to be essential, a delight made all the more nourishing by the absence of feeling essential in the hiatus between your child's young adulthood and their transition to the role of beginning parent.

There is a second, perhaps no less nourishing, aspect to being a viable grandparent vis-a-vis the context of feeling essential. What can also become replenished is your becoming essential all over again to your own child. If you are indeed proximate enough to become part of your child's caretaking system for their offspring, you can become relied upon to provide both physical care of the baby and emotional care to the parents as they struggle with their transition to parenthood. A graduate student of mine, holding her infant, whom she brought up to the student lounge for a "visit," smiled knowingly to me as I spoke of my longing to be a grandparent and said, "Don't worry, I'm closer now to my parents than I've ever been; I need them to help me raise my son." Talk about music to my ears! I, of course, have no idea as to when (or even if) I will become a grandparent, or if circumstances will permit my wife and I to be proximate to our grandchildren if they do come along. The almost visceral reaction I had to my student's comment told me a great deal about how the longing for feeling essential never fully evaporates. It should also be noted here that this discussion of the impact of grandparenthood on all concerned was depicted with the assumption that grandparent, parent, and child are all physically healthy. A prolonged illness on the part of any of the participants would likely have a profound impact on the nature of these relationships, including the degree to which the grandparent can maintain a degree of being essential.

Mentioning the impact of illness on the relationship between self and adult children and grandchildren raises the pervasive specter of the role of the fear of dying on the processes of being essential. It is beyond the scope of this chapter to explore this topic with any depth, but there is no doubt that as we age, the shadow of death becomes less easily denied and thus insidiously impacts our capacity for maintaining vitality. I would argue here that feeling essential to our adult children and grandchildren, being of value to them, may indeed be the sole, if only temporary, antidote that suffices to mitigate the fear of dying. If we define the fear of dying as the fear of losing all attachments, then we can see most vividly how our remaining essential to those we love is the prime bulwark in our fight to claim vitality for as long as we live.

MAINTAINING A SENSE OF GRACE

I have spent the majority of this chapter on the nature of the parenting process as it pertains to the development of, and then the reduction in, the feeling of being essential. I have also spent a significant minority of this chapter on the shift to potential essentialness and on the capacity to replace both types of essentialness with relevance and its vicissitudes through the lifespan of your now adult child. I then spoke of the remarkable manner in which being a viable grandparent can re-evoke a feeling of essentialness if one is close, psychologically and geographically, to the grandchild. I add here that even if one is not that close geographically, regular visits can evoke the anticipation of potential essentialness and a short spurt of full essentialness while visiting that can do wonders to mitigate the loss of self-as-parent that I have discussed throughout this chapter. It is also likely that as our video technology continues to evolve, "cyber contact" may serve to further maintain or even enhance the ties of grandparent to grandchild, even across vast distances.

There is one aspect of the title of this chapter that has not yet been mentioned. We have to address the *manner* in which we handle the process of parenthood. More specifically, it is worth examining the degree to which we master the processes of parenthood with *grace*. Everyone who becomes a parent, I believe, winds up addressing the vicissitudes of becoming essential. Some tragically never attain this state, even for short moments. Some attain the state but are terrified and/or depleted by it, setting it aside for much, if not all, of their offspring's childhood. But for those who feel blessed by being tamed by our children, we are continually faced with how well we can manage the burdens and responsibilities of this privileged connection. If you believe that children begin to develop their own autonomous self-states starting in very early childhood, then the very process of becoming essential is fraught with strain and mis-attunements. As our children wean us from our feeling essential to them, moreover, we must wrestle with not only the intense ambivalences and conflicts stirred up by our not being needed so exclusively but also the narcissistic injuries of realizing the limitations of our capacity to "fix" our child's problems. Can we handle these conflicts and losses with grace, and what allows us to do so?

There are several factors worth mentioning that may play critical roles in our degree of gracefulness. One is our basic mental health: how securely attached are we to meaningful others, including but not limited to our children? More specifically, what is our capacity for keeping our children in mind, even when our self-esteem is under assault by them? What levels of mutuality capture our modal way of being with others and how much satisfaction do we derive from these interactions? What is our capacity for being comfortable with our aloneness (Winnicott, 1958; Tuber, 2008)? Last, what is our capacity for playfulness, both within our own minds and with our children?

Each of these questions plays a significant role in the capacity to gracefully process the experience of parenthood. The more securely attached we are to others and to a stable and balanced representation of self, the greater the likelihood that we won't take our child's "rejection" of us as a fundamental narcissistic injury. This is especially likely to occur if our capacity for psychological-mindedness is fully operational even under affective duress, as is likely to occur in the process of raising children in an often chaotic, stressful world. The security of our own attachments grounds us in a manner that heightens our capacity to have access to our empathic selves, even when our children's behavior may make it extremely difficult to be sympathetic to their plight.

Our capacity for mutuality, for recognizing that our interactions with others, including our children, are bidirectional in nature, is also a major source of gracefulness in parenting. Knowing and admitting with humility that our behaviors may have evoked the behaviors in our children we are railing against is essential if we are to maintain the respective integrity of both parent and child (see Meehan and Zick, this volume). This mutuality enhances the child's feelings of being understood and maintains an effective and open line of communication between parent and child so crucial to ongoing feelings of essentialness.

Our capacity to be alone is a subtle but powerful part of our aptitude for grace while parenting. This capacity is a necessary but largely unsung hero in the process of parenting. It allows us to minimize our *need* to be essential to our children and replaces it with the much sturdier *wish* to be essential. *Needing* to be essential makes us vulnerable to needing our children to comply with our quest for closeness, even if this quest is not compatible with the child's need for independence at that time. Feeling at peace with aloneness, conversely, allows us to fully enjoy our connection to our child and to be eminently graceful when we return to that state of aloneness as the child turns her attention to others or other things.

Finally, our capacity for playfulness and humor is a large component of our succeeding at being graceful. There are so many, many moments during the process of parenting throughout the lifespan where a sense of humor provides the necessary perspective and resilience to maintain our presence with grace and aplomb. This is certainly true in the moments where our child may be at their worst. But it is especially true when our children's lives move away from ours for longer and longer periods of time. As we transition from essentialness to potential essentialness to relevance, our capacity to be playful eases the sting of loss, both in the moment and over time. If we don't take ourselves too seriously, then we also don't take short or even long-term losses of essentialness completely to heart. If we are truly lucky, we may even ride these bouts of loss and disconnection with dignity and grace. In that way, we maximize the seamlessness of our journey through parenthood and optimize our child's pathway to adulthood as well. This capacity for gracefulness is hardly a stable achievement, as aging is a most formidable opponent, but experiencing graceful parenting as a process to continually work on may well be the most useful and lasting gift we can give our children. My father's graceful gift of his "dance" has proven that to me many times over.

REFERENCES

Bowlby, J. (1983). *Attachment and loss*, vol. 1. New York: Basic Books.

Erikson, E. (1993). *Childhood and society*. New York: W. W. Norton.

Greenberg, J., and Mitchell, S. (1983). *Object relations in psychoanalytic theory*. Cambridge, MA: Harvard University Press.

Kohut, H. (1971). *The analysis of the self*. Chicago: University of Chicago Press.

Slade, A. (2014). Imagining fear: Attachment, threat and psychic experience. *Psychoanalytic Dialogues, 24*(3), 253–66.

Sroufe, L. A., Egeland, B., Carlson, E. A., and Collins, W. A. (2005). *The development of the person*. New York: Guilford Press.

Tuber, S. (2008). *Attachment, play and authenticity: A Winnicott primer*. Lanham, MD: Jason Aronson.

White, Robert W. (September 1959). Motivation reconsidered: The concept of competence. *Psychological Review, 66*, 297–333.

Winnicott, D. W. (1958). The capacity to be alone. In *Maturational processes and the facilitating environment*. New York: International Universities Press, 1965.

Winnicott, D. W. (1960). The theory of the parent-infant relationship. In *Maturational processes and the facilitating environment*. New York: International Universities Press, 1965.

Winnicott, D. W. (1971). The use of an object and relating through identification. In *Playing and reality*. London: Tavistock.

TWO

Not Your Mother's Identity

Good-Enough Parenting in the Age of Maximization

Lisa and Nick Samstag

Lisa and Nick Samstag, both practicing psychologists and parents of a preadolescent daughter, expand on Tuber's contributions by speaking directly to what
we know and don't know about parental identities. They posit the concept of the
internalization of the parent(s) as an essential object, permitting the parent's
actual, hands-on essentialness to be modified as the child grows. Their chapter
reviews the nature of maternal/paternal identities and distinguishes mothering
as a process that can subsume gender. They address the transition from feeling
essential to staying relevant from chapter 1 using relational theories, pointing
out limitations and gaps in existing theories, while providing examples from
their own parenting to buttress their conceptualizations.

———❦❦❦———

Given how central mothers are in psychological models of development,
and especially in psychoanalytically oriented psychotherapy, we know
relatively little about maternal identity. On the one hand, it is hard to
imagine any treatment that did not include at least a detailed history of a
patient's experiences with caregivers, and, depending on the treatment
model, understanding the influences of early relational patterns on the
therapeutic relationship is a fundamental mechanism of change in
psychotherapy. On the other hand, despite the enormous volume of writing on mothering, motherhood, and maternal subjectivity across disci-
plines, the subjective experience of being a mother and specifically how
nurturing a child impacts the sense of self, remains somewhat ineffable,

most especially in psychoanalytic treatises. This is, no doubt, a consequence of the complexity of the experience of mothering as well as the powerful social and cultural forces that both shape that literature and are shaped by it. It certainly tends to be a polarizing topic, with mothers presented in demonized as well as glorified ways (see Bueskens, 2014, for a recent review).

What is the psychological experience of being a good-enough mother (and father) in the twenty-first century? Parents have increasingly greater opportunities to integrate career and family, and as such, face more challenges to their omnipotence. Speaking more personally, parenting is *the* most challenging experience we have ever had as individuals and as a couple. As clinical psychologists and psychoanalysts, we thought we were well read, and thus well prepared, for our new roles. In fact, very little of the literature we covered captured the intensity and complexity of the experiences we had. Our daughter, such a small being, stimulated huge feelings about dependency and helplessness, things that were real about caring for a newborn and then growing child, and things that were about our own histories of being cared for. So why aren't mothers, and the experience of mothering, more central in writing about human development when the relationship with one's child is perhaps *the* most emotionally intense relationship one can have? This chapter addresses questions regarding maternal identity, what it is and why it seems to be such a difficult concept to capture. Drawing primarily from psychological and feminist literatures, we highlight a number of themes and problems in the field and offer a few suggestions for a contemporary model of maternal identity.

Perhaps the most basic problem regarding the nature of maternal identity is what the concept should be named. This relates to more complicated problems—namely, understanding gender development in our sons compared to our daughters and how mothers and fathers are thought to influence the separation-individuation process differently for boys and girls, as well as gender differences in the society at large.

Using a gendered term such as *maternal* identity, in line with what are called "difference" feminists (e.g., Carol Gilligan), where differences between men and women are highlighted, risks possibly regressing to an era when mothering was equated with femininity and got lumped in with domesticity, passivity, and dependency, as if mothering were the only relevant aspect of a women's self. Chodorow's (1978) early work on how mothering is "reproduced" across generations, due to what she described as the more intense relational merger between mothers and daughters and the grown daughter's wish to re-create that experience by mothering her own children is very relevant here. It began to shift the center of our developmental theories from mothers defined as doing only what the baby needed toward the mother's subjective experience of mothering, highlighting the importance of the *mother's* developing self.

Benjamin (1988) similarly emphasized the mother as a unique subject influencing her infant's developing subjectivity and how her uniqueness and authenticity were essential to the baby finding his or her unique self. Critical economic and racial issues have also been identified as themes and problems in this context, where theorizing by mostly white women who had the luxury of choosing to stay at home with their children was generalized to all mothers (Collins, 1994).

In contrast, using a gender-neutral term such as *parental* identity, which eliminates (or at least strives to minimize) differences between men and woman, perhaps does not capture the unique and nuanced experiences mothers and fathers have nurturing their children, including influencing the developing child's gendered self. In the end, separating the subjective experience of the mother from what the baby needs seems to be a useful way of working through the limitations of gender stereotypes and the conceptual confusion that has resulted from the definition of maternal identity perhaps covering too much ground. The influences of Erik Erikson and others in the adult development literature will be addressed later in this regard.

We ultimately decided to use the verb *mothering* to refer to child nurturing by either parent—mother or father—not the act of bearing a child, which is the first definition of the word in the dictionary. Of course, fathers also *mother* (i.e., nurture their children), so a relevant concept of mothering and a mothering identity should be distinct from pregnancy and the act of childbirth. The physical phenomenon of pregnancy is what initiates a maternal identity for *some* women, but it is a distinct phase of mothering that should be separated from a core concept of an identity as a nurturer. Winnicott's term, the "mothering one," referring to any caregiver in the nurturing role, captures this idea that the function of good-enough mothering—albeit privileging the child's needs and reducing caregivers to their roles as containers or mirrors—is not exclusive to mothers or even women (Winnicott, 1953).

The word *mothering* means being related to and nurturing a child in an essential and profound way that *fathering* and *parenting* do not similarly connote. Thus, the use of the term *mothering identity* for both men and women retains the importance of the essential, life-sustaining mothering function but also suggests that this is not primarily a biologically determined or instinctual experience of the self; in other words, one must actively choose to take on the role. This is also consistent with Ruddick's (1989) theory of mothering as a disciplined practice involving high-level cognitive thought processes and actions. Such a concept does not necessarily abrogate the gender problem in our theories (i.e., how gender differences are understood primarily from our Western emphasis on separation from mother and the implications of this, especially for female development), and is certainly beyond the scope of this chapter, but it does serve as a platform for further conceptualizing a more relevant model of mothering identity. Like Tuber (this volume), we consider these ideas in the context of healthy development.

Mothering is part of a couple and larger community, and it is also not synonymous with a prescribed social role, as in the institution of motherhood, although it is certainly impacted by it, and this should also be distinct from the concept of mothering identity. As de Marneffe (2004) has cogently argued, the "desire" to nurture children "is at once obvious and invisible partly because it is so easily confused with other things" (p. 3), and it must be a central component of a "truer model of the self" (p. 6). Developed from Tuber's (this volume) description of parenting as the capacity to gracefully move from a position where one is essential to one's child to being merely relevant, we present the idea of a parent not just as a good object but also as an *essential* object, a particular kind of self-involvement in the context of the relationship with one's child, that addresses a gap (or at least an underdeveloped area) in relational theories.

WHAT IS A MOTHERING IDENTITY?

In general, identity is defined as the conscious sense of self that we develop through social interaction. According to Erikson (1950), our identity is constantly changing in response to new experiences and information we acquire in daily interactions with others, and it does so across the lifespan. As we face each new stage of development, new challenges help enhance or hinder identity formation. Identity includes all of the beliefs, ideals, and values that help influence and motivate a person's behavior.

In *Identity and the Life Cycle* (1980/1959), Erikson defines three stages of adulthood, summarized as (1) intimacy versus isolation, (2) generativity versus stagnation, and (3) integrity versus despair and disgust, introducing parenting in the first of these three stages. As Erikson says, "When childhood and youth come to an end, life, so the saying goes, begins: by which we mean work or study for a specified career, sociability with the other sex, and in time, marriage and a family of one's own" (1959, pp. 100–101). It isn't until the next stage that "parental responsibility" is identified as part of the criterion for mental health, a "wish" to establish and guide the next generation (1959, p. 103).

Interestingly, Erikson described *parental* identity in a general way, rather than as separate psychological processes for mothers and fathers. We wondered why he did this and about the strengths and limitations of this idea. His choice of a term that could apply to either parent, even though he wrote more narrowly about opposite sex couples, is consistent with his overall theory of identity as responsive to changes in cultural and social values, and is, as a result, adaptable to the ideas we present here. He found a way to bypass the complications gender imposes by separating the mother (and father) from the child's gender development. As we write this chapter, the Supreme Court of the United States voted to make same-sex marriage legal in all fifty states (*Obergfell v. Hodges*, 2015). While Erikson could not have anticipated this cultural sea change, it is an exciting opportunity for our generation to reconsider a model of mothering identity that will be applicable to both same-sex and opposite-sex couples. Moreover, since the development of in vitro fertilization and the birth of the first healthy baby girl from this procedure in 1978, advances in reproductive medicine have allowed women and men to contemplate parenthood as single parents or in partnerships with same-sex partners using egg donors, sperm donors, and surrogate mothers (see Kamel, 2013). Since intercourse is no longer a requirement for having a baby, the concept of mothering identity must also uncouple itself from the sexual act. Of course, anyone who is a stepparent or an adoptive parent also understands this distinction (Waterman, 2003).

Around the time Erikson's major works were published, others *were* specifically addressing maternal identity, some taking first steps away from the mechanical, psycho-sexual Freudian view of women (and men) reduced to their biological functioning, and understanding the mother-child relationship largely as an *experience* of merger (e.g., Balint, 1949; de Beauvoir, 1949). Object relations theory represented an important shift toward the idea of separation between mother and infant, such as in Klein's (1952) description of the "depressive position," where the mother is internalized as an independent other, and Winnicott's (1953) ideas about the "good-enough" or "environmental" mother who appropriately balances loving attunement (e.g., holding, containing, mirroring) with separation and loss experiences (e.g., frustration).

A more complex understanding of the mother-infant relationship as incorporating elements of *both* merger and separateness has since been validated with the help of decades worth of research that demonstrates the infant's sensitive attunement to social cues, active efforts to keep caregivers close by, and the mutual responsiveness between a baby and caregiver, a moment-to-moment sharing of subjective experiences that shapes not only the *child's* identity and personality (e.g., Beebe and Lachmann, 2002; Stern, 1985) but also the *mother's* (e.g., Stern and Bruschweiler-Stern, 1998).

The attachment literature has addressed the centrality of both the baby's and the mother's desires in creating mutual satisfaction, linking a mother's internal representations of her own mother and her capacity to reflect on her own and other's minds with her child's security (Fonagy, Gergely, Jurist, and Target, 2002; van IJzendoorn, 1995), and between her expectations of her relationship with her own baby and resulting parenting behaviors (e.g., Slade, Belsky, Aber, and Phelps, 1999). Note that an attachment relationship, defined as a specific aspect of the relationship between a child and caregiver, in which the caregiver's attachment behaviors impact the child's experience of safety and security (Ainsworth, Blehar, Waters, and Wall, 1979; Bowlby, 1969), is distinct from merger, as the mother was described in earlier psychoanalytic writing as an extension of the baby rather than a subject in her own right. While a mother's capacity to reflect on her baby's needs are critical components of a mothering identity that are in place even before the baby arrives, these capacities and her sense of herself continue to evolve in the relationship with her child over time. The role of time is an interesting element of identity development that we will say more about later on in the chapter.

Expanding on Erikson's framework, Levinson described a developmental pathway that further divided stages of adulthood into eras, with transitions between eras, leading to the creation of an overall life structure (Levinson, 1986). This life structure, based on extensive interviews with middle-aged adult men (Levinson, 1978), was later generalized to adult women (Levinson, 1996). While the theory emphasized elements of the life structure that were common across genders, there were also compelling differences between men and women in terms of the aspirations or "dreams" reported in constructing goals for adult life. Young adult women's dreams, for instance, were far more complex compared to those of same aged men, and were characterized by concerns about both occupational accomplishments and interpersonal relationships (Roberts and Newton, 1987). Furthermore, such split dreams seemed to be linked to women later feeling dissatisfied with some aspect of their lives. Research on marital satisfaction indicates that for both men and women, the demands of parenting during early years of a child's life result in increased frustration, conflict, and dissatisfaction in their relationship (Shapiro, Gottman, and Carrère, 2000). In fact, marital dissatisfaction has been found to steadily increase over time (Hirschberger, Srivastava, Marsh, Cowan, and Cowan, 2009) and to decrease when children leave home (Gorchoff, John, and Helson, 2008).

Such findings suggest that couples pay a price for having and raising children, compromising (at least) marital satisfaction. This taps into one of the central paradoxes addressed in the feminist literature on maternal identity—namely, that the loving and caring we require from our mothers necessarily restricts them from engaging in other pursuits, and that ultimately, in a patriarchal society, motherhood is incompatible with selfhood (see Snitow, 1992, for a review). Of course, loss is inherent in any choice and choosing to mother does mean that other possibilities are not chosen (i.e., the choice to not have children, the choice to put one's energy into a career, etc.). But this way of thinking about the experience of being a mother neglects how being essential to the development of our child's self, shaping who that person becomes through one's own characteristics, fundamentally reorganizes and enriches one's own self. Again, de Marneffe's (2004) focus on the importance of the *desire* to mother is a critical element in pushing our understanding of mothering identity further. She describes mothering as a choice to work at being fully present with your child, to give up the defenses that are used with others and welcome the demands children make, demands that no one else makes, and to engage the best parts of yourself in the relationship with your child. These are active processes that require a kind of identity overhaul in response to a new "other," not simply an add-on to an existing identity or the dissolution of one's sense of self when one becomes a parent. An authentic, truer model of mothering identity must include this type of desire and pleasure, as well as the unique struggles that parents experience.

The experience of possessing everything your child needs is, by definition, a state of omnipotence that sets the stage for the development of the parent as essential. Considering mothering identity in this regard—the capacity to be an essential object—is different from what is required for one's identity as a partner, a wife, or a husband, thus suggesting a fuller meaning of Erikson's stage of intimacy versus isolation, if by "intimacy" we also take him to mean these kinds of relational experiences one has with one's child. Erikson considered the stage of intimacy versus isolation to be the first stage of adulthood, prior to parental responsibility; thus, we understandably interpret "intimacy" here to be specifically with another adult. Our perspective on mothering identity makes room for intimacy with a child and, as a result, for expanding our understanding of the impact of a wider range of relational experiences on self-development.

As stated previously, a contemporary view of mothering identity must also address time. While developmental models such as Erikson's, Levinson's, and others suggest a linear progression from one stage to the next, the interrelationship between the social and the psychological is not so straightforward, and this is where a focus on more specific identities may be particularly informative. For instance, while we all age in terms of chronological years in a linear fashion, the experience of time has been described as different and more complex for women, such as in the cyclical nature of menstrual cycles and reproduction in what Kristeva (1986) calls "woman's time." Chodorow (1978) emphasized the differential impact a mother has on sons compared to daughters in terms of her distinct identifications with her children, and that, as a result of a more intense identification with the same-sexed child, girls required a longer pre-oedipal period toward separation from the mother. This stronger identification a girl has with her mother, according to Chodorow, results in an incomplete resolution of the Oedipus complex, and the need to re-create this sense of unity is what motivates the grown daughter to mother.

Chodorow (2014) also considers time in a recent paper focused on two of her analytic patients for whom it was "too late" to have children. We include a lengthy quote here that captures these important links among gender, mothering identity, and time:

Motherhood is in conscious and unconscious fantasy first and foremost a gendered, bodily, object-relational, and cultural experience for women. But gender, here as elsewhere, also gains personal meaning and is constructed from phenomena that are not ostensibly gendered. In the women I am considering, this non-gendered phenomenon often involves a relation to time that itself has implicit cultural as well as psychological underpinnings. Many cultural commentators have noticed the contemporary cult of youthfulness and the flight from aging. . . . As people change careers in their fifties, as men remarry in their sixties and father children, as fertility treatments allow women to get pregnant in their forties and fifties, we can come to be fooled by time. For women such biocultural changes can contribute to the fantasy that there is no biological clock. (p. 231)

The theoretical and clinical implications of these ideas for a contemporary model of mothering identity clearly point to the importance of addressing time, loss, and the experience of omnipotence (or the fantasies of such). Maximization, included in our title, similarly refers to a cultural narcissism (Lasch, 1991) that prompts both men and women to strive for unattainable goals across all realms of living, including parenthood. Recent research on the concept of "maternal centrality," for instance, suggests links between a loss of self and grief in women who are unable to conceive (Levin, 2015). From a theoretical standpoint, Stone (2012) addresses the previously mentioned gender development problem through highlighting how the male-child-focused model that emphasizes separation from the mother creates a dilemma when applied to a girl's developmental trajectory—namely, for girls to successfully separate from their mothers, an identification with their father is necessary (the father as the critical "other" in the separation process), but they are not able to identify fully with the father and remain essentially female. Stone suggests that a meaningful maternal subjectivity emphasizes *difference*—how a woman is different from her mother, rather than "reproducing" mothering as described by Chodorow—as a way to open the possibility for development as a self-nurturer and for her child by transforming the past into a new present.

Time is also addressed as a central element of a mother's subjectivity by Baraitser (2009) who describes how the new baby, as a formidable "other," fundamentally changes the mother's intrapsychic and relational world. Maternal subjectivity develops through day-to-day experiences and responses to the rapid developmental changes within a particular child, what she calls the "raw materials" of motherhood: this mother struggles "to *bear* her subjectivity, not by gracefully juggling with constant tensions, but by tolerating very difficult and largely unconscious feelings—those of hatred, ambivalence, failure, shame, and remorse" (p. 52) and by tolerating constant "interruptions" to her competencies, her goals, her speech, her sleep. You name it, a baby will make it difficult to complete anything, and just when you think you have mastered a task as a parent, your child is onto the next developmental stage, requiring something different, a different *you*. Baraitser's description of motherhood as including a "newfound sense of clumsiness, slowness and delay" that "has its own sense of viscosity" introduces "maternal time" (p. 128) as unique to maternal identity, different from woman's time, described earlier. This mother is also transformed by a heightened sensitivity to everything around her and is now very present focused and hyper-vigilant to signs of danger, constantly scanning her environment for potential sources of threat to her child, reinterpreting the world as a result of her relationship to her child. Baraitser's maternal subjectivity is not a coherent self in the sense that a kind of fragmentation *is* characteristic of the phenomenology of mothering, such as feeling pulled in opposite directions when focusing on both self and other simultaneously. She warns us not to confuse maternal desire with maternal love, the latter being a feeling the "child stirs up in us" (p. 91): "the child's alterity offers the mother something. But contrary to the notion that in love we try to attain 'wholeness' by closing the gap between the self and other . . . perhaps we can work the idea the other way around and think about how, in moments when a splitting of the self is experienced, something we call love can emerge" (p. 99).

While Baraitser (2009) writes exclusively about *maternal* subjectivity, her anecdotal theory (Gallop, 2002) of how a woman changes her relationship to herself and others once she becomes a mother resonated for both of us as parents and seems easily applied to our concept of mothering identity for either parent. We now turn to the idea of the essential object.

THE ESSENTIAL OBJECT

Tuber's description of how parents can evolve from being essential to being relevant to their children, outlines a transitional path whereby both parties—parents and children—can potentially connect with one another in profound ways throughout life's developmental stages. Consistent with Baraitser (2009), Tuber employs anecdotal description in support of his developmental theory. We similarly delineate our conception of what we call the essential object, using our experiences as parents, to flesh out intersubjective and relational concepts that privilege a type of paradoxical relatedness between parent and child, validating the illusion of what is happening and its future implications. As will be further developed in this chapter, the essential object differs from the good object in that it is dynamic, not stable, and thus temporally bounded. The essential object describes a type of spontaneous dyadic interaction between parent and child whereby the parent temporarily puts aside his or her subjective state and creates the illusion of being empathically attuned to the child's fantasies and future projections. Now let us review what we know about objects.

What is critical for optimal human development over time includes both concrete and symbolic realms of experience that are always involved in dialectic tension, as Tuber noted. That is to say, the psyche and soma are mutually informing and impossible to recognize without the other. The dialectic tension between psyche and soma is of special interest here, as the infant comes into the world completely dependent on her caretakers for physical survival, as well as for psychological security. Just as dietary nutrients are essential for the infant's body, so, too, are good-enough parental interactions necessary for the formation of integrative object relations (Fonagy, Gergely, Jurist, and Target, 2002; Mahler, Pine, and Bergman, 1975). A sense of physical integrity allows for a greater possibility of psychological growth and a lack thereof reduces that possibility. However, what is essential for the infant's body and mind differs substantially from what is essential for the young child, adolescent, and adult. While the needs for psychic and somatic attunement are always intertwined, the older the infant and then child becomes, the more evident and specific is their need for complex psychological availability from the parent. The parent's capacity for availability will depend in large part on how the parent's own experiences of being cared for have become internalized (i.e., the particular meaning of dependency needs), as well as how aware the parent is of wanting or not wanting to imitate that parenting style.

As summarized in Greenberg and Mitchell's *Object Relations in Psychoanalytic Theory* (1983), developmental psychologists and psychoanalysts have acknowledged that the types of early interactions with caretakers that become internalized create the person's internal object world and form the groundwork for future relational possibilities. Greenberg and Mitchell averred that the different theoretical explanations for how these objects are internalized to form the relational world constituted "*the central conceptual problem within the history of psychoanalytic ideas. Every major psychoanalytic author has had to address himself to this issue, and his manner of resolving it determines the basic approach and sets the foundation for subsequent theorizing*" (italics in original; p. 4). Objects refer mainly to people with whom the infant and child interact in early life, although thoughts and feelings can also be considered objects to the extent that they are associated with early caregivers, and these experiences become internalized or symbolized as "a stable, structured set of images consisting of transformations of relationships with other people" (Greenberg, 1986, p. 93).

To become an object that is internalized by the child, it is necessary that this person be an interactive participant in the child's early life, in reality or in imagination. For example, parents, caregivers, imaginary friends, and transitional objects (Winnicott, 1971) are all viable inductees into a child's internal world. It is worth noting that the simplistic and bifurcating labels of "good" versus "bad" objects suggest the defensive mechanism of splitting that object relations theory has so eloquently articulated. As Klein (1952) stated, "I have often expressed my view that object-relations exist from the beginning of life, the first object being the mother's breast which to the child becomes split into a good (gratifying) and bad (frustrating) breast" (p. 1).

The defensive operation of splitting is the result of the infant and child not being able to integrate contradictory experiences of the parent or caregiver. For example, sometimes the mother will appear to nurse the baby just when he is hungry, while at other times, she will not arrive until the baby is in distress. This, according to Klein (1952), will produce the sense that there are two mothers, a good one and a bad one. If this inconsistent feeding pattern persists, the child will grow into an adult who has difficulty recognizing the inherent contradictions in human personality in both self and others.

Note that "good" and "bad" reflect an overall sense of goodness (as in satisfaction and comfort) or badness (as in frustration and pain). In order to be a so-called good or bad object, the caregiver has to be associated with satisfying or frustrating early life experiences. Assuming that child has had primarily neglectful and abusive early experiences with her caregivers, she will likely become involved in relationships as an adult that parallel these crucial early years. And, conversely, if her experiences were characterized by satisfaction and comfort, then she will associate primarily positive multisensory impressions with her caregivers and be more likely to forge an object relational web predisposing her to recognize mutually rewarding interpersonal possibilities.

The infant starts out in life as a chaotic bundle of unmet physical and psychic needs in which experiences of hunger, feeding, holding, and soothing occur as undifferentiated events (Fast, 1985). Over the course of development, the caregiver's capacity and willingness to meet these needs will determine, in large part, the way the infant comes to differentiate and organize self and relational experience. The internal organization of self-in-relation-to-other is how the infant and then toddler develops what psychoanalytic theorists call internal objects.

We consider the essential object an extension of a good object in that, similar to a good object, it provides a positive effect on the child. However, it is distinct from a good object in that what is stressed is the emergent nature or process of the interaction in which the parent is able to reflect and articulate the child's wish of who it is *she* wants to become (Thelen and Smith, 1994). An essential object is, thus, defined by a time-bound attunement that requires the establishment of previous good object internalization. In other words, given the fact that good and bad objects refer to the child's internalizations of impressions of relative goodness and badness of their early caregivers, and are not categorically distinct states of being, as noted above, it is possible that a typically misattuned parent would be able, in a particular interaction, to uncharacteristically respond to the child's needs to be recognized as the person she strives to become.

In *On the Therapeutic Action of Psychoanalysis*, Loewald (1960) comes closest to what we are describing about an essential object in terms of time:

> The parent ideally is in an empathic relationship of understanding the child's particular stage in development, yet ahead in his vision of the child's future and mediating this vision to the child in his dealing with him. This vision, informed by the parent's own experience and knowledge of growth and future, is, ideally, a more articulate and more integrated version of the core of being which the child presents to the parent. This "more" that the parent sees and knows, he mediates to the child so that the child in identification with it can grow. (p. 19)

Our way of thinking about how parents function as essential objects involves their capacity and willingness to *temporarily* put aside their own needs and reflect on what they intuit the child is asking for, *even if it collides with aspects of their own subjective experience.* In other words, it involves a willingness to be momentarily personally *inauthentic* in the service of responsiveness to a relational *process*, and the consequent willingness to lend oneself to a co-created parent-child *illusion*, of sorts.

Slochower's (1996) relational conceptualization of attunement as an illusion, elaborating on Winnicott's "holding" construct (1960, 1963a, 1963b), is relevant in this context. While Slochower discusses the relationship between an analyst and patient, we think the idea of an illusory attunement to be relevant to the description of an essential object, as well. Rather than being conceptualized as a concrete reality, Slochower argues that the holding experience between the analyst and patient is always a metaphor "describ[ing] the creation (by analyst and patient together) of an *illusion of absolute attunement* on the analyst's part"[1] (p. 326). It is this illusory quality of attunement with the child that the parent is able to effect that we are highlighting here in our delineation of the essential object, not the analogue of analyst-patient to parent-child relationships.

Slochower (1996) argues that this attunement "most centrally concerns the analyst's capacity to understand, and evenly and consistently to respond to the patient's needs or feeling states," and that *it is illusory in nature* because its existence and "maintenance requires that both parties temporarily bracket their awareness of the more complex aspects of the analytic interchange" (p. 326). In other words, this experience of seamless attunement actually involves a great deal of "emotional complexity for both patient and analyst" (p. 326). The implicit "bracketing," often in the context of struggle, conflict, and strain, of those aspects of the analyst's separate subjectivity that disrupt the patient's experience of the other as a subjective object, results in both the illusion of attunement and the absence of explicit knowledge of the patient's impact on the analyst.

Similarly, parents function as essential objects when they co-create with their children the illusion of attunement not only to the child's current experience but also *to whom the child is striving to become.* It is a version of attunement in which the Loewaldian parent, who, as noted above, relies on his or her subjectivity and experience and can (1) envision a more "articulate and integrated" version of what the child is reaching for, and (2) bring this vision into creative interplay with his or her child's strivings and desires. Obviously, the age of the child will determine how well formulated any image of the future will be.

Let us offer an anecdote of a parent functioning as an essential object from our own experience as an illustration of what we are trying to get at. One evening, after a particularly taxing day, Nick entered our apartment and was greeted (it's tempting to say "assaulted") by our eleven-year-old daughter, who insisted that he do nothing until he watched her dance routine: "Daddy, Daddy, stop. Look at this! Look at this!" What went through Nick's head at that moment were near simultaneous projections of possible next steps. The first association was to give voice to his discomfort and irritation and insist that he take care of his own needs before addressing hers. He then imagined our daughter both hurt and angry and the evening being ruined. He next considered saying nothing and not registering any emotion whatsoever—just standing there and impassively communicating his displeasure through his silence. This felt equally unpleasant. For some reason, he decided at that moment to just do as he was told. He put his briefcase down and said, "OK, let's see what you've got." Our daughter looked delighted, proceeding to crank up her iPod and throw her body around convulsively. He could feel the sweat running down his back, the day's many hours of frustrating and unhappy patients distracting him, and had to work hard to keep his mind focused and his heart open to our daughter's genuine and exuberant attempt to delight him with her performance. When it was over she asked, "Daddy, what do you think?" Once again, amid his fatigue, impatience, and intense wish to take a shower, he felt hooked by her hope and trusting anticipation in his response. What he said, with genuine pleasure, was "When I watch you dance, you make me forget my troubles. Thank you, that was terrific."

What Nick was aware of focusing on was not our daughter's dancing but her need for him to recognize her creativity, her spontaneity, her unself-conscious experience of her body, and her innocent exhibitionism. He wanted to acknowledge this as her gift to him, as a validation of the person she thinks she wants to become. In conflict with his desire to give into his exhaustion, his depletion, his impatience with the needs of others, and his conflicts about honoring our daughter's healthy exhibitionistic needs when his were so inconsistently met by his own parents *was his felt desire to be the person in that moment she needed him to be, and see the person, in that moment, she was striving to become.*

In the example just cited, for a variety of reasons about which we can only speculate, Nick was able to reflect to our daughter the dancer she felt she was and the one she hoped to become. He became an essential object in that moment. It involves an entirely different ego involvement by which parental self-satisfaction is garnered not by being idealized as an essential pragmatic provider of things (e.g., food, shelter) but *by reflecting the viability of what the child believes at that moment she ideally wants to become and that both parties know will inevitably make her distinct from them.* Both our daughter and Nick clearly saw and "bracketed" their awareness of the state Nick was in for a moment, while also appreciating each other's "bracketing." In a coercive play mode within transitional space, she demanded that he validate her dancing both for what it was and for what it was allowing her to dream she wanted to become. Similar to Tuber's father dancing with him, it was a paradoxical form of relatedness, a profound coming together and tacit recognition of growing apart.

This chapter began with a selective review of the literature on mothering and specific themes and problems that related to the issue of mothering identity. We can both attest to the fairly incalculable upheaval that parenthood is, and yet also recognize that reorienting ourselves and each other in the ever-evolving attempts to optimally care for our daughter—our formidable "other"—has brought us untold pleasures. It has demanded that we take a hard look at how we view ourselves and, perhaps more significantly, how we have redefined who we are. We are far less tempted to trust in our omnipotence, for instance, having survived the innumerable narcissistic injuries to which parenthood is heir. As Phillips (2013) stated, the problem with narcissism may well be believing in it in the first place. Self-involvement is part of being human: the question is, rather, how is one's self-involvement impacting one's life? Raising our daughter has definitely changed the nature of our self-involvement, often we think, for the better. As a result, we are far more tolerant of our own foibles, and those of our daughter. We continue to strive to be essential objects whenever we can, and recognize our good-enough status most of the time. As time races by at such a clip in this parenting phase of life, we both feel we are always catching up and striving to be gracious when saying goodbye.

NOTE

1. The idea that illusion constitutes much of what we mean by human perception at any age has long been established and is beyond the scope of this chapter to describe in detail.

REFERENCES

Ainsworth, M., Blehar, M. C., Waters, E., and Wall, S. (1979). *Patterns of attachment: A psychological study of the strange situation*. Hillsdale, NJ: Erlbaum.

Balint, A. (1949). Love for the mother and mother-love. *International Journal of Psychoanalysis, 30*, 251–59.

Baraitser, L. (2009). *Maternal encounters: The ethics of interruption*. Hove, East Sussex: Routledge.

Beebe, B. and Lachmann, F. M. (2002). *Infant research and adult treatment: Co-constructing interactions*. Hillsdale, NJ: Analytic Press.

Benjamin, J. (1988). *The bonds of love: Psychoanalysis, feminism, and the problem of domination*. New York: Pantheon.

Bowlby, J. (1969). *Attachment and loss, vol. 1: Attachment*. New York: Basic Books.

Bueskens, P. (2014). Introduction. In P. Bueskens (Ed). *Mothering and psychoanalysis: Clinical, sociological and feminist perspectives* (pp. 1–72). Bradford, ON: Demeter Press.

Chodorow, N. (1978). *The reproduction of mothering: Psychoanalysis and the sociology of gender*. Berkeley: University of California Press.

Chodorow, N. (2014). Too late. In P. Bueskens (Ed.). *Mothering and psychoanalysis: Clinical, sociological and feminist perspectives* (pp. 219–41). Bradford, ON: Demeter Press.

Collins, P. H. (1994). Shifting the center: Race, class, and feminist theorizing about motherhood. In E. N. Glenn, G. Chang, and L. R. Forcey (Eds.), *Mothering: Ideology, experience, and agency* (pp. 45–66). New York: Routledge.

de Beauvoir, S. (2010/1949). The mother. In C. Borde and S. Malovany-Chevallier (Translators). *The second sex* (pp. 597–648). New York: Vintage Books.

de Marneffe, D. (2004). *Maternal desire*. New York: Little, Brown.

Erikson, E. H. (1950). *Childhood and society*. New York: Norton.

Erikson, E. H. (1980/1959). *Identity and the life cycle*. New York: Norton.

Fast, I. (1985), *Event theory: A Piaget-Freud integration*. New York: Routledge.

Fonagy, P., Gergely, G., Jurist, E., and Target, M. (2002). *Affect regulation, mentalization, and the development of the self*. New York: Other Press.

Gallop, J. (2002). *Anecdotal theory*. Durham, NC: Duke University Press.

Gorchoff, S. M., John, O. P., and Helson, R. (2008). Contextualizing change in marital satisfaction during middle age. *Psychological Science, 19*, 1194–1200.

Greenberg, J. (1986). Theoretical models and the analyst's neutrality. *Contemporary Psychoanalysis, 22*, 87–106.

Greenberg, J., and Mitchell, S. (1983). *Object relations in psychoanalytic theory*. Cambridge, MA: Harvard University Press.

Hirschberger, G., Srivastava, S., Marsh, P., Cowan, C. P., and Cowan, P. A. (2009). Attachment, marital satisfaction, and divorce during the first fifteen years of parenthood. *Personal Relationships, 16*, 401–20.

Kamel, R. M. (2013). Assisted reproductive technologies after the birth of Louise Brown. *Journal of Reproductive Infertility, 14*, 96–109.

Klein, M. (1946). Notes on some schizoid mechanisms. *International Journal of Psychoanalysis, 27*, 99–110.

Klein, M. (1952). Notes on some schizoid mechanisms. In *Envy and gratitude and other works* (pp. 1–24). London: Hogarth Press.

Kristeva, J. (1986). Women's time. In T. Moi (Ed.), *The Kristeva reader* (pp. 187–213). New York: Columbia University Press.

Lasch, C. (1991). *The culture of narcissism: American life in an age of diminishing expectations*. New York: W. W. Norton.

Levin, K. K. (2015). *Psychological distress in women presenting for first-time in vitro fertilization: Relationships among maternal identity centrality, grief and psychopathology* (doctoral dissertation). Retrieved from ProQuest (3662561).

Levinson, D. J. (1978). *The season's of a man's life*. New York: Knopf.

42   *Lisa and Nick Samstag*

Levinson, D. J. (1986). A conception of adult development. *American Psychologist, 41,* 3–13.

Levinson, D. J. (1996). *The season's of a woman's life.* New York: Knopf.

Loewald, H .W. (1960). On the therapeutic action of psychoanalysis. *International Journal of Psychoanalysis, 41,* 16–33.

Mahler, M., Pine, F., and Bergman, A. (1975). *The psychological birth of the human infant: Symbiosis and individuation.* New York: Basic Books.

Obergfell v. Hodges, 576 U.S. 3, 2015.

Phillips, A. (2013). Narcissism, for and against. In *One way and another: Collected essays.* London: Hamish Hamilton.

Roberts, P., and Newton, P. M. (1987). Levinsonian studies of women's adult development. *Psychology and Aging, 2,* 154–63.

Ruddick, S. (1989). *Maternal thinking: Towards a politics of peace.* Boston: Beacon Press.

Shapiro, A. F., Gottman, J. M., and Carrère, S. (2000). The baby and the marriage: Identifying factors that buffer against decline in marital satisfaction after the first baby arrives. *Journal of Family Psychology, 14,* 59–70.

Slade, A., Belsky, J., Aber, J. L., and Phelps, J. (1999). Maternal representations of their relationship with their toddlers: Links to adult attachment and observed mothering. *Developmental Psychology, 35,* 611–19.

Slochower, J. (1996). Holding and the fate of the analyst's subjectivity. *Psychoanalytic Dialogues, 6,* 323–53.

Snitow, A. (1992). Feminism and motherhood: An American reading. *Feminist Review, 40,* 32–51.

Stern, D. (1985). *The interpersonal world of the infant: A view from psychoanalysis and developmental psychology.* New York: Basic Books.

Stern, D., and Bruschweiler-Stern, N. (1998). *Birth of a mother: How the motherhood experience changes you forever.* New York: Basic Books.

Stone, A. (2012). *Feminism, psychoanalysis and maternal subjectivity.* London: Routledge.

Thelen, E., and Smith, L. (1994). *A dynamic systems approach to the development of cognition and action.* Cambridge, MA: MIT Press.

van IJzendoorn, M. H. (1995). Adult attachment representations, parental responsiveness, and infant attachment: A meta-analysis on the predictive validity of the Adult Attachment Interview. *Psychological Bulletin, 117,* 387–403.

Waterman, B. (2003). *The birth of an adoptive, foster, or step-mother: Beyond biological mothering attachments.* London: Jessica Kingsley.

Winnicott, D. (1953). Transitional objects and transitional phenomena. *International Journal of Psychoanalysis, 34,* 89–97.

Winnicott, D. W. (1960). Ego distortions in terms of true and false self. *Maturational processes and the facilitating environment* (pp. 140–52). New York: International Universities Press.

Winnicott, D. W. (1963a). Psychiatric disorder in terms of infantile maturational processes. In *Maturational processes and the facilitating environment* (pp. 230–41). New York: International Universities Press.

Winnicott, D. W. (1963b). Dependence in infant-care, in child-care, and in the psychoanalytic setting. In *Maturational processes and the facilitating environment* (pp. 249–59). New York: International Universities Press.

Winnicott, D. W. (1971). *Playing and reality.* London: Tavistock.

THREE

On Being Essential

Parenting, Immigration, and Acculturation

Diana Puñales Morejon

In this third chapter, **Diana Puñales Morejon** *takes the broad theoretical brushes used in the first two chapters and applies them to the special complexities of immigrant parents.*

For the children of immigrants, the burden and joy of achievement is often a symbol of having attained the American Dream. Achievement by the immigrant child can therefore be perceived by the parent as indicative of emotional well-being and can come to represent parental pride as well as be infused with parental narcissism. The processes of assimilation, acculturation, and oppression intrinsic to immigration can also play a strong role in the ability of immigrant parents to be both essential and formative to their children. Being essential for immigrant parents can be a process that modifies the psychological phenomena of separation and individuation for the parent as well as the child and can be equally fraught with tension for both as they manage these developmental tasks in a culture that is new and unfamiliar. This chapter discusses how the process of being essential as well as relevant and graceful for immigrant parents changes dynamically over time with specific emphasis given to the acculturative process; journeys of migration and adaptation; the uprooting of meaning, religious, and health belief systems; safety nets and extended kin; and the Latino family across the lifespan. The author's personal narrative as a first-generation immigrant child and then as a bicultural mother of second-generation daughters highlights this particular form of essentialness in being a parent.

—◦∅◦—

Children learn more from what you are, than what you teach.
—W. E. B. Du Bois

Tell me and I forget. Teach me and I may remember. Involve me and
I learn.
—Benjamin Franklin

It is only with the heart that one see can rightly; what is essential is
invisible to the eye.
—Antoine de Saint-Exupéry

The experience of fear permeates my early memories of Cuba. The night
before we left to come to New York, I remember my grandmother telling
me to be quiet as we packed the one piece of luggage that we were
allowed to bring. She feared, so I feared as well, that the resident Communist Committee person who lived in our building would prevent us
from leaving Cuba because we were *gusanos* ("worms"). The Communist
government used this term to refer to Cuban citizens who did not embrace the ideals of the Cuban Revolution ("Fidelismo") and were seeking
exile in the United States. And so we packed in silence. I was six years
old.

The next morning, my parents, grandmother, and I would embark on
one of the "Freedom Flights," instituted by President Kennedy, that enabled Cubans to flee Communism and come to the United States. My
mother's sisters, who lived in New York, were able to sponsor us to
immigrate and secure us passage on a Freedom Flight. I later came to
learn that leaving Cuba was not an easy choice for my family. It was a
decision fraught with much tension, pain, and loss. My mother and
grandmother left many relatives behind, while my father left his entire
family in Cuba. My parents had created a life for themselves from the
abject poverty they had experienced as children. At that time, neither my
father nor my grandmother knew that this was the last time they would
see Cuba. They both died before ever being able to return.

At the Jose Marti International Airport, we had to pass security before
being allowed to board the Freedom Flight. I remember my fear, as if it
were yesterday, embodied in the argument that my father had with an
armed guard. This callous guard tore the only doll I owned from my
arms and removed all of its limbs, throwing them on the floor. He
wanted to ensure that we were not hiding *contrabando* in the arms and
legs of my doll, such as jewelry or cash that the Communist government
did not want leaving Cuba. I remember wetting myself in fear that something terrible was going to happen to my father if he kept arguing with
the guard. My grandmother held me in her arms while my mother held
my father back. We were finally cleared to leave our homeland—in fear,
humiliation, and dejection. Such was the start of our immigration to the
United States.

THE JOY AND BURDEN OF ACHIEVEMENT

Once my parents, grandmother, and I arrived in the United States, I was the first, and only one, to learn to speak English. After arriving in New York City, we relocated to Union City, New Jersey, where a community of Cuban immigrants was developing, creating the second largest concentration of Cubans outside of Miami, Florida. Both within my home and in my community, Spanish was the only language spoken, so learning English was not an easy task. I had no need to speak English except in school. Since no one at home spoke the language, it was left up to me to become fluent. I would practice for hours in front of a mirror, learning how to pronounce certain words, and working on my accent so that my English would sound "American." My mother, who to this day speaks limited English, would help me spell out words using Spanish-English dictionaries. I do not know how she did it or what it must have been like for her to help me learn something that she herself could not grasp. Without fail, she comforted and reassured me that I would learn even when neither of us could determine what was written or being said. In the parlance of this book, she was essential to me.

Shortly after arriving in Union City, my mother found a free program that had just started called Head Start. I was part of the first group of children in Union City to participate. The problem was that no one in Head Start spoke Spanish and that was the only language I knew. Bilingual education did not exist in 1965 in Union City and non-English-speaking students were expected to "sink or swim." That year was a blur. I dreaded going to Head Start because I could not understand anything. To support and comfort me, my mother would stay outside the school, waiting every day for the program to end. I was able to see her legs from the basement classroom window, sitting on a bench outside the school. Her constant presence was both comforting and grounding, especially when I could not understand what was going on around me. Only now, as a mother myself, can I imagine the uncertainty and fear that she must have endured when leaving me in school, not being able to communicate with anyone there. I marvel at her resilience and her desire to be essential for me.

My mother helping me learn English was one of the most formative experiences of my childhood. It was particularly poignant given her limitations with the language. However, my mother fervently believed that I needed to be fluent, both for myself and for our family. My father's lack of education and poor command of the English language greatly limited his employment opportunities. Like many immigrants at the time, my father found steady work only in factories. He was the primary provider in our family both because of traditional norms endorsed by Cuban culture and because of the realities of life in the United States for immigrants with limited education and language fluency. My father was essential for the livelihood of my family in a gendered and cultured way.

My mother, although being educated as a teacher in Cuba, was never able to renew her academic credentials in order to obtain her teaching certification in the United States. Her own fears and insecurities as an immigrant stood in the way of attaining employment. This fear was compounded by the need to care for her three young daughters and ailing mother. My father had his own set of insecurities and experiences of complex trauma. He was twelve years old when his own father died, leaving his mother a widow with eight children. My father's family was poor and became destitute after my grandfather's death. As the oldest, he dropped out of grade school and, at age eleven, worked to support his mother and siblings. He loved math and in his rare free moments taught himself geometry and algebra. My father's dream was to have been a mathematician—a dream he was never able to fulfill. I remember telling my mother that I was embarrassed by my father's public praise of my academic accomplishments. I now understand his pride to have been, in part, a narcissistic attempt to regain all that was lost when we left Cuba. My father never obtained the level of employment that he had in his homeland. In the United States, he shied away from risk because of his familial responsibilities. For many years, he worked two factory shifts in order to financially support us while we all lived in a one-bedroom apartment. He replaced supporting his mother and siblings with caring for his wife, mother-in-law, and three daughters.

The messages that I received from my family were therefore very clear. Early on, I learned that in order to be successful, and for my family to advance socioeconomically, I needed to be educated. My parents fervently believed that academic achievement was vital for economic success. They feared that it was too late for them, as immigrants, to attain this reward, but it was one that they wanted for their children, especially given what they had left behind and lost in Cuba. This way of thinking sustained my parents and allowed my family to tolerate, and to some extent rationalize, the prejudices and discrimination we experienced. As the oldest daughter, it fell on me to negotiate life in the United States on behalf of my family.

For many immigrant children, becoming a language and cultural broker is par for the course and can be critical for the sociocultural adaptation of the family. Lahey (2003) posits that effective communication is a requisite in assisting immigrants to be able to have even their basic social and personal needs met in the host country. Without having access to the means for quickly learning the new language, parents may find themselves in situations where their children become their prime means of communicating with the "outside" world. Children have the ability to become linguistically proficient at a much faster pace than their parents and thus it is easy to understand why they can end up serving as translators for their families (Suarez-Orozco and Suarez-Orozco, 2001). As such, an immigrant or first generation child may be asked to negotiate housing and employment, coordinate travel, and address medical needs on behalf of their parents. This parentified role can develop for children in immigrant families and/or in families that have experienced extreme levels of discrimination and oppression (Boyd-Franklin, 1989).

This parentification process has many strengths. It often results in increased family cohesion and stability, as the child's prowess facilitates the coping of the entire family. Children who have this role are often able to apply problem-solving skills developed throughout their lives. For the purposes of this chapter, it is crucial to note that in order for parentification to develop adaptively, parents must remain an essential part of the child's development. Only with the parent's recognition and validation of their child's accomplishments in this arena can the child make the parentified role more feasible (Dorner et al., 2008; Winton, 2003).

Given the Cuban immigrant community in which I was raised, many of my peers also grew up as parentified. This normalized role for children, combined with my parents continued involvement in my life, left me feeling validated, supported, and loved. While some parentified children feel that they are the sole caretakers of their family, I never had this experience. Because of my structured family life, I felt that I was able to share caretaking responsibilities with my parents. While I was essential on the "outside," they remained essential to me across all the other aspects of my "inside" life.

Much research has validated my own familial experience. Minuchin (1974), in his seminal work on Latino families, posits that parentified children can appropriate parental roles as long as child/parent relationships are clearly delineated. Byng-Hall (2002) believes that families often share internal working models of caretaking and care-seeking that inform and modulate the child's parental role. Conger et al. (2009) propose that when children are able to solve family problems related to the acquisition of social and technical skills, parentified adolescents feel capable, proficient, and self-efficacious. Hooper (2007) maintains that performing instrumental tasks allows a parentified child to feel accomplished and decreases stress for the parent.

In immigrant families, the parentified child inevitably has more interaction with the host culture, adapts more quickly to their surroundings, and exceeds their parents' social and cultural skills. These dynamics *can* create significant and seemingly insurmountable acculturation gaps between parents and children. Titzman (2012) concludes that parentification can be disruptive to the parent-child relationship whereby the parent becomes dependent on the child for survival. The parentification of the child may also thwart a parent's ability to stay essential for their child. On the whole, however, researchers maintain that despite the potential for drawbacks to the parent-child relationship, the role can strengthen a child's ego, allowing them to develop resilience and adaptability while creating and maintaining a privileged status within their family.

As I became fluent in brokering linguistic and cultural experiences for my family, I felt valued and appreciated for this contribution. My success became their success. Yet my mother and father maintained their role as the parents. I was fortunate in that I was a quick learner and did well in school, receiving recognition for my accomplishments from both my family and my teachers. Their emotional availability and support allowed me to thrive. My parents never missed an awards ceremony—my father going so far as to rush to my school between factory shifts. The memory of my parents' pride, especially that of my father, remains poignant even today.

IMMIGRATION, ACCULTURATION, ASSIMILATION, AND OPPRESSION

While raised in the traditional Cuban culture of my family and community, I became immersed in American culture through my socialization and education. In helping my family to negotiate life in English, I was acculturating and adapting to life in the United States. Valdes et al. (2003) state that even when non-English-speaking immigrant parents gain sufficient understanding of the language, parentified children may continue in that role as a way to build redundancy in understanding. Through language brokering, parentified children help parents understand American culture linguistically and socially. Lahey (2003) stipulates that if immigrants are able to communicate in the language of the host country, it is more likely that they will be able to acculturate. Communication in a host country can be self- or third party–facilitated and involves both language and cultural negotiation.

Growing up, I spent many mornings imploring my mother to make me American lunches. In a thermos she would pack *arroz con pollo* and plantains and other Cuban dishes. My American friends' lunches consisted of peanut butter and jelly or bologna sandwiches on white bread. Those foods were foreign to Cuban immigrants, especially my mother. She could not understand why having an "American lunch" was so important to me, but eventually she began packing grilled cheese sandwiches for me.

As I revisit those memories, it becomes clear that my parents intuitively understood something as immigrants that I, as a child, also knew but couldn't articulate. They understood that if I did not connect in some meaningful way to my peers—and, more important, to the culture of the United States—I would be at an enormous disadvantage. I was lucky that my parents understood the importance of my connectedness to our new environment. It was part of what made them essential as parents. It seems clear in hindsight that they did not allow their fears to dominate my experience and thus they encouraged my acculturation out of the security of their attachment to me. I was lucky. My much younger sisters, both born in this country, were also lucky, as I was able to model healthy acculturation for them. For my sisters, though, growing up was a different experience, largely devoid of my familial responsibilities.

My experience as the bridge between my family and the external world served another purpose—it also reinforced my ethnic identity. Tse (1995) was one of the first researchers to postulate that language brokering can be a means of preserving heritage, language competency, and positive relationships within a family. Umaña-Taylor et al. (2009) discuss how language brokering helps parents instill cultural values and healthy identity development in parentified children. In the process of becoming linguistically fluent, I began to internalize American cultural practices and norms. Many educators and social scientists recognize the importance for immigrant children of mastering English as it springboards academic success and provides viable opportunities for future employment. Sam (1992) explains the challenge immigrant children face when their family values, norms, and customs diverge from those of the host country. For my parents, integrating Cuban and American cultural values was challenging and often unsuccessful. I, however, had an advantage that they did not have: I was being socialized in American schools. I had no choice. As the oldest daughter in a Cuban immigrant family, I served as the sole language and cultural broker—assuming more responsibility and family obligation than my sisters. Morales and Hanson (2005) posit that birth order and gender greatly influence who will serve as the language broker, a role that carries over into adulthood.

In addition to the stress of being my family's cultural and language broker, I also faced the everyday racism of growing up as a young Latina in the United States. I became conscious of my race and ethnicity, most poignantly when I ventured outside of the protective enclave of Union City. Social scientists have recognized that early experiences of discrimination can serve to deepen identification with an individual's culture of origin. Such intense involvement with one's ethnic community facilitated my development of a bicultural identity.

Going away to college was an incredibly eye-opening experience for me. I struggled to balance my family's pride in my achievements with the isolation and inferiority I felt as a Latina and an immigrant. Yet, as painful as this process was, I developed an ability to move more fluidly between my two worlds while maintaining the essence of who I was. In graduate school, I became empowered as I embraced my bicultural identity despite oppressive experiences. One example that has stayed with me occurred in a weekly class that I taught. A white male student (who was failing the class) confronted me publicly about his grade. Before I had a chance to respond, he stated, "I just can't accept this. Who are you, anyway? I'm used to having people like you clean my home." It almost goes without saying that his grade did not get changed! My parents' emotional support and understanding kept me grounded during my college years and allowed me to forge my identity as a bicultural Latina. Their essentialness was critical to my growth.

JOURNEYS OF MIGRATION AND ADAPTATION

In their pivotal work on acculturation, social identity, and social cognition, Padilla (2003) argues that immigrants, undergoing cultural transitions due to migration, manage unfamiliar social and cultural pressures as they assimilate. My family met this transition with tremendous resistance. My parents never intended to permanently reside in the United States. While my parents experienced abject poverty in their childhoods, by the time they married in Cuba, both were gainfully employed. My father was a clerk in an electrical company and my mother was a teacher. After the revolution, my father lost his job when the business he worked for was confiscated and nationalized by the Communist government. After refusing to teach literacy to Fidel Castro's *barbudos* (the term used to refer to bearded revolutionary soldiers who emulated Fidel Castro), my mother also became unemployed. Our economic situation in Cuba became dire, and both of my parents took on small jobs whenever they could. My grandmother was a seamstress and did piecemeal work repairing soldiers' uniforms. The unstable unemployment and increasing poverty caused discord in our home. My parents often went without food to ensure that I ate every day. Our journey to the United States became inevitable in many ways.

As my family did not support the Communist government, they experienced decreased work, but, more than that, they became greatly concerned for my future. Before the revolution, two of my aunts had immigrated to New York, seeking economic advancement. Although my aunts were originally supposed to return to Cuba, this was no longer an option for them. Several years after Fidel Castro took power, my aunts were able to sponsor my family to come to the United States. While the move to the United States was seen as necessary and temporary, my family did not adjust well. For example, my grandmother did not unpack her luggage for two years after arriving in the United States. She claimed that she wanted to be ready to return to her homeland at a moment's notice. Such thinking and feeling compromised my family's ability to readily adapt to a new country. My parents and I did not become U.S. citizens until I was in high school—ten years after we moved to the United States. Gaining American citizenship seemed like a betrayal of our Cuban identity. As my family and I adapted to life in the United States, returning to Cuba became a wistful dream and stopped being a reality.

THE UPROOTING OF MEANING

Sam (1992) was one of the early social scientists to identify immigration as a family affair. This theory of dynamic migration argues that what affects one member of the family, affects all. Halperin (2004) posits that the specific cultural meanings of a community impact the interactions between child and parent. When families are socially uprooted, as in the case of immigration, both physical separation and intrapsychic upheaval occur. More specifically, the meanings associated with being uprooted center on the collective and subjective experiences of a person's thoughts, fantasies, dreams, wishes, fears, hopes, and disappointments. For the person who immigrated, their worldview has changed to include culturally determined constructions of reality, patterns of attachment, affect regulation, emotional expression, and conflict resolution (Halperin, 2004). A person's age at immigration, socioeconomic and cultural background, linguistic ability, migration experience, documentation status, and ability to return to the home country all contribute to the multiple meanings attributed to being uprooted. For many immigrants, the migration experience is one of unraveling and rebuilding. Issues of mourning, separation/individuation, guilt feelings, and fear of further loss can often be present. It is especially salient for immigrant children to experience those who are responsible for their well-being as essential during this uprooting. Thus it is crucial to note that the "typical" experience of parents ceding their essentialness to their children in the face of their emerging autonomy may not be nearly as ubiquitous in immigrant families or families who have undergone systematic oppression in their country of origin. It may indeed be a luxury only some can enjoy.

The meanings that my family created for their uprooting have been fluid. Our leaving Cuba was initially justified by an escape from Communism. But as time elapsed, and hope of returning evaporated, my family developed more of an exile identity. The meaning given to being uprooted became more ideological and self-preservative. Perez Firmat (1995) describes immigrants and exiles as two groups that go through life at different speeds. The immigrant is in a rush to do everything—get an education, obtain employment, learn the language, settle down, and eventually seek citizenship. If the immigrant arrives as an adult in the host country, they may create a second lifetime for themselves. The exile, however, waits. For the exile, life does not speed by, but rather passes one day at a time, even one hour at a time. There is a sense of hopelessness and loss in the exile that is not found in the immigrant.

A few years ago, I was invited to teach at the University of Havana and returned to Cuba with my husband and children. Many members of my family disapproved of my going. This return trip came to signify betrayal and support for an oppressive regime. My trip to Cuba, in some ways, invalidated my family's reasons for immigrating to the United States. It gave yet another meaning to our original uprootedness.

RELIGIOUS AND HEALTH BELIEFS

Yet parents are not the only ones who can be essential in the life of a child. Religious figures and health care providers can step into caretaking roles and become essential for immigrant children. Growing up, religion and spirituality were central to my existence. I was raised Catholic and attended Catholic schools until I entered college. For my family, Catholicism was, and continues to be, very important. Growing up, the school system in Union City was abysmally poor. Given my parents' strong desire that my sisters and I be properly educated, they made the decision for us to attend Catholic school. In both elementary and high school, I was fortunate to find teachers and administrators who cared about me and my academic achievement. My high school calculus teacher, for example, was instrumental in enhancing my self-worth and providing me with the tools necessary to go to college. This teacher, and others like him, was my "protective factor." The friendships and mentoring relationships that I was able to develop have survived long after my high school graduation. My calculus teacher is the godfather of both of my daughters.

The guidance my calculus teacher was able to provide offered more than protection—he was essential to my growth and development. My parents made many financial sacrifices in order for my sisters and me to receive a Catholic education. Our education often came at the cost of forgoing simple luxuries and even necessities. For my family, having their children attend Catholic schools also represented the religion that they practiced in Cuba; it was an opportunity for our religion to survive the trip to the United States. The religious community came to be essential for my sisters and me as we negotiated life in our new home. The structure and constancy that we found there instilled in us a sense of value and care outside of our home.

Our faith was a source of support and community in this country and fomented a potent connection to Cuba where our remaining family practiced Catholicism hidden from the Communist government. Those who openly practiced any religion were harassed, and even jailed, by the Cuban government. Communism did not tolerate any religion but their own dogma. Yet Catholics were not the only ones to be persecuted. In the 1970s, the Communist government expanded their attack on religious practices to include any religion, including Santeria. Since the time of slavery in Cuba, Santeria had emerged as a way for slaves to be able to uphold their African religious and spiritual beliefs within the Catholic faith of their Spanish masters. My mother's older brother and his wife were well-known *Santeros* in their community. As the Cuban government became more oppressive and intolerant of religion, my uncle and his wife began to consider immigrating to the United States. My uncle's wife was previously married and did not want to leave her children behind by immigrating, so they stayed in Cuba. However, the Communist government made it harder to practice any religion and remain living on the island. Not long after my family boarded the Freedom Flight, my uncle and his wife had to make the much-resisted journey. Once in the United States, they were able to reestablish their Santeria practice in Union City and later in Miami, Florida. Their forced migration caused great upheaval, as they lost their original Santeria community when they went into exile. Interestingly, not having children of their own in the United States, in part, contributed to my uncle and aunt's difficulties in adapting to mainstream American life. They did not have a child to serve as a language and cultural broker.

Similar to other racial and cultural groups, Latinos have varied religious beliefs. However, many Latinos have been exposed to and/or practice an organized Christian religion, with Catholicism being the most prevalent (Delgado, 1998). In Latino culture, religion is central to family life. Religious groups and organization often have a pivotal role in Latino communities and in the lives of their congregants. In particular, the Virgin Mary is highly revered, and the cultural phenomenon of *Marianismo* is a natural outcrop of reverence to the virtues of the Virgin. Prayer and miracles are commonly held beliefs, as is the notion that bad spirits and bad luck exist. Santeria, for some Latino Caribbean subgroups, is a way to embody and act upon these beliefs in miracles and spirits. The incorporation of Afro-Caribbean practices into one's religious faith can include seeking help to heal the sick from a *Santero* who is imbued with special powers and the gift of sight, the use of incense and herbs in ceremonies for spiritual cleansing or communing with other spirits, and the making of special offerings or sacrifices for saints and family members who are deceased. In many ways, religious and spiritual expressions represent the intersection of Christianity/Catholicism and indigenous beliefs.

In practice, religious beliefs can often bleed into health practices. The intersection between Christianity/Catholicism and indigenous beliefs informs a fatalistic worldview of physical illness and contributes to an external health locus of control (Arrendondo, 2014). For some Latino immigrants, the combination of fatalism and an external locos of control leads them to believe that no doctor can assist them. For other Latino immigrants, faith and a belief in the powers that be lead them to rely on doctors and health care providers as agents of change. As health care providers understand, and act upon, the collective nature of Latino culture, they become essential to their Latina/o patients. Cordova and Chiprut (2011) discuss how some Latinos/as are able to combine traditional health care practices or home remedies with Western medicine. This mixing of traditional and Western health practices can occur for financial reasons and also as a means of connecting to the culture of origin.

Often in my own work with patients, time is spent, especially in group psychotherapy, discussing *remedios* that can enhance mental health. My experience of this has been one where patients feel empowered to take more ownership of their psychological treatment and not feel dismissed. For some of my Latino patients, health and religious beliefs can intersect. Illnesses or poor health may be attributed to punishments from God or *mal de ojo* (evil eye). However, health and good fortune are rewards for having faith; it is to the unfaithful that bad things happen. Kemp and Rasbridge (2004) found that the majority of Latinos/Latinas endorse the idea that faith and God are central to their lives and that both play a key role in illnesses and healing.

SAFETY NET AND EXTENDED KIN

One of the most essential values in Latino culture is *familismo*: the importance of the family, including friends and extended kin. While many differences exist among Latino families based on national origin, ethnic background, and immigration histories, the pervasive nature of *familismo* is an enduring value (Falicov, 2015). For many Latinos, family needs and concerns override individual ones. Family support and relationships greatly contribute to an individual's self-confidence, worth, security, and identity (Delgado, 1998). Specifically, *familismo* provides a concept of family that allows individual members to overcome difficulties and stressors that they experience throughout life. Thus, being essential as a parent is an ingrained aspect of *familismo*, where first the parent and then the extended family play an essential role in the development of the child. Parents and family hold, protect, instruct, support, and provide structure for children. As a result, individual resilience develops through a collective essentialness in the face of adversities and/or oppressive experiences.

THE LATINO FAMILY ACROSS THE LIFESPAN

Latino families, like others, are anchored in beliefs and values that are passed down over time. The Latino family in particular emerges from a collectivistic culture that values cooperation and harmony among members (Arrendondo, 2014). Halperin (2004) presents that the family is the active agent that mediates the relationship between the individual member and the larger cultural systems. *Respeto* is a Latino cultural value that enables parents to remain essential to their children. *Respeto* requires that individual members defer to those who are in a position of authority because of age, gender, social position, title, economic status, and so forth. Being essential as a parent calls for the child to acknowledge the position of the parent as having authority and worthy of respect. Another Latino cultural value that allows parents and family members to be essential is *simpatia*. This refers to an individual being polite and pleasant even under stress. The quality of being essential is one that requires parents to be particularly *simpatico* with their children, as it allows the child to feel loved and grounded.

Although traditional Latino values allow parents and family members to be essential for immigrant children, when these values too strongly anchor family life, acculturation and assimilation can become an unattainable goal. Traditional values can at times conflict with those of the host country or mainstream culture, making assimilation difficult (Sonderup, 2010). Acculturative experiences, as well as that of being essential as parents, can vary across the lifespan of the Latina/o.

BEING ESSENTIAL AND STAYING RELEVANT
AS A BICULTURAL MOTHER

García Coll and Magnuson (1997) describe being bicultural as having several dimensions that encompass the culture of origin and that of the host country: knowledge of cultural beliefs, the ability to communicate effectively, positive attitudes toward both cultures, role repertoire, a sense of efficacy in both cultures, and feeling grounded with social support systems that extend across cultural boundaries. In a sense, the bicultural individual has to be able to manage two or more cultural realities with fluidity and effectiveness. These authors also discuss that factors such as child temperament, developmental age, gender, parental reactions and support, coping skills, cognitive abilities, and the cultural context of the host country play a role in the developmental process of acculturation. Immigrant parents, grappling themselves with biculturalism, can facilitate and shape the bicultural development of their children. Winter (2009) discusses this development in *A Judge Grows in the Bronx*, a children's book about Supreme Court Justice Sonia Sotomayor, which is available in both English and Spanish. In the beginning of the story, he writes about Sotomayor's blossoming as a result of her mother being essential to her:

> You never know what can happen. Sometimes the most beautiful moonflower blossoms in an unexpected place—on a chain link fence, near broken glass, next to an abandoned building—watered by someone whose name you might not even know.
>
> And sometimes the most amazing person blossoms in just such a place as well. So it was with a little girl named Sonia. Her blossoming began with her mother's love and hard work.
>
> Oh, how Sonia's mother loved her! She worked night and day, day and night, as a switchboard operator, just so she could pay for Sonia's

and her brother's private schools. She had never made it past the third grade when she was a girl, but she sure wanted her children to!

As a parent myself, I understand the concerns that my own parents had regarding their children developing a bicultural identity and the fear that my sisters and I would trade our "Cubanness" to become fully "Americanized." It is a concern that I share, to a lesser degree, in raising my own daughters. I comprehend my parents' fears and feeling of impotence when I have not been able to protect my daughters from discrimination and prejudice. Now that they are young adults, I often question whether my husband (who was also born in Cuba and immigrated to the United States) and I exposed and immersed our daughters enough in Cuban culture. In an ironic twist, it is language and the upkeep of our native tongue that my husband and I most worry about with our bicultural daughters. While my parents felt urgently that I needed to master the English language, forty-seven years later I worry about my daughters' mastery of Spanish. Do they speak Spanish well? Will there come a point when they refuse to speak Spanish? If they partner with someone who does not speak Spanish, will my unborn grandchildren speak only English?

The meanings of language fluency can change in less than a generation. Because the issue of language is so closely tied to culture, I attribute lack of language fluency with loss of cultural identity. Growing up, language was the ultimate mediator between my two cultures. Fluency in English and Spanish has allowed me to fluidly navigate both worlds. I clearly recognize that being grounded in my Cuban identity as a child allowed me to cope with the psychological consequences of entering a new culture. My parents, family, peers, and academic role models all proved to be essential in the development of my bicultural identity. I now ask myself if I have provided a substantial enough model of biculturalism for my daughters to internalize and make their own. But most critically, I am keenly aware of how important it is for my daughters to identify as bicultural, as it is a connection to my own past and history. It is no surprise that both of my daughters studied sociology and ethnic and gender studies in college.

My husband and I tried to be essential as parents in raising our daughters. Being essential has been one of the most rewarding (and tiring) experiences of my life. It is also the one experience that has changed me in innumerable ways forever. Once you are essential to your children, there is no going back.

Now that my daughters are starting their own adult lives and do not need their parents to be essential, my husband and I struggle with our new roles in being relevant as parents while missing the days of being essential. In the midst of the many deprivations and oppressive experiences that my parents endured as non-English-speaking immigrants to this country, being essential as parents gave them a sense of joy and accomplishment. It made them feel valued and acknowledged and by their very act of being essential, I came to feel the same. But it was not something that they were ever able to shift from easily given the profound significance that being essential played for them. It would have left them feeling too vulnerable. Being essential was a need for my parents as much as it was a need for me as a child. My daughters often tease and say "Mama, you and Daddi are becoming just like Nana and Lele [my parents]." I get it. They are not children anymore but young adults and need my husband and I to be more relevant and less essential or, at the very least, to be more seamless in our transition from essentialness to relevance. Kids get it, they really do, but how do we?

TREATING LATINO IMMIGRANTS AND THEIR CHILDREN

As society continues to become more diverse, a greater understanding of multiple family systems and parentification is needed for the provision of culturally responsive psychological treatment. This is especially relevant for children of immigrants or exiled parents whose voices need to be privileged and made visible. Such work will provide clinicians with opportunities to determine culturally normative practices. Culturally responsive psychology must also take into account the paradox of a parentified child in an immigrant family. It is dangerous to assume that a child who succeeds academically is well adjusted to mainstream culture and society. When working with immigrant parents and parentified children, factors that must be taken into account include identity, loss, grief, opportunity, hope, temperament, resilience, and reconciliation. As psychologists, we need to review these critical aspects of acculturation and not stop until we know them better. Why do some immigrant children adapt successfully while facing tremendous adversity, and other children do not? As many can attest, the process of "growing up in America" is not an easy one. What makes some children resilient or relatively invulnerable to the stressors of immigration and oppression? How do experiences of oppression and discrimination impact a person's ability to acculturate? How does the act of immigration contribute to an adult and child's acquisition of coping skills, provide access to opportunities, and impact their world views? What variables can be seen to mediate the stressors of immigration, adaptation, adjustment, and development over time for these children? How do political, historical, social, and economic variables impact adjustment and acculturation? And following the theme of this book, how does this process affect the nature of being essential and relevant to one's children across the lifespan? Can the shift from being essential to becoming relevant seamlessly occur when confronted with all of these permutations? *Should* it occur at all given the needs of a bicultural child?

My parents were adults socialized in another country by the time they immigrated. I was a child. Our experiences of negotiating life in United States were radically different. Even my own experience of acculturation varies greatly from that of my sisters who were born in the United States. The way I was essential for my daughters growing up and the way I am relevant now is also different from that of my own parents. More in-depth understanding and exploration of how parents can be essential and stay relevant in the lives of their children allows for growth and health. Understanding the particulars of this process through the lenses of immigration and oppression are especially vital going forward.

Even now, years after I immigrated to this country, or, as my father would have said, "*viviendo en el exilio,*" I continue to feel lucky. I left fear behind in Cuba. A lot has happened since then. I have learned to use my clinical work to embrace what is familiar to me. I have the privilege of working with immigrant communities whose members experience discrimination and oppression on a daily basis—even at the hands of those entrusted to care for them. My patients live racialized, gendered lives while battling psychiatric problems. In practicing culturally responsive psychology, I am able to bring the experiences of a parentified child to the clinical relationship. However, as their psychologist, I am both the parentified child, brokering language and culture, and the essential (aiming to be relevant) parent, facilitating the patient's growth and change.

I work mostly with immigrant monolingual patients who, in addition to experiencing mental illness, also have quite severe and chronic psychosocial stressors in their lives. I treat their mental illness and I help broker the culture and language of the systems within which my patients exist. I feel valued and appreciated. As I broker linguistic and cultural experiences for my patients, I become more in touch with my own bicultural identity. I set limits and maintain boundaries that separate our roles. My patients bring me fruits and pictures of their families as payment. When family members visit, my patients want me to meet their relatives. I see my father's pride in my patients when they want to "show me off" to their families and friends. It is a different way of working with patients than what I was taught. Way different. I feel essential as their therapist when my patients begin treatment. My goal with them is not to remain essential but to become relevant as they heal. It is also what I hope my students will learn from me. They have found, as I have, that it is not easy. It is a lifelong journey, one that uses humor and perspective in the attempt to achieve gracefulness.

REFERENCES

Arrendondo, P. (2014). *Culturally responsive counseling with Latinas/os.* (2014). Washington, DC: American Counseling Association.

Boyd-Franklin, N. (1989). *Black families in therapy.* New York: Guilford Press.

Byng-Hall, F. (2002). Relieving parentified children's burdens in families with insecure attachment patterns. *Family Process, 41*(3), 375–88.

Conger, K., Williams, S., Little, W., Masyn, K., and Shebloske, B. (2009). Development of mastery during adolescence: The role of family problem solving. *Journal of Health and Social Behavior, 50*(1), 99–114.

Cordova, D., and Chiprut, R. (2011). *The art of healing Latinos: Firsthand accounts from physicians and other health advocates.* Los Angeles: UCLA Chicano Studies Research Center Press.

Delgado, M. (1998). *Social services in Latino communities: Research strategies.* New York: Haworth Press.

Dorner, L., Orellana, M., and Jimenez, R. (2008). It's one of those things that you do to help your family: Language brokering and the development of immigrant adolescents. *Journal of Adolescent Research, 23*, 515–43.

Falicov, C. (2015). *Latino families in therapy.* New York: Guilford Press.

García Coll, C., and Magnuson, K. (1997). The psychological experience of immigration. In A. Booth, A. Crouter, and Landale, N. (eds.). *Immigration and the family: Research and policy on US immigration.* Mahwah, NJ: Lawrence Erlbaum Associates.

Halperin, S. (2004). The relevance of immigration in the psychodynamic formulation of psychotherapy with immigrant. *International Journal of Applied Psychoanalytic Studies, 1*(2), 99–120.

Hooper, L. (2007). The application of attachment theory and family systems theory to the phenomenon of parenting. *Family Journal, 15*, 217–23.

Kemp, C. and Rasbridge, L. (2004). Mexico. In *Refugee and immigrant health: A handbook for health professionals* (pp. 260–70). Cambridge: Cambridge University Press.

Lahey, P. (2003). Acculturation: A review of the literature. *Intercultural Communication Studies* XII-2: 103–18.

Minuchin, S. (1974). *Families and family therapy.* Cambridge: Harvard University Press.

Morales, A., and Hanson, W. (2005). Language brokering: An integrative review of the literature. *Hispanic Journal of the Behavioral Sciences, 27*, 471–503.

Padilla, A. (2003). Acculturation, social identity, and social cognition: A new perspective. *Hispanic Journal of Behavioral Sciences, 25*(1), 35–55.

Perez Firmat, G. (1995). *Next year in Cuba: A Cubano's coming of age in America.* New York: Anchor Books.

Sam, D. (1992). Psychological adaptation of young immigrants. *Migration World, 20*, 21–24.

Sonderup, L. (2010). Hispanic marketing: A critical market segment. *Advertising and Marketing Review.*

Stevens, G., and Ishizawa, H. (2007). Variation among siblings in the use of a non-English language. *Journal of Family Issues, 28*, 1008–25.

Suarez-Orozco, C., and Suarez-Orozco, M. (2001). *Children of immigrants.* Cambridge, MA: Harvard University Press.

Titzman, P. (2012). Growing up too soon? Parentification among immigrant and native adolescents in Germany. *Journal of Youth and Adolescents, 41*, 880–93.

Tse, L. (1995). Language brokering among Latino adolescents: Prevalence, attitudes, and school performance. *Hispanic Journal of Behavioral Sciences, 17*, 180–93.

Umaña-Taylor, A., Alfaro, E., Bamaca, M., and Guimond, A. (2009). The central role of familial ethnic socialization in Latino adolescents' cultural orientation. *Journal of Marriage and Family, 71*, 46–60.

Valdes, G., Chavez, C., and Angelelli, C. (2003). A performance team: Young interpreters and their parent. In G. Valdes (Ed.), *Expanding definitions of giftedness: The case of young interpreters from immigrant countries* (pp. 63–97). Mahwah, NJ: Lawrence Erlbaum.

Winter, J. (2009). *A judge grows in the Bronx/La juez crecio en el Bronx.* New York: Atheneum Books for Young Readers.

Winton, C. (2003). *Children as caregivers: Parental and parentified children.* Boston: Allyn and Bacon.

FOUR

We Are Always Essential

Kenneth Barish

Kenneth Barish concludes this introductory section by taking on Tuber's paradigm from the point of view of the child. He specifically asks the intriguing question "What is the nature of parental pride and parental generosity?" He thus explores parenthood from a different, complementary perspective. Even as the magic of early childhood fades and we become a less visible influence in our children's lives, in another sense, he avers, we remain essential. A child's need for an affirming parental response—for a parent's pride, generosity, understanding, and forgiveness—matures, but it does not go away. A parent's inner presence in the life of his or her child, at any age, is a source of emotional support that is more than relevance; it is a vital nutrient of psychological health, strengthening their own capacity for generosity and joy. Through offering clinical and personal examples to illustrate this ever-present aspect of parent-child relationships, Barish notes the explicit contrast between how the parent and child experience the nature of their shifts as they move together across the lifespan.

—◈◈◈—

In the introductory chapter of this book, Steven Tuber offers a profound and moving meditation on the experience of being a parent as we cope, more or less gracefully, with the transition from being essential to being just "relevant" in our children's daily lives. Steve's discussion goes to the heart of parenting, especially when he asks, "What is the nature of parental pride and parental generosity?"

It is all true. As our children become more autonomous and "experience life on their own terms," they need us less. At least, we are no longer essential in the same way, as we were when they were infants and young children. Certainly, they no longer look up to us as they once did. Disappointment and disillusionment are painful, but inevitable, in the emotional lives of all children.

But even as the magic of early childhood fades and we become a less visible influence in our children's lives, in another sense, we remain essential. A child's need for an affirming parental response—her need for a parent's encouragement and pride, generosity, understanding, and forgiveness—matures, but it does not go away. Our inner presence in the lives of our children, at any age, as a source of emotional support is more than relevance; it remains a vital nutrient of psychological health, strengthening their own capacity for generosity and joy. At the same time, from the perspective of the parent, this inner presence in our children can still signify a shift from a "hands on" experience of necessity that can be fraught with emotional struggle. The present chapter focuses instead on the experience of the child, and how, for children, an experience of their parents as emotionally essential never has to wane.

TWO FATHERS: REAL AND FICTIONAL

My favorite anecdote in the parenting literature comes from a letter written to Tim Russert following the publication of his memoir, *Big Russ and Me: Father and Son: Lessons of Life*. The letter, included in Russert's subsequent book (*Wisdom of Our Fathers: Lessons and Letters from Daughters and Sons*),[1] was written by Beth Hackett, daughter of Roger Hackett. Here is an excerpt from Ms. Hackett's letter:

> I was an only child. Mom said I was plenty; Dad said I was perfect. He worked hard to support us: twelve-hour shifts with thirteen days on and only one day off, because overtime paid the bills. He left early in the morning, long before mom and I were awake. He came home exhausted and slept until it was time to do it all over again. It was hard on him because he had so little time with us. It was hard on us too.
>
> We all found little ways to compensate. Mom would pack his lunch and take one bite of his sandwich, so he would smile when it was time to eat. I would put my favorite toy in his lunch box so he had something to play with at lunch.
>
> Dad's special time with me was morning coffee. He would get up at 4:00 AM, start the coffee brewing, and get ready for work. When the pot was ready, he would come into my room and wake me up. I would sit at the kitchen table as he poured two cups of coffee. His was always black. Mine was barely brown, full of milk and sugar, sweet to the taste. Dad would tell me about his day and ask about mine. When the cups were empty, he would tuck me back into bed and kiss me good night before heading out to work. It was our special time together, and we never missed. . . .

> He died in 1995, and I still miss him. Every morning I make a pot of coffee and sit at the kitchen table. . . . When I raise my mug . . . I see my dad sitting across from me, a smile on his face and a cup of coffee in his hands. . . . It's always special. I'm having coffee with my dad.

I have briefly discussed this moving story in a previous publication.[2] Here, I would like to consider, in greater detail, some of the lessons Ms. Hackett learned from her parents—and that we can learn from the Hackett family. Mr. and Mrs. Hackett, I believe, understood something of the essence, the soul of being parents, a quality that is often lost in our contemporary culture and current parenting debates.

They have, of course, given their daughter a feeling of being loved, deeply and unconditionally. And their love, in return, evoked in Beth lifelong feelings of love and gratitude. Beth has come to know the feeling of a parent's love and generosity—the feeling that she was special (or, as her father said, "perfect"). She has experienced the almost ineffable good feeling of being in the presence of a man she looked up to, admired in a way and with a depth of feeling that is hard for us to recapture, or even recall, as adults.

Over time, these feelings will be modified and transformed. Ms. Hackett will no longer believe that she is perfect (and she will not demand to be treated as if she were). She will no longer regard her father with the kind of awe she did in early childhood. But she has learned that these feelings are possible. As parents, we need to remember that every child looks to us for this feeling; when they find it, we have given them something invaluable, what Simon Baron-Cohen has called "an inner pot of gold."[3]

The feeling Beth describes is not a momentary pleasure. As her letter attests, the memory of her father's love has stayed with her. As I noted in a previous publication, "She will have with her, in moments of sadness and loneliness, in childhood and in her adult life, a deep and indelible feeling of inner support."[4] And, I would now add, she will try to re-create this feeling, in some way, as a source of meaning in her adult life.

But Beth has learned even more. She has learned how to care about the feelings of others. She knows that with small gestures of love and concern (by leaving a toy for her father to play with and a sandwich with a bite already taken) she can make her father smile, even when he isn't present. There are few lessons more important for all her future relationships throughout her life.

I would note, as a passing comment on contemporary culture, that Mr. Hackett's parenting was not derived from a parenting philosophy or learned as a parenting "strategy" or "technique." (I doubt that Mr. Hackett would have understood the word "parenting." Only in our time have we turned a good noun into a mediocre verb.) I imagine that, in these moments, Mr. Hackett did not believe that he was parenting. He was, more simply—and more profoundly—being a father. I also cannot help wondering, how often do today's parents, in our over-scheduled, over-stressed, and over-tired lives, take the time to create these moments? And what is our excuse?

The novelist Mary Gaitskill tells a different story. Toward the end of Gaitskill's short story "Tiny, Smiling Daddy," a middle-aged man, now retired, recalls the distance he felt in his relationship with his own father ("a distance . . . so great and so absolute that the word 'distance' seemed inadequate to describe it"). He remembers a moment when, as a young boy, he was looking admiringly at his father, eating breakfast. His father suddenly and inexplicably looked up and said, "Stop staring at me, you little shit." This memory comes to mind as he ruminates, angrily, about his troubled relationship with his own, now adult, daughter. He remembers, still with bitterness (and now some regret), how he was unable to accept her adolescent rebellion, how he had disowned her when she told him she was gay ("You're a lesbian? Fine. You mean nothing to me. You walk out that door, it doesn't matter. And if you come back in, I'm going to spit in your face. I don't care if I'm on my deathbed. I'll still have the energy to spit in your face"), and their only partially successful efforts at reconciliation in the years since. Gaitskill mocks the pop psychology advice to find "the good parent in yourself." In the depressive, masochistic world of Gaitskill's stories, there is no inner "tiny, smiling daddy who appears, waving happily, in a secret pocket in your chest. Some kinds of loss are absolute. And no amount of self-realization or self-expression will change that."[5]

A NEEDED FEELING

In moments of anxiety and discouragement, or of loneliness and self-doubt, and in moments of joy (for example, at the birth and rites of passage of their own children) our children will turn to us, throughout their lives. They will continue to turn to us, no matter how independent and self-reliant they have become.

If, as parents, we remain a source of emotional support, they will live better lives. A child's confident expectation, at any age, that her parents will offer comfort and solace, or share in her pride and joy, is an essential, perhaps the most essential, constituent of her emotional health.[6]

We all know this, of course. These ideas are basic tenets of a psychoanalytic theory of internal object relations.[7] Often, however, we do not think this way. Today, so much advice to parents (including my own) focuses on helping children learn to cooperate and behave well, or to develop better social skills, or solve everyday family problems. It is important work, helpful to many families. At our best, we are able to improve communication and understanding between parents and children, and strengthen family relationships. Still, even when we are able to ameliorate family conflict and improve daily family life, it is easy to overlook deeper sources of children's motivation and emotional health.

OUR CHILDREN LOOK UP TO US

There is a picture in our home of our son, about one year old, looking admiringly at his grandfather, who is reading to him. In the photo, he is looking up, literally as well as figuratively. Most families have similar pictures, and many fortunate children have memories, from a somewhat older age, of these experiences, sharing simple pleasures—reading, cooking, playing games—with an admired adult. The activities themselves are not very important; what matters is the feeling of being in the presence of an admired adult. Heinz Kohut understood this and referred to these experiences as "merger with an idealized selfobject."[8]

A young child's idealization of her parents and grandparents is one of childhood's most deeply felt emotions. Recall, for example, the look on the faces of Scout and Jem as Atticus addresses the jury in *To Kill a Mockingbird*. Or think of Beth Hackett, drinking morning coffee with her father.

Our developmental theories, with some exceptions, do not adequately convey the unique quality of feeling and inner motivation—the feeling of "wanting to be like"—that accompanies these experiences. A child's idealization of admired adults, as Kohut taught, becomes a guiding influence in her life, a source of ideals, especially her ego-ideal—the kind of person she aspires to become—and a needed inner support throughout life. The emotion that best captures this aspect of parent-child relationships is the feeling of pride.[9]

"I'M PROUD OF YOU"

Pride has a distinctive place among human emotions. It would be difficult to overstate the role played by feelings of pride in the lives of children, in the development of character, and in human relations more generally.[10]

Despite its obvious importance in our everyday lives, pride plays a surprisingly small role in most theories of child development. All developmental theories acknowledge the importance of parental *approval* in shaping a child's behavior and character. But praise and approval are not the same as pride. Pride is deeper; it is about who we are, not just what we do.[11]

In recent years, developmental psychologists have begun to study the emergence of pride in young children. We know, for example, that children begin to show unambiguous expressions of pride at two years old.[12]

I have been able to find very little research or discussion, however, on the importance of parents' expressions of pride in their children. This omission is unfortunate. My own belief, based on my experience as a son, a father, and a child therapist, is that the words "I'm proud of you" are among the most important that a parent can say.

In contemporary emotion theory, pride (along with shame, embarrassment, and guilt) is understood as a "self-conscious" or "self-evaluative" emotion. We feel sad, anxious, or angry about things that have happened (or may happen) to us in the world. We feel proud (or ashamed) of ourselves, especially how we feel about ourselves in the eyes of others.[13]

Like other self-evaluative emotions, pride is also an interpersonal emotion.[14] When children feel proud—when they have built a tower, drawn a picture, scored a goal, or won a game—they instinctively turn to others, especially admired others, to share in their pride (and when they feel ashamed, they look away). It may be difficult for any of us to sustain an inner feeling of pride without some affirming response from others. The affirming response does not always have to be spoken, but it has to felt. This basic fact of our emotional life has important implications for understanding depression and narcissism.

Feelings of pride also seem to require a special kind of relationship, something like a parent-child relationship (a relationship with someone we regard as an authority or a person we look up to and admire). In this respect, pride may be unique among human emotions; other basic emotions (for example, anger, anxiety, sadness, or even shame) do not depend on this kind of relationship. We may look to friends and colleagues for understanding and emotional support, but we look to parents and teachers (and, later, spouses) to be proud of us. Even as adolescents, when children increasingly turn to peers, they will not look to their peers to feel proud of them. This is a feeling that only parents and admired teachers can provide.

A child's feeling that her parent is proud of her is more than a momentary good feeling; it is a deep and intrinsic emotional need, essential for her present and future emotional health.

It is a need, not a wish. When we look to share a feeling of pride (especially in childhood) and do not find an affirming response, we do not simply feel disappointed or sad. We feel a more acute pain and, over time, a more profound loss.

I therefore think of parental pride as a basic nutrient of emotional health, required for the growth and maintenance of healthy emotional systems. Analogous to the role played by biological nutrients in a child's physical health, this feeling may be most needed in early development, to prevent permanent malformations of character and resilience, but it remains necessary throughout life, when deficiencies in basic nutrients may still cause disease.

When children know that their parents are proud of them, this feeling resonates throughout their emotional life. Parental pride acts as a protective factor and a sustaining influence, an inner psychological resource in moments of discouragement and defeat. A child's belief that her parents are proud of her strengthens her emotional immune system and opens a pathway toward emotional maturity. When this nutrient is present, her needs will feel less urgent, and she will recover more quickly from setbacks and disappointments of all kinds. When she is angry, she will be less absorbed in defiant thoughts and attitudes, and less insistent in her demands. She will also be more open and more generous toward others.

When a feeling of pride is absent, this absence (again, like a missing nutrient) is destructive, in a pernicious way, to our emotional health. A deficiency of parental pride seeps into our personality and character, influencing our feelings, attitudes, and behaviors, often in ways we are not aware of. We may experience a lack of parental pride as a tendency to feel resentment or envy, or as self-doubt, or cynicism, or as a vague feeling of "something missing." [15] Or we may feel all of these emotions and attitudes, more or less, depending on the challenges we face and our emotional needs at different times in our lives.

And we will look for it elsewhere. Because it is a needed feeling, we will seek substitutes for this missing nutrient, often in hedonism or narcissism. (I would offer the tentative hypothesis that self-aggrandizing narcissism, whether overt or disguised, is a substitute for normal parental pride.) But these are poor substitutes, because they create only a fleeting and fragile security and, unlike the real thing, do not foster openness and emotional maturity.

If, as parents, we fail to express pride in our children, no amount of success or recognition among their peers, or even their teachers, can fully compensate for this missing nutrient in their emotional lives. And if children become too deeply or traumatically disillusioned—if we are no longer, in some way, admired or respected—we will have forfeited our ability to provide this source of meaning in their lives. In this way, parents remain essential. The feeling that our parents are proud of us remains a needed feeling and, when present, a deep and lasting form of emotional support. When things go well, pride flows in both directions; our children know that we are proud of them, and they continue to feel proud of us. This mutual experience then becomes, for parents as well as children, a lifelong source of inner sustainment. [16]

Pride, of course, is the feeling Steve's father joyfully expressed when Steve received his college acceptance. And this moment of pride, as Steve tells us, has stayed with him as an inner presence throughout his adult life.

The feeling that our parents are proud of us is also a generative feeling. It is generative because it strengthens in us, as it did for Steve, a sense of what is possible between parents and children—our belief in the possibility of these good feelings and, with this, our desire to create similar moments of pride (and joy) in our own lives.

Of course, like everything else in our emotional life, pride is double edged. Parental pride, after early childhood, is not unconditional. When we express pride in our children, we also, implicitly, set a standard, often a moral standard, to live up to. Living up to this ideal is a healthy form of self-esteem (and, when we fail, a source of shame and guilt).

A TELLING CLINICAL VIGNETTE

My patient, Jane, did not have this feeling. As an adolescent and young adult, Jane struggled in many aspects of her life. Jane was a good student; however, she had few interests or passions, few commitments, and few goals. In all her relationships — with family, friends, and lovers — Jane had great difficulty expressing gratitude or joy.

Jane's father believed in "tough love." He was an arrogant man, scornful and contemptuous of his wife (who, in Jane's memory, did not challenge his denigration and contempt). He was not a man to express pride in his children. They should expect from him only the basics. He would pay for their education; they would pay for their mistakes.

Jane recalled many efforts, as a young child and early adolescent, to elicit her father's attention and interest, but she found him self-absorbed and aloof. As an adolescent, Jane became anxious, defiant, and depressed. She came to New York to go to college, seeking a new start, but was unable to focus on her work. With friends, she was often envious and resentful, acutely sensitive to feeling excluded. Jane would hold on to grievances, stuck in angry ruminations against people who (she believed) had treated her unfairly. There seemed to be no inner calming voice to assuage these hurt feelings.

Jane told me, "I have to make an effort to be interested in other people; it's hard for me to be spontaneous and playful." Over time, I also became aware of a lack of generosity in her relationships. She sought emotional support from others but did not offer to help, even when her younger brother became seriously ill. Jane seemed to lack an inner standard, an ego-ideal. She succinctly described the clinical syndrome of identity diffusion: "Growing up, I had no idea of the kind of person I wanted to be." I offer this brief vignette as a description of some of the problems in living that commonly occur when children grow up without a feeling of parental pride.

PRIDE OR NARCISSISM?

In this context, I'd like to return to some of the questions Steve Tuber raised in his chapter: Is the pride we feel as parents an expression of our own narcissism? Are we, as today's "helicopter" parents are often accused, living vicariously through our children?

My own answers to these questions are fundamentally in agreement with Steve's. Yes, our narcissism is always present when we feel proud of our children, but (within limits) it is *normal* narcissism. And the absence of this narcissistic investment is more deeply pathological and far more harmful to children's emotional health.

In his essay "On Narcissism," Freud famously observed,

> If we look at the attitude of affectionate parents towards their children, we have to recognize that it is a revival and reproduction of their own narcissism, which they have long since abandoned. . . . [T]hey are under a compulsion to ascribe every perfection to the child—which sober observation would find no reason to do. . . . The child shall fulfill those wishful dreams of the parents which they never carried out—the boy shall become a great man and a hero in his father's place and the girl shall marry a prince as a tardy compensation for her mother. . . . Parental love . . . is nothing but the parents' narcissism born again.[17]

I first read this passage when I was a young (and affectionate) parent. But I did not feel reproached. Freud understood that the narcissism of affectionate parents, "which is so moving and at bottom, so childish," was a normal part of parental love.

Consider an example from contemporary popular culture. An episode of the television comedy *The Big Bang Theory* features a visit by Leonard's bizarrely intellectual and unempathic mother. In a conversation over lunch, Dr. Hofstadter matter-of-factly recounts the professional success of Leonard's siblings. Leonard's friend Howard, impressed by their achievements, comments, "Wow, you must be very proud." Leonard's mother responds with puzzlement: "Why? They're not *my* accomplishments?" We laugh (and cringe) at the coldness of this response—because it is normal for parents to feel proud (and express pride in) their children.[18]

PERSONAL

My father was a warm and generous man. As a boy, I looked up to him with admiration, even awe. His passing, over twenty years ago at age eighty-five, remains a profound loss. When I was an adolescent, we often argued. I lost my belief in God, which has never returned. I accused him of hypocrisy. (It was the 1960s; I believed that he was too cautious in his support for civil rights and in his opposition to the Vietnam War.)

Still, even during this time, I regarded him as a wise and good man. On his eightieth birthday, I praised him with the lyrics of a song by jazz pianist Horace Silver: "If there was ever a man who was generous, gracious, and good, that was my dad." As an adult, and especially after I became a father, we were good friends.

When he died, I felt deep regret for the brief period in my life when I had let him down; when, in my youthful rebellion, I had been unable to understand what was important to him and to appreciate how much he sacrificed for me. And I wished that I had known him even better.

I knew, however, that he was proud of me, how much I wanted him to be proud of me, and how deeply important this feeling was in my emotional life. I can still recall my feeling when he told me, "You're a great dad." Again, this was not a momentary feeling. It has stayed with me over the years, resonating, as a source of meaning and support, and a standard to live up to.

PARENTING

To many of us, the importance of a parent's expressions of pride may seem self-evident. How often, however, in our work with troubled families, do we focus explicitly on this dimension of parent-child relationships?

The understanding I have presented suggests some modifications in our clinical focus with many child and adolescent patients, and in the advice we offer parents. If we view development as a process of increasing independence and individuation (which, of course, in many respects, it is), we will implicitly encourage a child's initiative and effort, as we should. But if, at the same time, we appreciate a child's need to internalize a feeling of pride, our focus subtly changes. We will work to clear away impediments, and then actively promote the expression of feelings of pride.[19]

When parents recognize their children's effort, not just their accomplishments (especially their kindness toward others), they will find many more opportunities to express pride. Even when children are (seemingly) stubbornly defiant or withdrawn, if we look hard enough, there is always something to be proud of. In this way, we set in motion a process of repair, a process that begins with the restoration of hopefulness, a child's renewed belief in the possibility of these good feelings.

From this perspective, the development of insight or even improved mentalization and emotion regulation, are not the essential mechanisms of therapeutic change. The most lasting impact of our work takes place, instead, in the repair of parent-child relationships, especially the restoration of moments of pride. Insight or changes in a child's patterns of thought and behavior are helpful, but subsidiary, goals.

A MEANINGFUL LIFE

All of these ideas come together in a deeply moving children's book by Montzalee Miller, *My Grandmother's Cookie Jar*.[20] Miller tells a story of a young Native American girl who listens every night to the stories her admired grandmother tells her about "her Indian people of long ago" as they eat cookies together from a special jar. When the grandmother dies, the girl's grandfather consoles her. He brings her the empty cookie jar and gently explains, "The jar is full of Grandma's love and Indian spirit. When you are grown and have children of your own you will put cookies in the jar. The cookies will be dusted with Grandma's love. If you tell one of Grandma's stories with each of the cookies, then her spirit and the spirit of those who went before her will live on." The young girl resolves, "I will keep the spirits alive. I will tell Grandmother's stories."

I have previously discussed this book in the context of helping children cope with sadness and loss.[21] But I cannot imagine (along with Beth Hackett's morning coffee with her father) a better description not only of a child's admiration and a (grand)parent's love but also of how a child's effort to preserve these good feelings becomes a core aspect of her identity and values, and the creation of meaning in her life.

NOTES

1. Russert, T. (2004). *Big Russ and me, father and son: Lessons of life*. New York: Perseus Books; Russert, T. (2007). *Wisdom of our fathers: Lessons and letters from daughters and sons*. New York: Random House.

2. Barish, K. (2012). *Pride and joy: A guide to understanding your child's emotions and solving family problems*. New York: Oxford University Press.

3. Baron-Cohen, S. (2011). *The science of evil: On empathy and the origins of cruelty*. New York: Basic Books.

4. Barish, *Pride and joy*.

5. Gaitskill, M. (1997). Tiny, smiling daddy. In *Because they wanted to*. New York: Simon & Schuster.

6. The opposite, of course, is also true—a parent's scorn, as in Mary Gaitskill's story, is a deeply destructive force in the emotional life of any child.

7. See especially Sandler, J., and Sandler, A. M. (1998). *Internal objects revisited*. London: Karnac Books. This understanding of children's inner lives has been demonstrated experimentally in Robert Emde's classic observations and many subsequent experiments on the phenomenon of social referencing. (For example, if an infant is placed on a "visual cliff" or a toy robot is placed in her crib, the child will look at her parent's face to see whether it is safe to explore.) Emde defines social referencing broadly as occurring when "an individual of any age encountering a situation of uncertainty looks to a significant other person to resolve the uncertainty and regulate behavior accordingly." (Emde, R. [2001]. Positive emotions for psychoanalytic theory: Surprises from infancy research and new directions. *Journal of the American Psychoanalytic Association, 39*, 3–44.)

8. Kohut, H. (1971). *The analysis of the self*. New York: International Universities Press.

9. There are few analogous experiences in our adult life. For most adults, with the exception of a religious person's experience of God, these experiences are rare. We may have some glimpse of this feeling when we are in the presence of a deeply admired person—for example, a president, cardinal, or pope. Although I am not a Catholic, I experienced some version of this feeling as a young adult standing in Vatican Square; a musician I know can still recall the night, over fifty years ago, when he sat in with Dizzy Gillespie's band; and the novelist Roy Hoffman recently wrote about the inspiration he felt when, along with his teenage daughter, he spoke briefly with Harper Lee.

10. Recall, for example, that Hitler promised to restore greatness (pride) to a humiliated German nation. Or consider a more recent (and more benign) example: Brazil is reported to have spent $550 million to build a soccer stadium for the 2014 World Cup games, a stadium that will be rarely used, in an effort to promote national pride. The evolutionary psychologist Glenn Weisfeld offers this succinct assessment of the role of pride (and shame) in our everyday lives: "We anticipate pride and shame at every turn and shape our behavior accordingly." (Weisfeld, G. E. [1997]. Discrete emotions theory with specific reference to pride and shame. In N. L. Segal, G. Weisfeld, and C. C. Weisfeld (Eds.), *Uniting psychology and biology: Integrative perspectives on human development*. Washington, DC: American Psychological Association, p. 426.)

11. Only in the past decade has pride been correctly understood as a universal human emotion, present and recognized by people in all cultures. The original list of universal emotions developed by Paul Ekman was based on facial expressions of emotion common to all human cultures. It is difficult, however, to distinguish pride from happiness based on facial expressions; the postural expressions of pride, however, are highly distinctive and now recognized as universal.

12. Stipek, D. (1995). The development of pride and shame in toddlers. In J. P. Tangney and K. W. Fischer (Eds.), *Self-conscious emotions: The psychology of shame, guilt, embarrassment, and pride* (pp. 237–52). New York: Guilford Press.

13. Many emotions have some component of self-evaluation. When we are angry, anxious, or sad, the intensity of these feelings depends, in part, on our intuitive assessment of our ability to cope with the opportunity or challenge presented. Pride and shame, however, are intrinsically self-evaluative.

14. Lagattuta, K. H., and Thompson, R. A. (2007). The development of self-conscious emotions: Cognitive processes and social influences. In J. L. Tracy, R. W. Robins, and J. P. Tangney (Eds.), *The self-conscious emotions: Theory and research* (pp. 91–113). New York: Guilford Press.

15. In her extensive research on Christian evangelical sects, psychological anthropologist Tanya Luhrmann identified this feeling—the feeling of "something missing"—as a core component of evangelical conversion. Luhrmann, T. (2012). *When God talks back: Understanding the American evangelical relationship with God*. New York: Random House.

16. On the concept of inner sustainment, see Saul, L. J. (1970). Inner sustainment: The concept. *Psychoanalytic Quarterly, 39*, 215–22.

17. Freud, S. (1914). On narcissism: An introduction. *Standard Edition*, Vol. XIV, 67–112 (quotation, pp. 90–91).

18. A recent, influential school of thought in parenting and education warns against praising children, including expressions of pride. Alfie Kohn has been the major proponent of this idea. Kohn believes that praise and other "extrinsic" rewards undermine children's intrinsic motivations and their confidence in their independent judgments. He argues that when parents praise their children, they create an "addiction" to praise—a hunger for external approval and a long-term sense of insecurity and inner pressure. (Kohn, A. [1993]. *Punished by rewards: The trouble with gold stars, incentive plans, A's and other bribes*. New York: Houghton Mifflin.) I have presented a critique of this flawed philosophy. Praise from admired others, especially expressions of pride, is not an extrinsic reward; it is a deeply intrinsic human need. See Barish, K.

(September 2012). Should parents praise their children? *Psychology Today*; Barish, *Pride and joy*.

19. Self-psychology, in the years since Kohut's death, has increasingly recognized that individuation and emotional maturity are not end points achieved once and for all; instead, we all have lifelong needs for affirmation and emotional support.

20. Miller, M. (1987). *My grandmother's cookie jar*. Los Angeles: Price, Stern, Sloan.

21. Barish, *Pride and joy*.

Part II

Parenting and Its Impact on Clinical Work

FIVE

The Therapist's Experience as Parent

*The Complex Interaction Between Parent
Process and Clinical Work*

Leslie Gibson

*In this chapter **Leslie Gibson** examines the complex interaction between our
clinical work with parents and the parent-clinician's experience of parenting and
development as a parent. She asks how vulnerable we are as clinicians as our
own experiences as parents are tapped by working with the parents of our child
patients. She speaks to the inevitable dialectic between our own experiences as
parents and its contributions to our conceptualizations and actions in our clinical work with parents and children. Just as raising children creates an opportunity for growth and resolution of past conflict, the potential for the re-creation of
earlier conflicts and/or the reenactment of unresolved experiences from the past,
working with parents as we are raising children creates interesting possibilities
and liabilities for growth. Working closely with parents allows us a different
window into understanding our experiences and identifications as parents. And
just as our children's struggles challenge our sense of self as a good-enough
parent, so, too, can our work with the parents of our child patients challenge our
experience of self as a good-enough parent/good-enough clinician. Finally, she
looks at how we are seen by the parents we work with and how this introduces
another layer of complexity not only to the clinical process but also to the parent-
clinician's sense of self, particularly as our parenting role shifts over time. Are
we the idealized perfect parent? Or are we the naïve, or perhaps aging clinician
who doesn't have a clue about how things really are? How do we avoid either the
all-knowing or the judgmental parent-clinician roles? As we confront our shifting centrality in the lives of our own children, Gibson lastly notes that we must*

find ways to incorporate, respond to and/or make sense of how we are seen by the parents we work with as well as our own shifting identity as parents.

—◁◉◉◉▷—

My work with parents has been profoundly impacted by my own growth and development as a parent. From typical parental experiences navigating life with my two infants, toddlers, school-age children, adolescents, and now young adults to elements specific to my family (raising fraternal twins and the impact of sudden, unforeseen events), my sense of self as a parent and my experience of myself as a clinician have influenced one another in a mutual process unfolding over time. Both roles, as parent and as clinician, take time to grow into. One's sense of self in each role evolves over time and moving from feelings of inadequacy (or at least feeling like a neophyte) to competence is part of the process of becoming both parent and therapist. This chapter will address these changes from a personal as well as a clinical perspective with an eye to explicating the ways in which this interaction has shaped my thinking about parenthood and clinical practice.

For me the role of therapist came first, though the view toward parenthood was always on the horizon. As a first-year graduate student, I was already in a relationship with the man I would marry and my imagined family was vividly present for me as I began my journey as a clinician. In my early clinical work with children and their parents, I felt the greatest comfort in working with parents when I discussed development and the emotional, cognitive, social capacities of children at different ages, when I helped parents to understand the importance of play, and when I worked with parents to respond to conflicts, address emotions, and support changes in their relationships with their children over time. I was less familiar with and less comfortable addressing the process of change each parent was engaged in. I was also profoundly aware that I was not a parent, that I was young, and that I was just learning how to be a clinician.

My first child case was that of a six-year-old boy. The primary parent figure in this family was a robust, formidable grandmother largely responsible for the ongoing care of her grandson and son, a young man in his early twenties. Neither parent of this boy served in any consistent parenting role, nor could they see him as an individual with needs and a mind or heart of his own. As often as not, my patient was experienced by his father as a burden and a rival for the grandmother's (and mother's) attention. In this family, where traumas were multiple across generations, I was to the grandmother a child myself, ill suited to provide guidance regarding the emotional needs of her grandson and even more ill suited to address her own needs and those of her son. As a playmate like the parents, yes, I was fine. But what life experience did I have that could hold, know, or contain the trauma, experiences, and multiplicity of life challenges they had all faced? How could my book knowledge or my graduate student experience as a clinician be of any use to her, her son, and her grandson? She was direct in her challenges to me, particularly when I did not validate her authority or when my work with her son posed a threat. I asked my supervisor: Wasn't she right? Where could I gain the authority, knowledge, and awareness of the kind so needed by this family?

Over time I learned to address such challenges and understand what lay underneath them. I learned to listen differently, less anxiously, to parents' experiences, needs, and the vulnerabilities they shared, showed or worked to hide. In working with this grandmother and the parents of other child patients, I explored the ways in which parents' own developmental trajectory, attachment history, past difficulties, fantasies, expectations, and internal working models of themselves as parents and of their children, influenced how they parented. By the time my children were born I felt more skilled, if not exactly seasoned, as a clinician. I was confident in my capacity to work with children and their parents and naively hopeful that this confidence would carry me into my role as a parent.

Then I became a parent.

The experience of being a parent shifted forever my experience of the work and my understanding of the parents with whom I have worked. Of course, it is not necessary to be a parent in order to work successfully with children and parents. There are many clinicians who serve in caregiving roles who may identify with many of the experiences I will address here. However, I wish to highlight that the magnitude of this shift in my life significantly changed my experience of working with parents. What flooded into my experiences clinically was the emotional experience of being a parent.

When I gave birth to my children, exhausted by the physical experience, joyous and overwhelmed by the emotions and newness of it all, nursing babies whom at times I felt too weak to hold, the joy, fear, awe, and weight of responsibility of caring for two tender, fragile, little beings sunk in. At the hospital in the bed next to mine was a mother who had also just given birth. When not nursing, she spent her time socializing with visitors and the nurses on the ward who seemed to know her well. She chatted incessantly on the phone—not just about the birth of her baby but also about the news, politics, family gossip, and other elements of daily life that had faded from my awareness overnight. Who was this woman? She seemed to relish the opportunity that having a baby had afforded her to have a break from the ongoing-ness of daily family life and childcare. She was like an alien being to me. She was a mother in a completely different stage of motherhood. I was flummoxed and thankful when my father-in-law brought me earplugs so I could sleep.

After the months of anticipation, I was suddenly a parent. I saw the world through a different lens, much as I did some years later when my father died. The newness was like a fog at first, and, thankfully, in the hospital it felt like there were plenty of others around who seemed to know what they were doing. Suddenly, however, we were heading home. The nurses who had changed my babies' diapers and clothed and swaddled them seemed oddly absent as my husband and I set out to dress them for the journey home. Slowly, very slowly, we began to tackle what felt like a near-impossible task. Excitement flooded in as we got our daughter dressed and snuggled safely in her car seat. Marvelous! If memory serves me right, she mostly slept through our largely incompetent actions. Feeling ever so slightly encouraged, we did the same with our son—a much squirmier soul than his sister—and settled him into the car seat. Bravo! We might get home before midnight! We turned a bit more confidently to work on the straps of the car seat. Suddenly, clearly in response to our actions, there was an intense cry. AHH!! The fog evaporated. Laser-sharp fear followed. My husband and I looked at each other in panic. I'll never forget his face. In that moment I felt a profound shift in my basic perspective. *I* was the parent (and luckily not alone). I was no longer the child (albeit in my thirties)—that is, someone whose parents figured these things out. *I* had to act. We altered the strap. He stopped crying. It had taken a second, but I saw the world through very different eyes. I felt profoundly imperfect and suddenly unprepared. My journey was just beginning. There would be many more such moments—not so easily sorted out. That moment, that shift, that awareness has informed my work with every parent I have worked with since.

THE ROLE OF IDENTIFICATION WITH OTHER PARENTS AND ITS IMPACT ON THE CLINICAL PROCESS

No doubt becoming a parent allowed me to be in the room with parents in a new way. My identification and experience of self as a parent did not stay out of the therapy room as I worked with parents but filtered into the room in ways both subtle and explicit. I found that the shift in my role and identity as a parent were aspects of myself no less knowable to my patients than, for example, my style of engagement as a therapist or changes in my physical appearance. I could often feel a shift in the parents I worked with as they incorporated an awareness of me as a parent as well. This would emerge in subtle ways—for example, when intimate knowledge regarding a wide range of early childhood cartoon and pop culture characters, or a more than casual familiarity with the latest serialized chapter book (knowledge that at this stage of parenting I no longer have), indicated that we shared experiences that shaped the cultural backdrop of raising children in a similar period of time and location.

It is difficult, and I would argue not so useful to parents, to mask one's response or recognition of the experiences referenced by parents. Parents need to talk about the intimate details of their experiences raising children and some may be helped by knowing that the therapist may have a firsthand knowledge of some of the daily details that frame their days and nights. Often parents are not prepared for the shift in attention to the minutia that absorbs their time with little ones or the difficulty some may find staying connected to their children in particular moments or in ongoing ways. If the therapist can be present and even acknowledge similar experiences—for example, playing a game beloved by a child but mind-numbing to a parent (what *was* the appeal of *Pretty, Pretty Princess?*) or feeling the pull of the evening schedule and the desire for sleep when kids are wanting to be deeply engaged with us—this can be very meaningful to parents. It may allow them to explore somewhat differently their experiences about themselves as parents, their child, and the issues that brought them into treatment.

Looking back at my experience as a clinician and parent, I can see how elements of my experiences as a parent and the recognition of the needs addressed above filtered into elements of my practice in ways I was not initially aware of. Early on in my private practice I had the fortune of sharing office space with some dear colleagues with whom I trained. They were also parents of young children, and the presence of these colleagues in the suite was a welcome support when the stress of the work or parenting was high or the days long. My colleagues also saw children, and as the waiting room evolved, books for kids and parents appeared, as well as a desk where kids and parents could work and where games, paper, pencils, and markers were stored. Patients played with their parents, siblings, and other children as they waited for their appointments. Some sat quietly reading or observing others. Parents sought out information and resources from books and other parents with whom they formed a familiarity over time. The waiting room had organically become an extension of the treatment room and allowed for a continuation of the work as parents bonded, kids developed social skills, and relationships evolved. Sometimes the waiting room became a place for negotiation or for working through issues related to separation, attachment, learning disabilities, and a myriad of other issues.

The form and function of our waiting room developed, I believe, in large part because each of us in the suite were parents of young children, balancing work and time with our children. No one was unsettled by the sight of kids playing on the waiting room floor or the need to walk around a game in progress or the negotiations that sometimes occurred. While at times there was more or less of what a given clinician may have wanted, each of us knew the value of a desk for homework or parent's work, for toys and books while waiting, and the value of a child- and parent-friendly environment. Everything in the waiting room supported elements of the therapeutic work that extended beyond the therapy room and addressed the needs, stressors, and realities of parents or caregivers and the children they brought for treatment. All of us were aware of the impact and value of the connections adults and kids made with others during this period. For some, the waiting room became a space for calm, reflection, or bonding. For others, it provided an opportunity not to feel judged as social interactions unfurled in ways unwanted but available for therapeutic intervention. It was a holding environment for parents, care-givers, child patients, and their siblings in tow.

Over the years, my needs as a clinician and a parent have changed. As my children grew older, I increased my days at work, requiring a change in office and new suitemates who do not see children in regular weekly therapy. Though a desk, toys, books for adults and children, paper, pen-cils, and markers are all still present, the opportunities for the sort of interactions that took place in my old waiting room are fewer in my new suite. Parents, caregivers, patients, and siblings still play, read, or do homework, and treatment still sometimes extends into the waiting room space, but the sociology of my waiting room has changed. While I like to think that these changes were largely circumstantial, there is some truth to the fact that my own changing path as a parent has played a role in this. While valuing the opportunity for the kinds of interactions that un-folded at my old office, my own needs for breaks and a slightly slower pace took precedence in my new space. My books for kids have not been replenished with newer stories or characters that my patients might know, though they are still carefully selected, meaningful, and, in their oldness, new to many. I miss the days (as do some of my long-term patients) when adults and kids were able to make connections and en-gage with one another in ways that often extended the work of therapy into an unconventional space. Some of the vitality of the space is gone from the room as well, as it has morphed back into a space of privacy and waiting for many. I have to ask myself whether my shift from a period of intensive parenting has played a role in how these organic shifts took hold. The work is no less fruitful—just shifting in some of its forms and with a reduced feeling of mutuality with respect to being in a parallel and more active stage of parenting. With this transition, I have had to watch for ways in which parents react to these shifts within me and have had to learn to attend more to the stressors that were so easy to hold uppermost in mind when my own children were younger.

THINKING ABOUT THE THERAPIST'S EXPERIENCE AS ONE WORKS WITH PARENTS

When my children were younger, during parent sessions, suddenly I could be aware of wondering how our conversations and interactions might be different if we were sitting on a park bench or at a barbeque and not in a therapy office. What pearls of wisdom might I be free to receive? How might I engage differently in a dialogue about a given parent's experience with children older than mine? What information might I pursue with my own children in mind? As the therapist, it was easiest to acknowledge to myself what I gained from practical information shared by parents in our interactions. What activities, materials, games, books, or programs had I not known about or thought to introduce to my children? Over time these intrusions lessened, but they did not disappear. They might surface in a given conversation when a parent discussed a child's interest that one of my children shared, when one of my children also had difficulties similar to what a parent was discussing, or during periods of developmental change and transition in my family. Noting these moments and then readily returning to the work at hand was usually not difficult, though often I sought to hold these in mind as something that I might wish to pursue for my family later or research as a resource. Such moments were helpful for me to track with respect to my own process as a parent.

Other times more interruptive thoughts came to awareness during sessions with parents, especially when I felt unsettled in my own experiences and process as a parent. At times I found myself comparing my parenting to a given parent in my practice and noticed a range of different responses, from negative judgments that surfaced defensively to relief that difficulties in my own family paled in comparison, to feelings of admiration and inspiration. The therapist who is a parent must be attuned to such feelings as they emerge so as to better understand the source of these responses in themselves, their patients, and their ongoing experience of self as a parent.

Prior to becoming a parent, my style as a clinician had been to be rather bounded and to limit disclosures. This felt comfortable and fairly easy to do but was suddenly much more challenging as a parent. Before children I rarely had the need to reschedule a session, to inform a patient that I might need to take a phone call, or to establish a way of being reached in case of an emergency. But children get sick, doctors will call only when they can, babysitters cancel, flat tires occur, and we fear for the well-being of our children, even if sometimes a call from school is from a child about a missing book or a playdate, and not from the nurse's office. I could no longer be so opaque in my role. At times my anxiety, distraction, or agitation was evident at work in ways that I did not wish to be seen ("This is not an emergency—I will call you later . . ."). Often such moments would engender fruitful conversations with parents about their own experiences managing the conflicting demands of parenthood and other aspects of their life. Many seemed relieved to see how these moments unfolded for the therapist as well and served to reduce feelings of idealization, shame, or guilt. Often, I scrutinized my own feelings of being observed and perhaps found wanting as a parent or my feelings of concern about how a parent experienced my shifting focus away from them and their children. How these moments entered into and impacted various treatments became important in how I thought about and worked with each family affected. Before having children, I felt more capable of being clinically true to my training; after children, I had to accommodate a new way of thinking about being known as a parent in my role as a therapist and had to address the tension I felt about how I was trained and how I, and how other parent therapists I knew, was beginning to practice.

FEELINGS ABOUT WORKING WITH OTHER PEOPLE'S CHILDREN

Complex emotions can arise when the day-to-day demands of parenting balanced with work life eclipse the opportunity to be with our children with the kind of protected time and fullness of attention we provide our child patients during sessions. The relationship with our children is, of course, different, and there is a need for us to be with our children in ways that we are not when we do child therapy. In the need to rush home to cook dinner, attend to homework, get everyone to bed on time, and perhaps find a quiet moment for oneself or with one's partner, we can find ourselves in the position to envy the time we have with our child patients and feel guilty that we might not have this kind of time with our own children on given days or in moments when we or they so wish for it. We must be alert to feelings that stir when time with parents focusing on the needs of their children keeps us from bedtime with our own. While difficult, it is important to watch for ways in which feelings of competition, resentment, and camaraderie can sit side by side as we work with parents.

The very nature of clinical work with children and their parents also makes it difficult to think about how to help our own children understand what we do and to process the many emotionally complex meanings it may have for our children. What does it mean to share your mom or dad with other children and their parents? How do you share elements of your day while guarding confidentiality and being sensitive to your children's feelings and the potential meaning they may ascribe to your role as a therapist to other children and their parents? For me, as I tried to balance these conflicts, I found ways to talk with my children about my work in ways that I hoped would minimize any experience of feeling left out. I would take them to play at my office and found a way to speak in generalities about what I did on a given day. I would reference a particular activity from an earlier stage in their development ("I got to play with finger paints today") or tell a story about one of their old toys that, once outgrown, had found a new life in my office ("Mrs. Mouse was in trouble today"). Sometimes I would share something to bring a laugh ("I got walloped in chess again"). And other times I would highlight things that felt more serious ("I met with some parents about school stuff that's not going so well"). As they grew older and notions of privacy seemed more relevant in their own lives, I would talk about confidentiality. Looking back on this, I am aware that my solution was as much about managing my own feelings about the tension about being away from my children while addressing the needs of other children as it was about being mindful of a range of possible meanings the nature of my work might have in the emotional lives of my children.

VULNERABILITY AND THE WISH FOR VALIDATION AS A PARENT

As personal experience and awareness of the difficulties and vulnerabilities of being a parent filtered into my experience as a clinician, I became more attuned to the felt struggles of the parents with whom I worked. I found that the more I could begin the work with parents in their experiences of difficulty and be alert to feelings of fragility or shame felt in their experiences as parents, the better I could provide the ever important holding environment for them and to better know, reflect and time ways of supporting and intervening with them.

Following the work of Benedek (1959, 1970) and others (Furman, 2001; Lieberman and Van Horn, 2011; Steele et al., 2014), I have come to see that the wish to be validated in our capacity and actions as parents is a central aspect of the emotional experience of being a parent. I see this clinically time and again. I also know it to be true for myself and see this expressed in various ways with parents I meet in life outside of my office. As parents we often look to our children, to their successes and failures, to our painful feelings of acceptance or rejection, and to our attempts to soothe, guide, and love our children, as a means of determining how effective we are. We also look to see how others (e.g., relatives, teachers, parents, and even random individuals on the checkout line) perceive our children and our capacities as parents and in so doing measure ourselves against how we imagine others see us. This, in turn, impacts our valuation and sense of self as a parent.

Our work with parents often centers on addressing these feelings and helping parents to come to accept what it means to be a "good-enough" parent. This construct, so readily and easily referenced by therapists and admirers of Winnicott's great clinical wisdom (Winnicott, 1960), can be a very difficult concept for parents to truly incorporate into their experience. This is especially true when the child's behavior, as well as their play at home and in sessions, involves considerable expressions of anger, violent themes, and aggressive acts toward siblings, parents, or other children.

With families where there are fewer emotional resources and where the parents' and child's deficits, behavioral difficulties, emotional variability, and/or the needs of the family are overwhelming or comprehensive, it can also be difficult to recall the near universality of a parent's wish to do well by their children and their healthy desire to feel supported and validated in their experiences as parents. Families with these sorts of struggles can present a significant challenge to the therapist who may be thrust into a range of overwhelming feelings of their own as the therapy moves from crisis to crisis and the fragility of the parent is as much a focus of the work as the fragility of the child. With such parents, it is easy to activate feelings of shame or blame inadvertently as we seek to address the needs and deficits of either the child or the parent. As we respond to feelings of narcissistic injury surrounding the parent's experience of their child, we must also address moments when such injury is (or has been) evoked by others' responses to the parent and others' assessments or reflections regarding the child's behaviors, needs, or deficits. Parents thus affected may experience even more rage and injury in response to how this information has been addressed and whether they feel their own experience of raising a difficult child has been acknowledged with sufficient regard.

I will now briefly present aspects of two clinical cases, cases in which each parent's feelings of vulnerability in their capacity as a parent was impacted by the intersection of their concerns for their child and their own emotional responses to challenging behaviors and emotions. In both cases, the different emotional capacities and histories of each parent (as well as other elements that I will not address here) significantly differentiated the complexity and experience of the work with each family. However, an essential component in each treatment involved moments when my emergent recognition of the parent's experience, as well as my own awareness of what each parent evoked in me *as a parent*, allowed the treatment to move forward in necessary directions.

THE CASE OF H

H was a delightful four-year-old girl whose behavior and mood significantly changed after the birth of a brother. Initially loving and kind, and proud of becoming a big sister, H became sad, angry, and aggressive as her brother moved into toddlerhood and became a more significant presence in the family. In dyadic sessions with her mother, this girl would enact the birth, destruction, return to the womb, rebirth, hiding, finding, and destruction again of a tiny infant figure that could fit in the palm of H's hand. Her play was animated, repetitive, aggressive, exuberant, angry, and gleeful at times. She did not engage her mother in this play but would check in visually and physically, seeking a hug or a snuggle, or attempting to curl up under her mother's shirt. She sought comfort and reassurance even as she expressed joyful shock that her feelings and wishes could be represented, narrated, and tolerated without retaliation or rejection by her mother.

This play can be understood from various paradigms, but I wish to highlight the role of the mother's presence in the room. Comfortable in my role as child therapist, I fell fully into the potent meaning of the play. In parent sessions we had discussed the importance of her presence for her daughter in these sessions. Initial attempts by the mother to redirect this play when it first emerged indicated her discomfort, though she was able to allow this play to unfold as we processed the meaning and function of the play during parent sessions. Even though initially aware of her discomfort, I often forgot her quiet presence as she sat engaged in a project she had brought and took cues from her child as to the level of involvement that she wished from her.

As the intensity of the aggressive play increased and H repetitively played out murderous fantasies regarding her baby brother, thoughts of my children began to surface in sessions. My own experiences as a parent dealing with expressions of anger and jealousy between my children at home had perhaps surfaced, allowing this awareness to emerge. It may also be that it had kept me from being available to this mother's experience in the room earlier or more consistently. Once aware of this, I could redirect my attention to her needs and engage the significant emotional resources and strengths she had as a parent not only to process her response to the play and respond to the aggressive behaviors at home but also to explore how this experience with her daughter had challenged her experience of herself as a capable, good, and loving mother. My own discomfort with H's play as it unfolded had led to an important shift in the treatment that both mother and daughter could benefit from. That this little girl skipped out of each session with a smile on her face, happily holding her mother's hand, helped this mother as well as this therapist to continue the dyadic work that felt painful but was so necessary for this pair.

THE CASE OF B

B was a volatile young boy who lived with his mother and whose father was not engaged in decisions regarding his needs. Significant learning deficits, attention and executive function difficulties, impulsivity, and aggressive behavior were components of his clinical picture. Battles at home could rage for long periods and included physical escalations that were increasingly serious. Mother and child were embroiled in a painful cycle of rage, lashing out, recriminations, and despair. Cycles of aggressive behavior by B would fuel angry recriminations and blame by the mother. These became more intense when family members and others acknowledged or attempted to address the difficulties, fueling the mother's experience of shame and intensifying feelings of blame and rage at her son. Clearly, this was a very difficult pair to be with in the room.

This mother's sense of self as a mother had been deeply wounded by her experiences of others' responses to B. Often unavailable to parenting work, this work could only progress when topics or areas of focus were first generated and then carefully titrated and controlled by the mother to prevent feeling flooded by experiences of either herself or her son being judged as damaged goods. Despite these limitations, this parent continued to seek out professionals who could see past the behaviors, rage, and extremely challenging family system to understand the deep love and commitment she felt for B. This parent was clear in her awareness that she needed this support from others so that both she and her son could feel held, contained, and helped to move toward growth and change.

Initially, as I focused on the significant needs of this young boy, I felt blocked at every turn. Every intervention suggested had been tried and failed, new avenues for understanding struggles were rejected as naïve formulations, and offers to engage others were rejected as likely to backfire in unpleasant (if not dangerous) ways. As I fought against the desire to lay blame at this mother's feet and experienced a rising tide of helplessness and anger, I became more aware of feelings of being a failure as a therapist. The feelings of "not-good-enough-ness" of this mother were filtering through to similar feelings of my own "not-good-enough-ness" as a therapist. Furthermore, they were beginning to make me question my feelings of being a good-enough parent as well. I found myself wondering what I would do if my children were similarly wired. The feeling that I would not be up to the task continued to grow. Uncharacteristically, the phrase "there but for the grace of God go I" continued to intrude into my awareness.

Eventually, during a parent session when these feelings were particularly intense, I found myself holding my arms up in front of me, crossed at the wrist, saying, "I feel as if my hands are tied." (I have subsequently found this phrase and action useful in moments with other parents.) It wasn't until we could explore this experience over and over as it passed between this mother and myself in parent sessions, and also in dyadic sessions with her son, that this mother could feel seen and understood in the struggles and helplessness she experienced with B. When words could not be tolerated, this gesture served to connect this mother to feeling understood in her struggle, in her profound feelings of "not-good-enough-ness" as a parent, in her rage at B for his badness and for making her feel bad as well, and in the simultaneous desire deep down to help the child she so identified with and deeply loved.

Despite the different level of needs, experience, and deficits in the parents in these vignettes, each was able to do their best work and shift most when their own needs as parents and experiences of vulnerability in their capacity as parents could hold the equal (at times dominant) attention of the therapist. For both, a shift in treatment occurred when this therapist became aware of how her sense of self and experiences as a parent became activated during dyadic sessions with parent and child. This awareness allowed the therapist to shift focus to the needs of the parent while in the presence of their child, which was extremely meaningful to each parent. In being acknowledged and known and not abandoned by the therapist in these moments of great vulnerability and anger, each found the capacity to engage (in the case of H) and develop new (in the case of B) capacities to meet their child's needs.

COMPLEX REACTIONS TO THE THERAPIST AS PARENT AND THE IMPACT ON TREATMENT

Earlier I noted some very general ways in which a parent's awareness of the therapist's role as a parent can have a positive impact that sits in the background of a treatment. However, the therapist's visibility as a parent can also serve as a backdrop for more complex reactions that impact the process of and become entwined in our work with parents. Positive and negative transference to the therapist as a parent can stir us in ways that interfere with the parent's capacity to feel adequate, solid, or skilled as a parent. A parent's idealization, envy, dependency, competitiveness, need, feelings of inadequacy, and a range of other reactions to us can be starkly expressed, enacted, noted in an offhand way, or disguised playfully. Comments such as

"You make it sound so easy."
"Can you move in please?"
"Your kids are so lucky to have you as a parent."
"Where were you last night when things were out of hand at home?"
"You have no idea what it is like for me."

may slip into sessions with parents in ways that require us to stop and listen even as parents toss them out in an offhand way. In these moments, we are rarely seen in a realistic light as the parent we know ourselves to be. Of course, unpacking and understanding these comments and what they reflect about the treatment, a parent's transference reactions to us, and their own history as a child and as a parent is part of the work in any therapy. As a parent, however, balancing one's experience as a parent while having the lens turned on us as a parent may complicate how readily one takes in, sees, and responds to such comments. The therapist who is visible as a parent and highly identified in this role must be attuned as much to their own needs to be seen as a good parent and skillful clinician as to what these statements can mean for parents struggling at home. For example, a parent's idealization of us may be very gratifying or may trigger feelings of wishing to hide behind this way of being seen when the therapist may be experiencing times of transition or difficulty in a treatment or at home. Gratifications of this sort may interact in complex ways with the various dynamics parents bring to treatment. Parents who feel inadequate or at fault for elements of their child's difficulties can engage the therapist in repeated requests to learn how to better respond to their child's needs. Successful changes can feel gratifying to both parent (who feels success but also may be seeking validation and approval from the therapist) and therapist (who feels success in their comfortable role as a clinician engaged in parenting work). However, the feelings of success and validation provided may inadvertently create a cycle that maintains the parent's feelings of inadequacy and dependence on the therapist and the therapist's experience of self as a skilled clinician. Layer in feelings of competition, envy, transference, countertransference, and the parent's and therapist's attachment histories, as well as the therapist's own experience of parenting, and the dynamics enacted between parent and therapist can become complex very quickly. Such patterns of interaction may continue unobserved for some time until therapist or parent sees the cycle or perhaps a comment by the child or another individual in the parent's life may suddenly highlight the pattern. Successes and change in how a parent meets their child's needs and positive changes in patterns of interaction in the relationship must come to be owned by the parent. The therapist must be alert as much to the parent's dynamics, history, and sense of self as parent as to their own and the ways these may be impacting the treatment as it unfolds.

Once known in our role as parents, our children, too, are abstractions and ready figures for projection, parental assumptions, and transference reactions. As parents, clinicians may suddenly need to address a range of reactions and complex feelings about how or when one's children become a focus for a parent we work with. As therapists who are visible as parents, we must develop ways of responding to patient queries regarding our children. Warm queries and curiosity will be received differently, of course, from others that feel intrusive, that cause distress, that are uncomfortable to hear, or that raise feelings of alarm. As a parent, I came to pay particular attention in moments when I responded to generic queries regarding my children with a strident need to maintain a rigidly firm boundary, as if needing to protect my children from projection or the unwanted attention of some parents. Once clear, such awareness almost always brought me back to focus on the issues of boundaries in the treatment for the parent, the child, and their relationship. With these same families, I might also notice times when my attention turned to my children in uncharacteristic ways (for example, feeling preoccupied as to whether I should adopt some activity or style of engagement important to a parent-child dyad that on the surface seemed lovely but on closer examination served more to meet the parent's emotional needs and less the interests of the child). In each situation, what first eluded my awareness surfaced as I learned to track my responses to parents vis-à-vis my children.

OPPORTUNITY FOR REPAIR AS BOTH PARENT AND THERAPIST

Over the decades, many have written about the powerful opportunity that becoming a parent provides for reworking (or repeating) past experiences, difficulties, trauma, and conflict from our past with our children (Benedek, 1959; Fraiberg et al., 1975; Lieberman and Van Horn, 2011; Slade, 1999; Stern, 1995). Or, in the language of attachment theory, our early attachment relationships and internal working models of attachment set the stage when we become parents for how we regulate affect, relate to, and engage with our children. New opportunities for reworking old patterns of attachment are possible when we address and work to fully process our early attachment experiences allowing us to be present in new ways of relating and engaging with our children (Bowlby, 1969, 1973, 1980; Coates, 1998; Fonagy and Target, 1998; Main, Kaplan, and Cassidy, 1985; Slade, 1999, 2014). As our children move through the various developmental stages of childhood, elements of our history, emotions, models of parenting, and experiences long ago forgotten may be evoked. In part this occurs because of the easy accessibility of the emotions, thought processes and felt experience of our past as we again experience, in the constant daily interactions with our children and our child patients, what it is like to be one, four, nine, or thirteen, and our experiences from these times in our lives may be emotionally accessible and vital (and behaviorally engaged) in ways they have not been in a long time (Pantone, 2000).

In fact, I would argue that generally the potential for change or repetition is always alive as the therapist-parent engages in clinical work with children. When a therapist's children are of similar age to the children we treat, or when difficulties experienced by our child patients and their families resonate with our experiences from the past or in our current experiences with our children, there may be an exacerbation of these processes that are already active for the therapist. Depending on circumstances, clinicians may also at times be blind to the ways in which their past experiences are being played out at home or in a given treatment until something alerts us to the presence of these difficulties. It is interesting to consider how reverberations of and connections to our past that remain out of our awareness may first be visible in relation to a child patient or their parent, as we may be less defended or not as consistently triggered as we might be with our own children. Therapists as parents may be most vulnerable in this way when confronting new situations, stages of development, tasks or challenges within their family, as these are times when all parents are likely to struggle the most.

THE THERAPIST'S DIFFICULTY AS PARENT IN HOLDING ONTO NOTIONS OF THE GOOD-ENOUGH PARENT BEING GOOD ENOUGH

All parents have moments when they wish they could turn back the clock, take back a comment, or do things differently. When feelings triggered by our own or our children's troubles challenge our sense of self and capacity as a parent, clinicians will struggle with tolerating the not-so-great moments of being a "good-enough" parent just as readily as the parents with whom we work. For clinicians, questions such as

"Aren't I supposed to know how to deal with this?"
"Should this really be this hard?"
"Don't I help others with this all the time?"

may readily morph into the corollary:

"Who am I to be doing this work when I am experiencing my own difficulties as a parent?"

In these moments, our desire to feel competent as parents and as clinicians may become linked. Feelings of competence that have developed over years of working with families can be called into question in the rawness of moments when one has not been at one's best as a parent. These moments, in turn, can filter into the therapy room in many different ways.

How does one acknowledge and address this in oneself when also working with others in this vulnerable space? How welcome are we to addressing these feelings with the parents in our practices as we address these feelings in our own experiences and process as parents? This is work we can best do if as therapists we confront in ourselves the moments when we have repeated history or unlocked an interaction pattern previously inaccessible to conscious awareness. Success in supporting parents in our practices may in turn give clinicians the strength to look at their own struggles as parents with the knowledge that healing and growth is possible and enriching.

As therapists who are parents, we must come to recognize our strengths and weaknesses as parents and must truly come to terms with what it means (and what it really feels like at times of difficulty) to be a good-enough parent. As we do so, we may also be better able to help the parents in our practices to integrate disparate experiences of themselves, to increase their ability to be aware of their positive and negative capacities as parents, and to tolerate moments of difficulty as parents. Therapists who have not adequately addressed these issues in themselves may inadvertently engage in a process in our parenting work that may replicate the style of helicopter parenting that is so damaging to children but may serve to preserve the parent's or therapist's desire to minimize the feelings stirred by difficult experiences. Parents must know that they are also allowed to make mistakes and learn to repair after moments with their children when they have not be at their best.

THE ROLE OF DIFFERENCES IN SOCIAL LOCATION BETWEEN THERAPIST AND PATIENT

In developing a parenting style and identity as a parent, individual parents live at the intersection of their broader cultural background, spouse or partner's background, community, education, race, class, economic resources, religious background and practice, family culture and traditions, temperament, and a myriad of other factors. As clinicians working with parents from different backgrounds, we must be particularly attuned in our work so that we do not superimpose a style of parenting that is culturally bound by our own experiences, beliefs, and expectations while disregarding or not attending to the cultural background and parenting beliefs of the parents with whom we work. We must also guard against uniformly presuming cultural knowledge or imposing notions of cultural difference that may serve to exclude an essential awareness of individual difference and diverse experience that exists in all cultures. Styles of parenting and patterns of engagement can vary across cultures and within families with many variations that support the healthy development of children. Our earliest interactions in our families form our most basic implicit expectations of ways of being in the world such that it may be difficult to step outside of our own experiences as we work with families from different backgrounds. In our work with families, the therapist must be ready to examine one's own parenting ideology, experiences, history, and cultural bias and be alert to moments when we may unintentionally attempt to replicate what is familiar to us in our family and in our experiences of being a parent.

WHEN A PARENT'S EXPERIENCE OF THEIR CHILD IS DISCREPANT WITH THE CHANGING NEEDS OF THE CHILD

As parents, we can at times be blind to the ways our children are ready to move forward to new stages of development and ways of engaging the world and with us as they age. Sometimes external forces and sometimes our children are needed to press on us as parents to recognize their growing capacities and need for us to alter how we see and respond to them. In thinking about the ways in which parents must shift in how they engage with their children over time at different ages and stages and how to help parents with this process, I have found it particularly valuable when I have been able to be in touch with experiences as a parent when I have been out of sync with the shifting needs and experiences of my children.

Years ago, at a meeting proposing a change in how science and math would be taught at my children's school, I got caught up in an anxious and angry dialogue about whether this change was developmentally appropriate. When I described these changes to my children, I was caught off guard by their responses. They were excited and a bit nervous about the change. It was a step toward independence. They did not need the grown-ups to dial it back for them. They needed us to help them to make the transition. As a consultant at a private K–8 school at the time, I used to sit with teachers and administrators as various elements of the school program were addressed and respond to parents' anxious queries. As a clinician in private practice, I have become attuned to helping parents recognize moments when they are out of sync with the movement of their children out into the world. As a parent over the years, I have been caught off guard by this more often than I would like. Each time this has occurred, I am reminded again of the naïve graduate student who thought that being a clinician would guide me seamlessly in my process as a parent.

Over time, parents catch up to their children—that is, until the next time we find ourselves lagging behind the changing needs and experiences of our children. As parents, we can also be caught off guard by the internal emotional changes in our children over time, until again something occurs to catch our attention.

Several years ago I went to my college reunion. Reminiscing and seeing friends who had shared in this transitional time in my life was uppermost in my mind. My children were in high school, soon enough to begin their college process, and when I arrived at my dorm for the weekend, I fell into easy conversation with the young college student at the registration desk. I felt as if I were chatting with my children's friends. Old memories felt more alive, and some were newly recalled as I took in the sounds echoing off the nearby stairways, the dim light of the entranceway that looked toward the living room, the sight of the old-fashioned, well-loved furniture and the sheen of the wooden window seats that I had sat on decades earlier. As I talked with this young woman, perhaps because my senses had brought my memories and experiences as a college student to life, I became aware that my children were on the cusp of an emotional shift and change, and that they were already more like this young women, alive and vital with the stirrings of maturity and independence that I had not yet been ready to fully recognize.

The connection, once it occurred, was immediate and visceral. It had required being removed from the ongoing ways of being with my children in our day-to-day interactions. It had also required being confronted simultaneously with a young woman whom I could associate with my children and suddenly having access to a flood of memories and feelings of being that age. The nature of my response felt in my body and without words guided my growing recognition of the changes my children were embarking on. It has since informed subsequent conversations with parents of late high school and college-age students struggling or reluctant to see their children as young men and women moving into the world.

This asynchrony between where children are heading developmentally and where parents are ready for them to be in this process is an essential part of the parent-child process. It often feels like a paradox that the continuity of our daily experiences with our children can make it difficult to integrate new ways of seeing or being with them as they shift into new stages of development. Conceivably, the opportunity to be caught off guard in the ways described above is necessary for both parent and child. With each transition and shift toward growing independence, parents must find a way to let go of cherished ways of being with the children they have come to know in a particular stage of life, so that they may come to know once again the new people they are becoming. Parents may trail behind their children in times of transition, holding fast to layers of awareness of the children they have been at different stages. Children may require us to hold onto these layers, helping them not to lose sight of elements of their past selves as they move toward new ways of being in the world. As we move through these moments and shifts in our day-to-day interactions with our own children, we may be more alert to these moments as they arise for parents and children in our work.

WHEN THE THERAPIST'S NEEDS AS A PARENT INTERRUPT TREATMENT

At times there are moments in the lives of therapists when our needs as parents may surface and we become known to patients in very significant ways. Major events in the life of the therapist, happy and otherwise (e.g., pregnancy or the birth of a child, illness of the therapist or a family member, death of a family member, etc.), have the potential to intrude on the therapy in ways small or large. At these times, the therapist must find ways to acknowledge, address, and process these disruptions, their meaning to our child patients and their parents, and the therapist's own response to these events.

Several years ago my practice was brought to a sudden temporary halt in the aftermath of a serious accident and injury to my daughter, who was in high school at the time. Surgeries, a long hospital stay, ongo-

ing questions regarding unfolding needs, home tutors, an additional sur-
gery, physical therapy, follow-up visits, and an eventual full recovery
after many months resulted in numerous disruptions to treatment as I
focused on the needs of my daughter. Immediately, there was the need to
cancel sessions with no knowledge of when I would return. The calm
reassuring words crafted with the help of several colleagues regarding
my open-ended absence and plan for coverage were hard to deliver, as I
sought not to alarm patients when I felt nothing but alarm. The parents
and patients I spoke to immediately expressed concern that was welcome
but also made it difficult to stick to my reassuring script. Many of the
parents I spoke with gathered in that first call that a child had been hurt.
One parent shared later that she had known in that first call that something had happened to one of my children from "that unmistakable voice
you hear" when something bad has happened to a child. Ultimately, I
disclosed this fact to all parents as we discussed my return and sorted out
how to talk with their children about what was happening.

When I returned to see patients, there were ongoing ways in which
my needs as a parent altered aspects of my practice. Changes to my
schedule were significant, beginning first with a shift to weekend hours
and a reduction of the frequency of sessions for some. For many patients,
there was a disruption in the regularity of sessions due to the complexity
of family schedules and weekend obligations. Another patient was unable to make this shift, unfortunately speeding up a planned transition to
finding a therapist closer to where they were currently living. Later,
when returning to a regular weekday schedule, I had limited flexibility
and continued to need to cancel or reschedule appointments. Of a different order, awareness of these events and my needs impacted my child
patients and their parents on an emotional level as well. Most were aware
of high levels of stress and worry that triggered feelings of worry and
concern in them. Many sensed my difficulty and at the time shied away
from asking questions or sharing worries that surfaced in response to
these events regarding their own children. Others quietly addressed fears
about potential injury to themselves or their children and what it might
feel like to be a parent confronting such a situation. More worried what it
was like for me as a parent confronting these difficulties.

Largely, parents shielded their children from too much information,
providing a simplified version of what I had shared with parents and
which I explained as well on my return. Most of my child patients settled
back into our work where we had been with minor impacts once the
regularity of our work was reestablished. Many expressed curiosity
about what had happened. Most were very comfortable with a simple
explanation, though some wished for more detail. Many expressed a
sense of reassurance that I did what moms are supposed to do when a
child is hurt (e.g., take care of one's child). For those with a history of
trauma or loss, however, the disruption was more unsettling, and the

event and disruptions played out in various ways in their treatments for some time. For one family, the disruptions were too much, and after working for a few months, the parents made the decision to stop treatment at the end of the school year, having been unable to process the impact of the events and the ways it evoked an experience of traumatic loss in this family's history. The intrusion of my needs (a return to more normalcy with a shift back to a weekday schedule) once again at the expense of theirs (they wished to continue weekend hours, something they had requested at the beginning of treatment) was something we could not get past.

Parents' responses to these events were intense almost across the board. In the immediate aftermath, the humanity of parents was most notable. Their empathy, kindness, caring, and nurturing responses were warmly received and helped me to maintain the capacity to work with them and their children during a difficult time. For some, the opportunity to express kindness, empathy, and support for me was powerful. Other parents, with a history of difficulty expressing emotions in their relationships, developed new capacities to express emotion as they processed their feelings and response to the events. My undeniable stress and worry in my initial phone calls and in later moments had a powerful impact in many treatments. A number of parents did not wish to process their responses for some time and others never did. Looking back, I am sure I felt some relief regarding this at the time.

Over time, it has been fruitful and very interesting to discuss parents' reactions and responses to what unfolded during that period. Perhaps for some, and certainly for myself, time was a helpful factor in being able to have these conversations. There is a manner in which parents of the children in my practice at the time engaged with me in ways that evolved in the aftermath of the accident that felt different from our ways of engaging before the accident. It also felt different than the ways of engaging with parents who entered my practice after that time. With the parents who were in my practice at that time, there is a feeling of a shared history and an alteration in their way of knowing me and my way of knowing them that can bubble up in moments of our work. While elements of this experience are different for each parent, for many there is meaning in having come to see me as a parent experiencing difficulty. In momentarily being able to step out of our usual roles in response to these events, we shared a mutual experience of acknowledging and being acknowledged as a parent preoccupied in the aftermath of a trauma to one's child. Over time, follow-up queries have slowed down, though they surface from time to time. By and large it is an event in the past for my child patients. But for some parents in my practice, it remains an event that has taken on meaning in our relationship or with respect to their own experience of being a parent. As my needs receded into the background, it has become another way I am known and not known, and our work has returned to the more typical feel and rhythm of an ongoing treatment.

With my daughter's accident, the unfortunate substrate of an accident in my own history was activated and highlighted ways in which this experience had gone unprocessed despite considerable attention to these events. Over the years, I had come to recognize moments where current experience triggered an awareness of my accident and provided the opportunity to process this experience anew. In graduate school, we had to practice giving the Rorschach test. One of my responses struck me in my association to the Road Runner cartoons where Wile E. Coyote gets flattened in various ways in each episode. The image, but also the childhood form of the content, pointed me to address an event from when I was nine years old and I was hit by a car. Later, when my niece was almost this same age, I had a daydream in which I saved her by tackling and rolling with her out of the path of an oncoming car (like Jim from *Mutual of Omaha's Wild Kingdom*, who tackled wild animals from the back of a moving truck on the African plains every Sunday night in my living room for years). Still later, the first year of going house-to-house trick-or-treating with my children at dusk, the triggers were the cold, the waning light, and the drivers who carelessly sped home past my excited and distracted children. This is what we talk about as therapists when we say to parents that raising children can provide opportunities for reworking or processing experiences from the past that help parents to heal and that allow them to be in the present with their children in new or more flexible ways.

As I made links to my history and addressed these triggers, I was able to move forward in ways that helped me to not bind my children to me for fear of events that were out of my control. They grew. I was mostly less neurotic. I had rescued my niece in my daydream. My children were safe. All lay relatively dormant for some long period. After my daughter's accident, when she had healed and there was space and time to process what she and we had all experienced, I could see how my history had layered with hers and the events surrounding her accident. Once again my history was open and active but with a new layer. I had not saved my daughter from a terrible accident. It did not go as it did in my daydream. I understood my parents' experience of my event. I had more work to do—for her, for me, and for our family.

AS THE THERAPIST AGES

As therapists, we also move through our own stages of parenthood and the inevitability of getting older and having children who have left the nest. In this section I wish to think about the ways in which this transition out of active parenting may impact our work as clinicians and our work with parents who are younger than we are. Gone may be the immediacy of each earlier developmental stage that felt alive for us as our own children moved through them. As with childbirth, when the memories of pain fade with time, as our children age we may be prone to feel more distant from the felt stressors of the most difficult elements of parenting. When we do, or when others presume we have, we may run the risk of seeming less relevant to the parents we are working with—much in the way that Tuber describes this process for parents as their children grow and leave home (Tuber, this volume). The need to ask questions about a character or the latest collecting craze of middle childhood will highlight where on the path of parenting we are as will other clues that enter the consulting room. As we age, the nature of how parents see us is likely to shift. We may be seen as out of touch, less aware, wiser, or more "grand-parently." To remain relevant to the parents we work with, we must continue to remain connected to the rhythms of parents' shifting experiences as parents and to monitor and be in touch with our own feelings of moving into a new stage of family life.

Well into my writing process, I realized that the arc or narrative flow of this chapter was following my trajectory as a parent. Even as I noted in the beginning of this chapter that being a parent and working with parents and children have been intertwined in a process of mutual influence for me from the beginning of my experience in each role, a parallel process in the writing of this chapter was unfolding out of awareness until the trajectory of the narrative became clear to me. Now, at the end of writing the chapter, in part as a result of playing with these ideas, I am made aware of the ways in which the work is again changing as my children move out into the world and I have the opportunity to think about my own path as a parent from a bit of a distance. As I think about what feels vital or newly interesting to me about my work, I am becoming aware of the ways in which it feels refreshing to look back or reexperience periods of development and experiences in my work with children and parents and consider my process as a parent when not engaged in a time of being essential (Tuber, this volume).

As a therapist-parent, I feel lucky to continue to work with children and their parents as their children move through stages of development that my children have long ago (and not so long ago) moved through. I feel connected to the rhythm of this cycle of parenting even as I continue to incorporate into my thinking experiences in my role as a parent of young adults. I see in myself a new freedom to think differently about the work from a distance with a renewed curiosity and delight about the world of children as the pressing demands of day-to-day parenting are behind me. The thrill and joy of engaging in play as a narrative develops and provides a window into the inner world of a child is precious and hard to give up. It is a delight to play with kids long after mine have moved on. In play, I am connected to this vital link to my past—to memories of my children at play at home and in visits to my office when they came to play where Mommy worked.

REFERENCES

Benedek, T. (1959). Parenthood as a developmental phase—a contribution to the libido theory. *Journal of the American Psychoanalytic Association, 7,* 389–417.

Benedek, T. (1970). The family as psychobiologic field. In E. J. Anthony and T. Benedek (Eds.), *Parenthood: Its Psychology and Psychopathology* (109–36). Boston: Little, Brown.

Bowlby, J. (1969). *Attachment and loss,* vol. 1: *Attachment.* New York: Basic Books.

Bowlby, J. (1973). *Attachment and loss,* vol. 2: *Separation.* New York: Basic Books.

Bowlby, J. (1980). *Attachment and loss,* vol. 3: *Loss.* New York: Basic Books.

Coates, S. (1998). Having a mind of one's own and holding the other in mind: Commentary on paper by Peter Fonagy and Mary Target. *Psychoanalytic Dialogues, 8,* 115–48.

Fonagy, P., and Target, M. (1998). Mentalization and the changing aims of child psychoanalysis. *Psychoanalytic Dialogues, 8,* 87–114.

Fraiberg, S., Adelson, E., Shapiro,V. (1975). Ghosts in the nursery: A psychoanalytic approach to the problems of impaired mother-infant relationships. *Journal of the American Academy of Child Psychiatry, 14,* 387–421.

Furman, E. (2001). *On being and having a mother.* New York: International Universities Press.

Lieberman, A. F., and Van Horn, P. (2011). *Psychotherapy with infants and young children: Repairing the effects of stress and trauma on early attachment.* New York: Guilford Press.

Main, M., Kaplan, N., and Cassidy, J. (1985). Security in infancy, childhood and adulthood: A move to a level of representation. *Monographs of the Society for Research in Child Development, 50,* 1/2 (Growing Points of Attachment Theory and Research), 66–104.

Pantone, P. (2000). Treating the parental relationship as the identified patient in child psychotherapy. *Journal of Infant, Child and Adolescent Psychotherapy, 1,* 19–37.

Slade, A. (1999). Representation, symbolization, and affect regulation in the concomitant treatment of a mother and child: Attachment theory and child psychotherapy. *Psychoanalytic Inquiry, 19,* 797–830.

Slade, A. (2014). Imagining fear: Attachment, threat and psychic experience. *Psychoanalytic Dialogues, 24,* 253–66.

Steele, M., Steele, H., Bate, J., Knafo, H., Kinsey, M., Bonuck, K., Meisner, P., and Murphy, A. (2014). Looking from the outside in: The use of video in attachment-based interventions. *Attachment and Human Development, 16*(4), 402–15.

Winnicott, D.W. (1960). The theory of the parent-infant relationship. In *Maturational Processes and the Facilitating Environment,* 37–55. New York: International Universities Press.

SIX

Parental Humility

Kevin B. Meehan and Elizabeth Zick

Psychologists and co-parents of three young children, **Kevin Meehan and Elizabeth Zick** *focus on the ways the humility evoked by being a parent can have a dramatic impact on the processes inherent in being essential to our children. Nowhere is this more evident than in the role parental humility plays in the development of parental grace. Without humility, and its close cousins humor and perspective, the all-too-common moments of parental frustration, vulnerability, and confusion over the course of any given day can quickly erode into blame and shame. They poignantly note how neither of them understood this as so viscerally true until they had children of their own. These challenges of parenting suggest shifts not only in theory but also in practice. The experience of parenting, they argue, has provoked a fundamental shift in their understanding of this formative relationship, with the tendency to pathologize parents being put in a new light. This chapter therefore directly addresses the complexities of conceptualizing the parent-child relationship once having had children of one's own.*

———❦———

These are many things that make a good parent: patience, love, empathy, consistency. These are qualities that at once can be so simple and so complicated. It is less complicated when viewed from the outside of a family, objectively, clinically, without the hidden ghosts of past relationships. But though we strive to be rational, and in our best moments achieve a vibrant balance between how our capacity to reason and our reflex to feel inform one another, when we are in the moment, when we are at our limit, this balance is lost and all the rationality and even training in the world doesn't seem to matter. At those moments, being a trained psychologist carries precious little added value.

Neither of us understood this as so viscerally true until we had children of our own. The challenges of parenting have shifted our thinking not only in theory but also in practice. As a field, in an attempt to understand pathology and suffering, we often trace its roots to how someone was parented, perhaps to understand how to undo the damage that has been done, and perhaps to find an outlet of blame to attenuate the pain and unfairness of those who suffer from mental illness. But the experience of parenting has been profoundly humbling, and it has provoked a fundamental shift in our understanding of this formative relationship, and the tendency to pathologize parents has been put in a new light. This chapter will address the complexities of reconceptualizing the parent-child relationship now from the vantage point of two clinicians having children of their own.

INDIVIDUATE, BUT PLEASE DO IT GENTLY

After I (KM) became an adult, my mother shared with me that after leaving to take the train back to my college dorm, she would worry about whether I had arrived safely. However, she did not want to intrusively call me, or ask me to call her, so she would call my phone around the time of my expected arrival, and if she heard my voice answer, she would quickly hang up, comforted that I was okay. Because this was before the ubiquity of cell phones and caller ID, I would not have known who tried to call me; as a result, I had no idea this happened. I was astonished to learn this as an adult, and with some degree of guilt, as I recognized that she felt the separation more acutely than I did.

Developmentally speaking, this is a remarkable turn of events; one of my earliest flashbulb memories is of visiting the Statue of Liberty with my parents at about four years old and experiencing a moment of terror upon realizing that the woman with my mother's sweater whom I was following was not actually my mother. My mother was in fact only twenty feet away, and therefore we were quickly reunited, but that moment of terror remains a crystal clear early memory. How did I go from that terrified child to that indifferent young adult? Further—and this is a question I never asked until having my own children—how did my mother go from soothingly bemused by our separation at the Statue of Liberty to panicked at my traveling back to college?

As infants, we begin life completely dependent on our parents. Infants are born with only the most primitive tools for self-regulation (Stern, 1985). A newborn child may reduce arousal by looking away and avoiding eye contact with stimuli, or may begin to cry, which will function as a distress call for an externally regulating "other" to approach. However, other than this limited repertoire, the infant has few tools to self-regulate in the face of distress or over-arousal. It is from this vantage point that we can appreciate the remarkable process that takes place during the course of development, whereby the child progresses from being almost wholly externally regulated to internalizing the capacity for self-regulation.

Central to understanding how we make this remarkable transition is the notion of internal working models, or mental representations, of one-self in an affectively valenced relationship to others. In normal psychological development, the infant's experiences, initially organized around moments of pain ("I am uncomfortable and in need of someone to care for me") and pleasure ("I am now being soothed by someone and feel loved"), become increasingly differentiated and integrated representations of self and other (Stern, 1985). Thus it is through the experience of being regulated that the child comes to internalize a representation of self in relation to a regulating other, such that at a later stage of development the child is able to draw internally upon this "self being soothed by a regulating other" representation. While at an earlier stage of development external contact with the m/other was primary in down-regulating affect, the child may now internally evoke a regulating representation, and thus concrete contact with caregivers becomes a less immediate need. This capacity has been termed "evocative constancy"—the capacity to retain and recall an object that is no longer immediately present (Blatt, 1995). Evocative constancy is central to individuation, because it allows for the individual's internal experience to be "populated" with loving and caring others, even when no one else is present. Thus the internalization of a consistently present and reliable other is what paves the way for the capacity to tolerate aloneness and begin to individuate (Winnicott, 1958).

When the child internalizes a secure internal working model of self in relation to caregivers, a remarkable thing can occur—the child can dare to turn their back on caregivers and walk away from them (Bowlby, 1973; Tuber, 2008). Because the child experiences the caregiver as a secure base with whom there is little doubt of their enduring presence, especially in times of distress, the child can begin to take the parent's presence for granted and feel unconstrained in exploring his/her external environment and later internal states (Fonagy et al., 2002; Winnicott, 1958). This exploration allows us to play and explore the minds of others, which allows for a more realistic blending of good and bad, such that positive and negative qualities of oneself and others can be integrated into a complex, multifaceted representation of an individual (Kernberg, 1975).

However, less emphasized is the experience of this process for the parent—as the child, rightfully, can begin to take the parent's reliable presence for granted and turn their back while feeling unconstrained in exploring the world, the parent must contend with the pain of having and letting that back be turned on them. In fact, this may be a key quality of the "good-enough" parent—the parent will allow and even foster the child's turning their back, and will internally tolerate any hurt or discomfort and not burden the child with those negative effects (Winnicott, 1949). When I headed back to college, there's no doubt that my mother felt the sting of my leaving; the remarkable thing is the lengths to which she went to not burden me with that pain.

To be sure, we all exit childhood feeling the weight of our parents' pain to some degree. Winnicott (1949) discusses how the greater the parent's capacity to grapple with and contain complex affects, the less likely the parent is to enact those feelings in ways that may burden the child. For the parent to not contain their anxiety about separation forces the child to direct resources toward monitoring distance from the parent. When contained by the parent, the child does not feel encumbered to vigilantly assess the parent's emotional states, freeing the child up to explore (Tuber, 2008). Therefore, if all goes well, the parent will be in touch with the pain of the separation more than the child ever will. Very often parents intuitively know this (and thus hang up the phone). Adolescents are supposed to reject their parents and turn to the world; parents may know this process is normal but still terribly painful. A benefit of secure attachment is that the child does not have to attend to the parent in the same way—the child's security affords them the freedom to not have to over-attend to the fact that the parent is sad about the child's leaving. Of course the child may be quite aware of the parent's pain, but that awareness is not encumbered by a sense of responsibility for *fixing* that pain. Being securely attached frees both parent and child from having to feel that the other's pain portends a threat to one's own survival. The child may very well see and even empathize with the parent's pain, not know how long it will go on, or if and when it will be resolved, and yet not feel that it is one's burden to bear. The ambiguity of another's affect states becomes more tolerable.

In these moments of loss and separation, the parent must tolerate not only pain and sadness but also a loss of a sense of control and knowing. Some of the easiest moments in caring for a distraught child are when as the parent you know that you can fix the distress, and that your warm closeness is the answer to that distress. Of course, my mother was not scared in the way I was at the Statue of Liberty; unlike me, she knew how quickly and easily resolvable my discomfort was. Now, as parents, when our daughter falls and lightly scratches her knee, it feels like such a simple thing to help her in that pain and panic because we know what it is and how to fix it, and we hold her close and that feels good to her. She is terrified, but we are not; we know, we are in control, and we are the solution. The pain of parenting emerges most acutely when you don't know how to fix your child's pain, and when your closeness is not what feels good or remedies their distress.

SAYING GOODBYE TO YOU—AGAIN, AGAIN, AND AGAIN

Raising a child is in many ways is a long process of saying goodbye. From the moment they understand that there is a world outside of you, it is their job to start moving away from you, and it is your job to help them figure out how to do it. Basically, your job as a parent is to teach your child how to leave you. This is an incredibly wonderful and painful task.

Mahler, Pine, and Bergman (1975) contributed significantly to the understanding of the early parent-infant relationship and the process of a child becoming a separate being out of that relationship. Their work was based on extensive observation, over the course of nine years, of thirty-eight mother-child pairs from six months to three years of age in a play-room setting. Based on their findings of the developmental change in mother-child interaction, they elaborated the process of separation and individuation of an infant from his or her mother, from the initial experience of symbiosis and oneness to an understanding that mother and child are separate beings. Mahler and colleagues identified stages in this process, the first of which, *hatching*, is characterized by the infant's increased alertness and studying of the environment alternating with checking back with the mother who serves as an orienting focus. The second sub-phase, *practicing*, coincides with the child's increased ability to move independently in the world and separately from the mother, though the child still experiences a psychological oneness with the mother. The third subphase, *rapprochement*, is characterized by the child's increasing awareness of his or her separateness from the mother. This can be a period of tentativeness and fear about mobility and separateness, necessitating continual reassurance that the mother is present, as the child negotiates this new experience of the recognition of being apart and independent in the world. In the fourth subphase, *consolidation and object constancy*, the child has internalized the mother as a separate object, and is able to feel more secure about venturing away from her to explore the world.

The process of separation and the move away from the family continues throughout childhood, and in many ways throughout life. We can know this as psychologists, and we can help parents normalize and brace themselves for this, but we have a new appreciation for the profound sense of loss and frustration that may accompany this very healthy and necessary progression. Perhaps most surprising to directly experience is the reality that the movement through these developmental phases is not a steady rise, but rather jarring hills and valleys of progression and regression (Cicchetti and Cohen, 1995). As our independent-minded five-year-old cycles into a clingy period in which she only wants her mother, and at no more of a distance than three inches, a feeling of frustration arises at the seeming dissolution of her self-sufficiency. It is grounding to remember that such moments are something to be savored; in ten years' time, her mother's embrace may be among the last things she wants as the pendulum swings and she asserts every ounce of her adolescent autonomy.

And yet the process of individuation implies a oneness that gradually unzips into greater separation and autonomy. However, that initial oneness is largely more fantasy than reality, and the dissolution of that fantasy is itself a loss. As clinicians who are steeped in the attachment and infancy literatures, we entered parenting with the expectation of seeing the fingerprints of our every decision on the budding personalities of our children. Their emotional lives would be those we mirrored, their joy would be moments we'd create together, their frustrations would reflect the needs we could not gratify.

Then, one day, we look at our unbelievably feisty boy, mercurial and at times intensely dysregulated from the start, and stare in puzzlement at where it all came from. Then we have a second child, who, despite some physical resemblances, seems to have not a single overlapping trait with the first. After intense efforts to discourage and shield her from the culture of stereotypically gendered clothes and games, we stare at our pink-loving ballerina in puzzlement. By the time the third child arrives with a strikingly different personality from the first two—feisty, yes, but also mischievous and loud—we throw up our hands and have to reassess everything our embraced theories told us about what aspects of personality we believed ourselves as parents to be actively shaping.

PERHAPS WE WERE SEPARATE FROM THE START

Loss does not come with the slipping away of a oneness; loss comes with the realization that the oneness was never there in the first place. Solomon (2012) notes that the term "reproduction" is misleading, in that it implies a copy of two people, an assumption that all observable traits that cannot be traced back to one parent will then surely be visible in the other parent. He says, "In the subconscious fantasies that make conception look so alluring, it is often ourselves who we would like to see live forever, not someone with a personality of their own. Having anticipated the onward march of our selfish genes, many of us are unprepared for children who present unfamiliar needs. Parenthood abruptly catapults us into a permanent relationship with a stranger, and the more alien the stranger, the stronger the whiff of negativity" (p. 1).

Solomon (2012) emphasizes that it's not that parents struggle with the fact that their children are different people per se, but that their needs are different. In the end, we don't really care if our daughter loves princesses; it's more a signifier of the fact that what we want for her only very loosely correlates with what she wants for herself, and that gulf will only be more apparent as she grows. It is often quite difficult for parents to come to terms with this fact, particularly because parents are often not conscious of these needs and the ways in which they are subtly communicated to children.

Based on our needs, values, and intellectual bents, we each chose to become psychologists. However, those same states of needs and values, given different life events and trajectories, could have led us toward medicine, journalism, law, and so on. We say we want our children to be their own individuals and do anything they want, but if we are honest with ourselves, we mean that we want them to take any of the different but equally plausible paths we might have taken ourselves. We want the reassurance of "knowing" what will happen to them and what life will be like for them and may cling to these future paths as a way of assuaging ourselves that they will be happy and safe.

Of course we want our children to be cerebral and creative and curious about the world, to develop passions and a commitment to social justice. And in many ways they do share our traits, such as stubbornness, silliness, and tendency to fixate (EZ) as well as curiosity, intensity, and oversensitivity (KM). But the temperaments that accompanied them into the world and the characteristics they display that we cannot see in ourselves leave us bewildered and at times disheartened. How can we raise children we don't always understand? And given our years of training and work, how is it possible that we don't fully understand our own children? Truth be told, at moments we feel like the blind leading the blind, but feeling such moments of uncertainty has allowed us to develop a much deeper appreciation of the struggle to attempt to know one's children as both such a part of and so separate from oneself. And the harrowing confusion of this deep understanding and simultaneous ignorance has given us a visceral understanding of yet another kind of internal struggle that is so characteristic of being a parent.

AM I EVEN MAKING SENSE?

Many parents have said in exasperation that their kid never came with an instruction manual, though since that phrase came into favor there have been quite a few people who have tried to write one. It is comforting to think that human behavior is something that is rational and explainable, but it is often not, and parenting books frequently overlook this hiccup in human design. As psychoanalytic theory has long understood, how we relate to others and to ourselves is largely set on course by our early experiences in our families, and this is certainly no more evident than in the partners we choose and the children we make. We can have the accepted and correct tools and strategies to raise children from little animals into responsible, kind, and productive adults, but without an appreciation of the irrational, unconscious, emotional experience of what is it like to be with and raise a child, the tools don't get us very far.

What makes parenting so hard, so crazy-making? The external realities of every parenting situation will shape the experience, and no doubt culture, class, social location, and financial support will have enormous implications for the day-to-day experience of being a parent. However, what unites us is the internal reality that we are parenting in the context of a legacy of someone having parented us. Fraiberg and colleagues (1975) wrote, "In every nursery there are ghosts." This often repeated phrase speaks to a deeper appreciation in the world of psychoanalytic theory of the profound impact of unconscious processes, and how the early experiences with our own parents that set these processes in motion impact how we parent our own children. These ghosts take many forms and cast influence to varying degrees on how we understand our children, how we relate to them, who we want them to become. We learn to parent first by how we ourselves were parented, and this is no more evident than in the attachments we form to and with them.

WHAT WERE WE THINKING?

Why do otherwise calm, regulated individuals lose it with their children? What is so dysregulating about being a parent? One of the byproducts of the deep attachments that we form with our children may be that they are able to stir emotions and block our thinking more than just about anyone else in our lives. We fall deeply in love with our children; the difficulty is that love sometimes makes it hard to think. Bartels and Zeki (2004) evaluated the neurocircuitry of social bonding and found that activation of the attachment system inhibits the capacity for mentalization. They measured brain activity of mothers looking at pictures of their own and unfamiliar infants; looking at their own infant was associated with comparatively higher activation of regions associated with pleasure and dense with neuropeptides related to affiliation and bonding, and a relative deactivation of regions associated with social judgment and deliberation. Parallel findings have been observed in adult romantic love as well, which they note makes sense from an evolutionary perspective—attachment and mating is facilitated by not thinking too hard about it. This is thought to be why there is so little mentalizing in the honeymoon phase of romantic relationships, during which time so much is expressed preverbally (Fonagy, 2008). This may also explain why couples struggle to say what they want in the midst of intense arguments—the threat of loss of the relationship may activate the attachment system in ways that inhibit the capacity to reflect on the emerging process within the couple.

Our children continually activate our attachment systems, often in ways in which we are not aware, and it may be a challenge to mentalize the experience of the child at moments of such heightened activation. Parents can probably call to mind instances in which the babysitter or an extended family member could see and sidestep an emerging dynamic or wave of emotion that eludes the parent him/herself. Grandparents often remark that, of all of their relationships, this is the most joyous, and why wouldn't it be—they are brimming with love for the child and yet unencumbered by the entanglements of the parental relationship that tax the attachment system and ensnare parents in conflict (see Meyer, this volume). Further, the more fraught the relationship, the more likely parents will struggle to mentalize the experience of that child. The capacity to understand the mind of another is sometimes regarded as a trait; some people are simply more skillful at it than others. However, emerging research confirms what we intuitively know—our capacity to be thoughtful and mentalize the experience of another is highly dependent on context, waxes and wanes with our emotionality, and is more challenging with those whom we are emotionally entangled. Such disparities in the capacity to mentalize have been observed in clinical contexts, with research demonstrating that a given therapist may differ in his capacity to mentalize the experience of different patients depending on how stuck in emotional enactments he feels (Diamond et al., 2003).

Findings from research on self-regulation further clarify why being a parent may at times be so dysregulating. Similar to mentalization, the capacity for self-regulation is often discussed as a trait that is stable across contexts. In fact, as adults our capacity for self-regulation is highly variable and often driven by contextual factors (Bauer and Baumeister, 2011). We have finite self-regulatory resources that we are continually shifting according to the pressures on us at any given moment. As a result, efforts to regulate one domain cut into our capacity to regulate others. For example, with a relatively sturdy capacity for regulation, in a moment of calm, I might show restraint in not reaching for a bowl of M&Ms that the secretary has placed on her desk next to my office. However, following a distressing conversation with a coworker, as I seek to regulate my anxiety and esteem, my capacity to refrain from eating the M&Ms will be diminished (Vohs and Heatherton, 2000). The capacity for constraint is not static but fluctuates according to what other domains are being regulated at a given moment. Therefore, much as we may try to hold it together, the regulation of a given stressor may lead to lapses in self-control elsewhere. A seemingly benign request for a snack may receive a snappy response as the baby is crying, the doorbell is ringing, and the pot on the stove is boiling over.

The capacity for self-regulation will be diminished in the context of not only heightened emotions (i.e., an upsetting event) but also prolonged emotions (i.e., an enduring stressor) and shifting or conflicting emotions (i.e., an exciting opportunity that arouses both joy and anxiety). Positive emotions, such as exhilaration and joy, also require some degree of regulation, and therefore may lead to lapses in self-control (consider the impulsive, reward-oriented decisions that people make at celebrations). Thus even good feelings may cut into our ability to self-regulate (Bauer and Baumeister, 2011).

The nature of self-regulation has direct implications for the experience of parenting, in that the intensity, endurance, and lability of emotional experiences are enormously taxing on parents, which may lead to "uncharacteristic" decision-making, lapses in judgment, and emotions that are difficult to restrain. Parents intuitively know this, often noting that "if I just had a break," a given calamity may have been averted. Those with young children often remark that even going to the bathroom is no longer a solitary activity, that there are periods within which one's personal space and emotional resources are continually being impinged upon. The lability of the emotional highs and lows can be destabilizing, with cycles of joy and exasperation all before a morning cup of coffee.

Parents may be caught off-guard by subsequent lapses in emotion and judgment, thinking of themselves as individuals with otherwise sturdy emotional control. As psychologists, we had always regarded ourselves as surely having good impulse control, as evidenced by the endurance to achieve in our careers in lieu of choices with more instant gratification. However, this conflates two kinds of self-regulation that are only loosely coupled. The self-regulation literature has focused on the notion of grit, or the persistent pursuit of long-term goals even in the face of stress and obstacles (Duckworth et al., 2007). Given years of schooling and professional hurdles, it is reasonable to suggest that as psychologists we have at least a moderate amount of grit. However, that kind of long-term regulatory endurance is different from the momentary capacity to inhibit a strong feeling or desirable behavior, which is often referred to as effortful control (Rothbart et al., 2003). Successful people may be high on grit and yet prone to momentary fluctuations and lapses in effortful control (consider Bill Clinton). As both parents and professionals who think of ourselves as having good impulse control, we find ourselves shocked and ashamed of "losing it" with our kids in ways that fly in the face of how we see ourselves. We often have moments in which we are exasperated with our kids and find ourselves setting a limit in ways that, from the standpoint of everything we know about attachment theory and behavior modification, is completely and utterly wrong. With us both being clinicians, we sometimes think that we should "know better"—surely at least one of us should be able to come up with something—but in these intense moments it's hard to know anything at all. (After a particularly poorly executed limit I sometimes wonder to myself, "Who would be more horrified by how that played out, Bowlby or Skinner? Not a secure base moment, and on an intermittent punishment schedule, no less.") Our experiences in parenting in these moments, in feeling such high intensity emotion, be it anger, sadness, or joy, that overwhelms our capacity for more rational and measured reasoning, have often left us bewildered and humbled by the capacity of our children to evoke these feelings with such force.

Complicating things further, self-regulatory lapses may compromise our capacity to be empathic toward those with whom we are embroiled. Eisenberg and colleagues (1988) have found that individuals high in effortful control tend to experience sympathy (an other-oriented response to another's condition) rather than personal distress (a self-focused response to another's emotion). Put differently, those who are internally well modulated are able to direct their resources more toward empathizing with and attending to the distress that others are experiencing. However, those less well modulated need to allocate all of their regulatory resources inward in the service of calming themselves down, and this may be at the expense of being able to see and identify with the distress of others. In fact, it may often be adaptive for those less well modulated to overlook another's distress when they are themselves distressed, out of concern that taking on another's distress might only escalate their own. Thus, someone sufficiently modulated can afford to identify with someone else's distress while maintaining a comfortable distance from it, allowing room to reflect on and reflect back that state of distress. When calm, another's distress is a shame; when upset, another's distress is a liability.

As parents, our capacity for empathic concern is therefore likely to fluctuate to some degree as distress rises and falls. Parents can quite easily identify with these findings—at times their child's distress breaks their heart, whereas other times (when juggling multiple stressors, when sorting through multiple emotional demands—negative or positive) their child's distress may feel more like a burden. This, too, may evoke guilt in parents, who feel like they should be able to evoke a more tender response than they are actually feeling at that moment.

AND YET YOU BRING ME SUCH JOY

All of this begs the question of why we chose to parent. Other than the obvious benefits of passing on our genetic material and having someone around to take care of us when we are elderly, it is a reasonable question. For those who become parents on purpose or accidentally, ideally, something more than just obligation or tradition or biological imperative keeps us tethered to our offspring.

The uncertainty and despair of parenthood is equally matched, if not outweighed, by the ecstatic joy and meaning that children bring to our lives. In an analysis of two hundred studies comparing parents to nonparents, the transition to parenthood, parents' experiences while raising their children, and studies comparing different types of parents, Nelson and colleagues (2014) begin by affirming that "children are the fount of our greatest joys and the sources of our greatest sorrows" (p. 1). They propose from their findings that the aspects of parenting that engender negative emotions and financial difficulties, that disrupt sleep and marriage, contribute to unhappiness. But if parents' basic needs are met—if they experience subsequent social connection, validation, and positive emotions through parenting and, importantly, experience the greater sense of meaning and purpose in life of raising children—there is great potential for happiness and joy.

As with the more challenging and destabilizing forces that parenting brings forth, we have been awed by the power of our children to evoke such intense joyfulness, delight, and satisfaction in us. It is the reexperience of the delight and innocence of childhood. It is the feeling of omnipotence at creating new life. It is the deeply felt sense of purpose and meaning in the privilege and responsibility of nurturing another life, a satisfaction of the drive to participate in the onward march of the human race. It is the promise of seeing the best parts of ourselves carry on and outlive us; as Solomon (2012) writes, "We depend on the guarantee in our children's faces that we will not die" (p. 2). But maybe it is not just being satisfied by the possibility of a replication of ourselves, and a sense of therefore achieving immortality, but also that we can cast aside the bad and pass on the good. We carry on in hopes that the fruits of our labor can triumph over the less desirable aspects of ourselves and can be realized in these people to whom we are so essential.

In the final analysis, having the grace to maintain humility while being a parent provides the foundation for having hope for their future, and hence in the future that you are helping to shape. This is what supports and drives us through the madness and doubt. And in many ways that is also the most important thing we can give the individuals and families we work with, the hope that there is always the possibility of change, of greater satisfaction and connection, even amid the anguish and confusion and discord. There is hope in our children's faces that the future may very well be better, and that sustains us.

REFERENCES

Bartels, A., and Zeki, S. (2004). The neural correlates of maternal and romantic love. *NeuroImage, 21*, 1155–1166.

Bauer, I. M., and Baumeister, R. F. (2011). Self-regulatory strength. In K. D. Vohs and R. F. Baumeister (Eds.), *Handbook of self-regulation: Research, theory, and applications*, 2nd edition (64–82). New York: Guilford.

Blatt, S. J. (1995). Representational structures in psychopathology. Rochester symposium on developmental psychopathology, vol. 6. S. L. Toth and D. Cicchetti (Eds.), *Emotion, cognition, and representation* (1–33). New York: University of Rochester Press.

Bowlby, J. (1973). *Attachment and loss*, vol. 2: *Separation*. New York: Basic Books.

Cicchetti, D., and Cohen, D. J. (1995). Perspectives on developmental psychopathology. In D. Cicchetti and D. J. Cohen (Eds.), *Developmental Psychopathology*, vol. I, 3–22.

Diamond, D., Stovall-McClough, C., Clarkin, J. F., and Levy, K. N. (2003). Patient-therapist attachment in the treatment of borderline personality disorder. *Bulletin of the Menninger Clinic, 67,* 227–59.

Duckworth, A. L., Peterson, C., Matthews, M. D., and Kelly, D. R. (2007). Grit: Perseverance and passion for long-term goals. *Journal of Personality and Social Psychology, 92*(6), 1087–1101.

Eisenberg, N., Schaller, M., Fabes, R. A., Bustamante, D., Mathy, R. M., Shell, R., and Rhodes, K. (1988). Differentiation of personal distress and sympathy in children and adults. *Developmental Psychology, 24*(6), 766–75.

Fonagy, P. (2008). A genuinely developmental theory of sexual enjoyment. *Journal of the American Psychoanalytic Association, 56*(1), 11–36.

Fonagy, P., Gergely, G., Jurist, E., and Target, M. (2002). *Affect regulation, mentalization, and the development of the self.* New York: Other Press.

Fraiberg, S., Adelson, E., and Shapiro, V. (1975). Ghosts in the nursery: A psychoanalytic approach to the problems of impaired infant-mother relationships. *Journal of the American Academy of Child Psychiatry, 14*(3), 387–421.

Kernberg, O. F. (1975). *Borderline conditions and pathological narcissism.* New Haven, CT: Yale University Press.

Mahler, M. S., Pine, F., and Bergman, A. (1975). *The psychological birth of the human infant.* New York: Basic Books.

Nelson, S. K., Kushlev, K., and Lyubomirsky, S. (2014). The pains and pleasures of parenting: When, why, and how is parenthood associated with more or less well-being? *Psychological Bulletin, 140*(3), 846–95.

Rothbart, M. K., Ellis, L. K., Rosario Rueda, M., and Posner, M. I. (2003). Developing mechanisms of temperamental effortful control. *Journal of Personality, 71*(6), 1113–44.

Solomon, A. (2012). *Far from the tree: Parents, children and the search for identity.* New York: Simon & Schuster.

Stern, D. N. (1985). *The interpersonal world of the human infant.* New York: Basic Books.

Tuber, S. (2008). *Attachment, play and authenticity: A Winnicott primer.* Lanham, MD: Jason Aronson.

Vohs, K. D., and Heatherton, T. F. (2000). Self-regulatory failure: A resource-depletion approach. *Psychological Science, 11*(3), 249–54.

Winnicott, D. W. (1949). Hate in the countertransference. *International Journal of Psycho-Analysis, 30*(2), 69–74.

Winnicott, D. W. (1958). The capacity to be alone. In *Maturational processes and the facilitating environment* (1979), 29–36. New York: International Universities Press.

SEVEN

Rage, Forgiveness, and Acceptance

Parenting Through Difficult Moments

Paul Donahue

*In this chapter, **Paul Donahue** speaks as both parent and clinician to the psychological burdens inherent in dealing with rageful and aggressive feelings brought out by both domains. Although there is a fledgling trend toward realism in our culture's depiction of family life, there remains a persistent image in the media and in our collective fantasies of the idealized, loving family to which many parents aspire. That imagery regularly clashes with the experiences of parents in the trenches—namely, that their day-to-day lot involves considerable blood, sweat, and tears, as well as negative interactions with their children. This chapter is intended to give voice and meaning to the rage and desperation that many of us have experienced in critical moments with our children. Rather than shun or deny feelings of anger or rejection, it will be suggested that parents can benefit from expressing their frustration more openly, to countermand feelings of shame and guilt that can lead to more toxic interactions and feeling of isolation and alienation from their children.*

The therapeutic process can facilitate a more realistic understanding of expectations in the parent-child relationship, and allow parents to be more forgiving of their own rage and their children's transgressions. However, the critical element in changing negative family dynamics often involves an acceptance of the inevitable clashes of will and desires at home. Parents can gain significant relief as they come to recognize that these need not be irrevocable moments that define the relationship with their children, or inevitably predict who they will become later in life.

—◦◦◦—

"This is why I didn't want to be a parent. I feel angry all the time. . . . Being a parent is forcing me into these feelings. It brings out the worst in me. I don't want to feel these things!"

These are the words of Sandy, just past forty, lamenting her inability to remain calm in the wake of her children's transgressions. Wracked with guilt and sadness over her failings, she had come to me seeking counsel on how to be a better mother.

Sandy's despair puzzled me at first. By her own account she was a dedicated mother who was juggling her part-time job in an advertising agency, managing her household, and caring for her two school-aged children. She was a hands-on mom who reveled in showing her kids how to plant vegetables, sew their own clothes, and play basketball. Sandy loved being on the road and outdoors with them, and she regularly sought out new adventures for the family. At home she taught her son, who struggled with anxiety and irritability, how to meditate, to breathe deeply and to find calming activities for himself. She soothed him after his tantrums and in our work together quickly learned how to effectively prep him for difficult situations. When her adolescent daughter began to challenge her more frequently, Sandy was taken aback but quickly recognized that her new defiance was a positive step for a girl who had always been well behaved and mild mannered.

What was most intriguing, however, was Sandy's description of her anger. She rarely lost her temper, at least not so far as I could tell. There was a good deal of bickering in her home and arguments over the kids completing their chores or getting ready for school. Of the few moments she described as "losing it," one involved yelling at her son for crossing the street without looking both ways, fearing he would be in danger of being hit by an oncoming car. Sandy's expressions of anger all appeared fairly typical, and it hardly seemed to warrant the self-loathing she felt so deeply.

Sandy's recriminations did give me reason to pause, however. If these outbursts were so damaging in her mind, what must I be doing to my own children? My two teenage daughters and I were often at odds during her first year of treatment. As the older one was preparing to leave for college, our battles were escalating. I had less inhibition in expressing my anger than Sandy did, and despite "knowing better," I was often caught in a cycle of defiance, rebuttal, and explosiveness with my children. The trigger could be small, like my daughter refusing a request to move the car in the morning before school, but my reaction could be outsized and instantaneous. I was struggling with thoughts of separation and what I felt to be a sharp reduction in my perceived authority, and I wasn't proud of the result. How could I help guide Sandy to tolerate and find expression for her anger when I had trouble containing my own frustration and rage?

THOUGHTS ON RAGE RESPONSES

Most psychodynamic clinicians work on the assumption that early humiliations and shame-inducing episodes often lead to feelings of narcissistic rage and expressions of destructive aggression in adolescents and adults (Nason, 1985). Despite contrasting views on the relative influence of developmental insults and the biological imperative of aggression, few theorists counter the widely held notion that less than optimal parenting, particularly as it involves overt expression of anger and rejection, is linked to predictable and pathological outcomes in children. Advances in infant and toddler research, most notably by Stern (1977) and his colleagues, has allowed for a more nuanced view of the caretaker's role in the development of aggression, and the interaction between temperament and parental attunement. Nonetheless, in boiled-down form, there persists a notion of the "disappointing or abusive parent" who induces his children to express their rage at "people who were not responsible for the original hurt and humiliation" (Ornstein, 1997). Even for theorists who tout the adaptive power of aggression, there remains a duality between parents' attempts to "squelch the child's anger," which tends to increase rage responses, and "parental reception, understanding and attuned responsiveness to the child's frustration, anger and aggression," which leads to more adaptive assertiveness and improved coping skills (Fosshage, 1998).

How does this attuned responsiveness look in practice, and is it a realistic expectation for most parents in most situations? Are there alternative, more direct and expressive responses that are valid in some cases and do not have such deleterious effects? We will struggle with these questions for the rest of this chapter. In no sense am I advocating an unbridled expression of rage by parents toward their children. The ability of mothers and fathers to tolerate and not act on negative affect is still a cornerstone of good parenting. My concern is that the emphasis on helping parents "remain calm, firm and unyielding" (Axelman, 2009) in moments of emotional tumult puts undue pressure on the family system, and the parents in particular, to live up to an idealized and largely unattainable image of modern family life.

The popular parenting literature does much to perpetuate the stereotype of the angry, hurtful parent who traumatizes their children. In an otherwise helpful guide on how not to magnify and overreact to children's transgressions, McKay and his colleagues (1996) begin with stark research findings that make a direct link between parental anger and a range of negative outcomes in children and adolescents, from depression

to delinquency to poor school performance. There is little effort to provide balance or distinguish chronically abusive homes from ones in
which angry responses and positive interactions exist side by side. The
popular book *Raising Your Spirited Child* (Kurcinka, 1991), which includes
some compelling suggestions for how to manage and engage children
who have difficult temperaments, takes a softer and less critical approach
to parents who lose their cool. The advice provided, however, still tends
toward helping parents avoid direct confrontation when angry, resorting
instead to calming self-talk, getting additional rest, and taking a break
from their children in the most heated moments.

   These are sound strategies, and it can be useful to remind parents of
their own capacity for aggression and their need to find other outlets for
their anger. Few parental observers will fully acknowledge the more profound moments of rage that are not so easily set aside. Winnicott (1947),
who as a pediatrician knew parents and young children well, remains
one of the few clinicians who does not shy away from the core dilemma
of parents: that they may (and in fact must) hate their children if they are
to truly love them. Parents' awareness of their own capacity for rage, and
their ability to check but not disown their aggressive impulses, are necessary for children to integrate a more complete object representation, and
to develop a more evolved sense of concern and attachment to their parents (Nason, 1985). Winnicott's challenge to parents is to provide a good-
enough holding environment, one that includes allowances for a range of
positive and negative emotions and intense moments of intimacy and
rage. How parents take up that challenge, and face their own fears of
aggression and potential loss of control, will largely define their relationship and help or hinder their children's mastery and expressions of their
own best and worst impulses.

                    THE ORIGINS OF PARENTAL RAGE

Many of us grew up in homes that are far different from the ones our
children occupy. The comparative luxury and opportunities afforded to
our kids can seem like a fantasy land from the vantage point of our own
childhood, even for those of us who grew up in comfortable middle-class
families. These material differences are noteworthy, but for many adults
the more compelling distinction lies in the range of emotional expression
that their children enjoy. Open expressions of love and affection, joy and
sadness, and anger and frustration, are marked contrasts to their own
more reserved and emotionally stifling childhood homes.

   While we can readily accept the overt displays of warmth and love,
it's the anger that often gets to us. As my children grew into teenagers, I
failed to catch myself on several occasions from castigating them in the
name of my own father: "I can't believe you said that to me. I would

never have spoken to my dad that way." Of course I wouldn't have. Although he was a warm and generous man with a twinkle in his eye, my father had a serious temper, and when you tripped the switch, you knew there would be a significant response from him. Usually it involved raised voices or threats of punishment and, on rare but not unheard-of occasions, a slap from the back of his hand. Mostly you learned not to cross that line and were careful not to disturb him after a hard day's work.

My story seems unremarkable and was no different in basic form from many of my friends and colleagues of a certain age, who grew up in places where traditional parental roles and authority were rarely questioned. It was not an abusive home, not filled with rage or rejection. We children were expected to be respectful and to work hard, and we were allowed to play and left to our own devices when there was no work to be done. Yet there was a clear distinction between the privileges of adults and the limited rights of the children, a mainly unspoken boundary that had to be observed, lest you suffer the consequences. This family model of control and parent's reacting with scorn and punishment when one bent the rules was not uncommon.

Though twelve years my junior, Sandy grew up in a similar fashion, but in a home that was more rigid and anger-filled. Her father left the family when she was still an infant, and her mother remarried not long after to a widower who had two daughters of his own. He was a mostly kind man and not overbearing, but he traveled frequently and spent long hours away from the family, at work or out with his colleagues. Her mother, who stayed home with Sandy, was a bitter woman who brooked no challenge. Extremely needy and domineering, she rarely asked Sandy about her own experience or consulted her opinion. "Growing up there was no discussion, no flexibility; I was not allowed to share my feelings or even to speak up." Her mother sometimes disciplined her physically and was often cruel and rejecting, especially if Sandy was not tending directly to her needs.

Sandy was determined not to be that type of mother. She opened up conversation with her kids, and allowed them to speak their minds. She set aside quiet times to talk, to inquire about her children's friendships and feelings about school, to celebrate their successes, and to explore their frustrations and disappointments. Much to her chagrin, they often had "nothing to say," at least not when it came to establishing an open dialogue about their desires and dreams that she so longed for.

When it came to anger, however, they rarely held back, and in the face of her children's rage Sandy struggled mightily. She prided herself on being "a lover, not a fighter," and worried that she could not handle "the total negativity" from her son: "It is awful all day long. I don't know what to do. I just feel so angry, frustrated. All the negativity feels like a cycle, like an addiction." Sandy had thoughts of hitting her children to control them, as her mother had done frequently to her, but she resisted the urge to do so. When she got enraged and lost her temper, she felt humiliated and engaged in bouts of self-loathing. Her anxiety tended to spike in these moments. Mainly she felt paralyzed and wished to withdraw into her own work and mind space.

This cycle that Sandy described of angry lashing out by the child, rage response of the parent, and subsequent feelings of shame and self-deprecation (often by both parties) cannot be easily undone. The rage adults feel can have multiple etiologies, including later-in-life trauma, but often it can be traced to early childhood experiences of frustration that "includes the sense of narcissistic injury, a wound to pride, a shaming and humiliation to the sense of self" (Lichtenberg and Shapard, 2000). I can recall jumping up from my seat at the head of the dinner table and rushing to verbally confront my youngest daughter, who had just cursed out "the whole f'n family" after an argument with her sister. I was not merely hellbent on explaining to her the rules or imposing a suitable punishment; I was reacting instinctively to what I felt were a series of minor insults to my sense of autonomy and freedom to speak my mind as a child. The rawness of having that wound touched, of the perceived threat to my own prideful position of authority, was too much to bear in the moment, and I lashed out at her. My subsequent apologies and regret over having "lost it" with my daughter did little to contain the sense that I was not in control of my anger, nor did it stymie the feeling that I was falling far short in my efforts to avoid replicating the pattern of control and shaming that was part of my family's legacy.

ANGER, LOSS, AND THE SUBJUGATION OF SELF

If touching early narcissistic wounds can arouse a rage response in parents, so, too, can reminders of later deprivation and loss. When parents are describing their struggles with their children, they often cite their child's self-involvement, lack of appreciation and the apparent absence of concern for others. Labeling children as "spoiled" or "entitled" remains fairly common in my office, despite the fact that these value judgments implicate parents as much as the child. Someone, after all, has to be doing the spoiling. Attempts to reconcile the misgivings over how children adapt to perceived abundance with the urge to give them a more comfortable life creates inherent conflict in parents who grew up in far more modest circumstances.

The mother of nine-year-old Antonio, an impulsive and intense boy who was acting out in school and at home, described him as "such a selfish kid, he doesn't do anything for other people; he never shares with his brothers." His father was more sympathetic to Antonio, and could relate to his temperament and high-energy level, but he still couldn't help recalling his own childhood, where family had to come first. He always had to pitch in and share with his siblings. Although he worked hard to control himself and regretted it mightily when he lost his temper, he would often erupt at Antonio on weekends that they spent together. Another father grew visibly upset in my office when describing how his eight-year-old son never showed any gratitude: "He doesn't realize how much we do for him!" As he elaborated further, it became clear that his son was a somewhat immature and egocentric child focused primarily on his own needs and desires, and this reframing, along with some changes in routines, helped calm things at home. But like Antonio's parents, he, too, felt a lingering sense of disappointment and anger that his son did not appreciate all that he had been given.

Children's listless response to material comforts and lack of appreciation for their family can incite angry responses from many parents. These reactions are typically far more intense when combined with a history of significant loss and self-denial. Such was the case with Sandy. She rarely complained about her children's good fortune. Her family lived in a large home in an upper-middle-class neighborhood. They traveled frequently and her kids had access to all the sports instruction and music lessons they desired. Sandy did everything she could to support and encourage her children's athletic and artistic interests, and to find creative ways to celebrate their talents. This was especially true when it came to her son Teddy, who was less adept socially and academically than his older sister.

What Sandy could not tolerate was her son's lack of responsiveness to all her efforts. She went out of her way to find ways to soothe and engage Teddy, and did things for him that she knew her mother would not have dreamed of doing for her. Early on in her treatment, Sandy described an exchange from the previous afternoon. It had been a particularly difficult mid-winter stretch for Teddy, and she decided that he and his sister Annie should have a break. She made a plan to take them shopping and then out to dinner at their favorite restaurant. As they were getting ready to leave, Teddy began sliding on the ice outside their house over and over, despite Sandy's warnings that it was "very dangerous" and that they needed to get going. After a few minutes of this, she grew enraged and abruptly announced that she was cancelling their plans. To me, this sounded like fairly typical high-energy boy behavior, and Sandy could see I was puzzled that it would feel like such an affront to her authority: "I know, I know, I just lost it, it was extreme." She felt a jumble of emotions—an intense (and somewhat irrational) fear for Teddy's safety and a wish to protect him, combined with disdain and rage over his lack of respect and appreciation for her good intentions and carefully arranged plan.

Her mother and extended family continued to ridicule Sandy for indulging Teddy, and for being overly solicitous when he grew irritable or needed breaks during large family gatherings. Sandy's mother frequently chided her by asking "Is this normal for Teddy?" after his meltdowns. Her husband was supportive and offered to intervene during the worst of these moments. His helpfulness, although welcome, further high-lighted Sandy's feelings of abandonment by her own father and raised her ire at her son's blatant disregard for the people who cared for him deeply and worked so hard to help him manage. Almost inevitably, after several attempts to make things right for him in these larger groups, Sandy would lose her patience and snap at Teddy for not acting appro-priately.

Perhaps most galling to Sandy were her son's lack of empathy and unwillingness to help out at home. Getting Teddy to do his chores was a constant struggle. Although she recognized that she expected more than most mothers, Sandy could not help but compare her expectations to the relentless wave of requests from her own mother when she was a child. From a young age, Sandy was expected to be at her mother's beck and call at all times and to comply with her wishes without complaint or regard for her own desires to play with her siblings or go out with friends. When Sandy asked Teddy to do her a favor and play with a younger boy in the neighborhood who idolized him, he refused, saying he only wanted to stay home and relax. Sandy was furious that he would not accommodate this small request to make someone else happy, a choice that she was never free to make.

As she grew older, Sandy was still expected to be the "good girl" who rarely raised her voice. It was also understood that she would work out-side the home and take care of herself. Listening to stories of her adoles-cence reminded me of my own family's similar expectations. My brothers and I were asked do odd jobs for my father at his business beginning in elementary school, and we were in charge of raking and mowing the yard and other outdoor work from around the age of ten. I was the youngest and often got the short end of the stick—namely, raking and garbage duty. As we reached high school, we were expected to work in the family business during summers and school vacations, an arrange-ment that continued through college. I enjoyed the camaraderie there, and I learned that my father could show his playful, less serious side at work and at home as long as he knew we were earning our keep. Al-though odd monies were doled out for special treats and occasions, we were largely financially independent from our parents by the time we were teenagers.

This seemed a fair and logical arrangement until my father became seriously ill with a life-threatening kidney disorder when I was fifteen. He recovered for a time but was forced to undergo dialysis several times a week, and within a year's time he had to be hospitalized again. He gradually declined and died the next summer, just after I completed my junior year of high school. Although we were all devastated by our father's death, we were not immediately uprooted. We remained in our home and payments from my father's share of the business supported my mother for several years thereafter. Despite this continuity and relative good fortune, by the age of eighteen it was clear to me that I was mainly on my own. My older brothers were supportive and helped me apply to college, but I had to work out how to pay for school and how to budget my summer earnings, student loans, and the social security payments that came after my father's death.

Throughout most of my adult life I looked upon this early fiscal responsibility and independence with pride. Although I wished no such trauma upon my own children, I was determined to teach them the value of working hard and pitching in for the family. They each had chores from a young age and were expected to help out in a number of seasonal projects, like cleaning out the garage or shoveling the sidewalks after winter storms. As he reached age thirteen, my son begrudgingly obliged my requests to mow the lawn, knowing full well he was one of the few teenagers in the neighborhood required to do so. My wife Jenny and I were proud of them—they were hardworking kids, and despite some complaints and feet dragging, they normally complied when we asked them to help out.

That arrangement worked smoothly for quite some time. But as they became older teens, our kids became less than thrilled with our expectations of assistance, and tales of the hard lessons from their mother and father's younger days grew more tiresome. I was disappointed with my son when he failed to find a full-time job the summer after his senior year of high school and became infuriated when he did not display any particular urgency to remedy the situation. When my oldest daughter was seventeen, she asked to travel to Africa to work in a school for orphaned girls during her summer break. I was proud of her and impressed by her wish to help such a disenfranchised group. However, when the trip was condensed from a several-week commitment to a far shorter time period due to logistical constraints, I grew uncomfortable. It began to feel precious, and an indulgence to travel so far at such a high cost. My daughter knew she could not go without the financial backing of her parents. In the end she went, and the experience left her enriched and more aware of the public health and educational disparities in the developing world.

Still, I felt a nagging sense of frustration at her privileged position, as a child who felt few qualms in asking her parents to support her biggest dreams. I knew the next year would be difficult. We were very close and had similar temperaments, and the thought of her leaving for college saddened me. She was the same age that I was when my father died, and I was now fifty-three, his age at death. I admired her spunk and intensity, but her increasing requests to support her activities in and out of school and to provide money for the escalating cost of her social life and athletic trips fueled my anger. After she turned eighteen, I was determined not to tolerate it any longer. She surely had the means now to support herself. When she asked me for pocket money for one last out-of-state track and field trip, I exploded at her: "You are off the payroll! You can pay for yourself; don't ask me for any more money."

With my wife's help, I quickly realized that my outburst was absurd, over a relatively petty and familiar request that had never before troubled me. I went to my daughter and apologized and gave her the money, which she reluctantly accepted. I ultimately decided to travel with the team to watch her race one final time, and we had some great moments together that weekend. I remained, however, deeply troubled by my resentment and anger toward her. I could not easily shake the feeling that she was the victim of my own incomplete mourning process for the death of my father, nor the fact that my rage reaction was so easily triggered by her blithe request for help at an age when I had no recourse to do the same. My resentment and envy led me to rail against her, to chastise her for her self-advocacy and assertiveness, two of the things I most admired about her.

FUTURE SHOCK

Like most parents, my wife and I worry about what will become of our children as adults, a prospect that now seems much closer than it did just a few years ago. How will they support themselves? Will they have the drive, the work ethic, and the good fortune to find successful and fulfilling careers? Will they form lasting intimate relationships based on trust and kindness? Will they live in communities where they have the ongoing support of friends and family? These concerns can give rise to significant worry when parsed among groups of like-minded parents.

This is a well-worn tale, but anxiety about what the future holds for their children also fuels much of the anger parents feel toward them. Visions of raising adults who lead less than satisfying lives can lead to immense fears of failure, particularly if parents feel a sense of disappointment with their own lives (Barish, 2009). Parents who witness early signs of idle activity often cannot help but extrapolate from the present. If they disagree with the way their children spend their free time, they may combine their expressions of concern with thinly veiled disdain. One mother of an avid middle-school gamer described her worst fears: "I'm afraid he's going to be the loser in the basement his whole life. I can't stand it." For the mother of another introverted child, his computer obsession was further proof that he would "always be with the nerds." She would frequently fight bitterly with him to turn off his electronics and do something else. It is not difficult for the parents of an older child who avoids the mainstream social scene in high school to draw a straight line in their minds to future isolation and unhappiness. Their efforts to active-

ly intervene are typically (and predictably) met with resistance and escalating arguments.

Children who struggle with impulse control and anger instill other
worries in their parents. A mother of a sixteen-year-old boy whom I had
treated years earlier came to my office anxious and enraged over his
behavior. Now a high school sophomore, he was doing well academically
and much better socially, but he continued to struggle with frustration
and explosiveness, particularly during and after his sporting events. She
stated bluntly, "He must correct this now; what kind of boyfriend or
husband will he be later on? Would he hit a girl?" Her concern and
subsequent anger had escalated as her son had gotten older, despite the
fact that he had not been in any physical confrontations and would mostly rail against himself in his darkest moments.

A third fear that fuels parents' anger lies in the perception that their
children's lack of ambition or more passive disposition will limit their
possibilities later in life. Sam, the father of eight-year-old twin girls, felt
strongly connected to one of his daughters but could not relate well to
her sister: "I can't deal with her weepiness, with all the neediness and the
fact that she always copies others. It's so hard to relate to, I am an independent person, I don't follow along with others." I had known Sam to be
a caring and invested father, as well as a successful businessman. He was
clearly ashamed at how angry he could get with his daughter when she
passively acquiesced to the wishes of others, and embarrassed to admit
that he would frequently snap at her in futile attempts to stop her from
acting "so insecure."

It is not unusual for parents who come in for help to describe their
children as "lazy" and unmotivated. Ten-year-old Danny was a pretty
good student, but his mother Lydia, a hard-working immigrant woman
who worked her way through college and graduate school, could not
accept his lackadaisical attitude: "There's a real lack of effort. He never
goes for the extra credit!" She often screamed at Danny if she felt that he
had failed to do his best work. Like many parents who had endured early
hardships, Lydia worried that she had indulged her son too much and
was now paying the price. Her dilemma reminded me of the father of
another patient, a physician who had grown up in poverty and had
learned to be resourceful and fend for himself from a young age. Reflecting on his own children's much more comfortable lives, he wistfully
entertained an uncomfortable notion: "I sometimes wish my children had
the same disadvantages I had." He knew that his resilience and determi-
nation to overcome adversity had led to a successful career, and he worried that the ease of their existence would do little to prepare them for the
working world.

Sandy worried on all fronts about her son. She, too, feared that Teddy
would "end up alone in the basement." After a mildly negative teacher
conference, she reported that he was a "bright kid but lacked ambition,"

and that he was "coasting" in second grade and never gave his best effort on the soccer field. Sandy also saw how Teddy lashed out at her and his sister, and she openly questioned how he would handle his future relationships. Despite the fact that he was just seven years old, she grew increasingly concerned that he could someday mistreat his girlfriend or wife. After watching a movie depicting the tortured life of a young man with bipolar disorder, Sandy talked about her darkest fears about Teddy: "How will this troubled kid turn into a good man?"

Sandy mainly blamed herself, that somehow she had not been a good mentor or coach for her children and had been unable to transmit the values of hard work, self-reliance, and grit to her son, lessons she was forced to learn early in childhood. She was angry at him and all the negativity he had brought to their lives, but she was more frustrated by her own failures. Like many parents of challenging children, she felt that she was squandering precious time to make things right (Crown, 2009). Although she was desperate to have her own life back, Sandy felt destined to a "lifetime of worry" with Teddy.

RECOGNIZING PARENTAL VULNERABILITIES

In the early phase of treatment Sandy began to understand how her early experiences had left her feeling ill-prepared to be a parent. Familiar feelings of inadequacy, self-blame, and despair had resurfaced repeatedly as she lamented her attempts to curb her son's behavior and manage her own frustrations with him. Teddy's anger and aggressive lashing out were particularly troubling for his mother, who was given no such room as a child and could not conceive of the idea that emotional outbursts like his could exist in a "normal" functioning family. Having been taught to please others and ignore her own desires, she could not initially relate to or tolerate his egocentric demands and irrational tantrums. Sandy invariably felt that she was falling short of her own expectations to stay calm all the time, and she worried that she could not help her son reach his potential or grow into a well-adjusted adult if she remained angry with him.

Sandy's struggles call to mind Lerner's (1980) seminal article on female anger. She argued that girls who are not permitted to contradict or countermand their own mothers, or to express anger and aggression as children, are likely to be less assertive as adults. The women she treated who worked hard to remain even-tempered and to placate others as adults were usually thwarted in their attempts at separation as children. Viewed as disloyal or self-aggrandizing if they spoke out, their independent strivings were typically met with disdain or rejection by their mothers. Many had learned to avoid confrontation as they grew older, and after becoming mothers they worried that angry exchanges could do irreparable harm to attachment bonds with both their husbands and their children. Although the cultural imperative that places unspoken limits on women's expressions of assertiveness (Turkel, 2000) appears to be abating, mothers (and fathers) who experienced early separation anxiety are still prone to difficulty with expressing anger. Sandy's favorite catch-all phrase, "I'm a lover, not a fighter," elegantly captures this dilemma. When conflict arose she sought to appease Teddy and her daughter. She worried constantly about the potential long-term damage to her relationships with them that could result from episodic angry outbursts on either side.

Although less frequently commented upon, fathers often struggle with feelings of aggression toward their children. Despite the stereotype of the angry, punitive dad who unleashes a torrent of anger ("wait until your father comes home"), many men seek to avoid confrontation and retreat from limits with their kids. This hesitance can stem from guilt over working long hours, often combined with the strong desire to be an involved and concerned parent, not primarily a disciplinarian. Some wish to share in the fun and to play and hang out with their kids when they come home, sometimes to the chagrin of their wives ("Oh no, Daddy is home" is not an uncommon lament in my office). For others, there is a conscious wish to do it differently, to not succumb to the same cycle of reprimands, punishments, and harsh criticism they experienced from their own fathers. These attempts to de-identify with the aggressor are usually only partially successful, and the flashes of anger that seep out in interactions with their children can lead to intense self-reproach and self-loathing. Although boys may be allowed to separate more readily from both parents, they frequently carry a burden of a different sort as they grow up. If they are charged with carrying on the tradition of independence, hard work, and success in the family, they may have little patience with their own children's ambivalence about doing the same. Despite expressed desires to be supportive and understanding, fathers can be quick to point out academic failings, criticize any perceived lack of ambition or willingness to contribute to the family, or respond irrationally to minor shortcomings in their children. Although this is not uniquely a male phenomenon, men tend to worry about teaching diligence and respect, in part to carry on the legacy of their own fathers.

As a father I have felt vulnerable to all of these competing impulses. Having wanted children since I was a young adult, I resolved to be an involved dad from early on. Though not usually afraid to step in if my kids were misbehaving, I was conscious of not wanting to be pigeonholed as the limit setter in our family, and I resented being thrust into that role at times by them or my wife. Much preferring the role of rabble-rouser and fun-starter, especially after long hours at work, I could easily overreact when these efforts were thwarted or met with passive resistance by my son and daughters. With vivid pictures embedded in my mind of moments my father lost control with us, I had vowed not to relive those scenes with my own children. Although largely succeeding in avoiding physical confrontations with them, I could lose my patience much more easily than I cared to admit, especially as they grew older and began to challenge our authority more regularly.

When our children became teenagers the arguments escalated, and I became aware that certain signals from them were particular triggers for me. If any of the three of them were disrespectful to their mother or me, I was liable to react in a volatile way. It was not hard to recall in the aftermath of those incidents how much disdain my father had for that kind of behavior. Despite knowing that my interventions would likely backfire, I could also not easily tolerate a lack of effort or focus in school by my kids. Although I tried to be diplomatic in my feedback to them, my profound distaste for taking the easy way out was hard to disguise. Perhaps most troubling, any hints of entitlement or a lack of appreciation for the things we had worked hard to provide for our children could draw my intense ire. My wife Jenny would understandably grow impatient with me in these moments, often chastising, "If we don't want to feel badly, then we shouldn't take them on these trips (or buy these gifts, or go to this event)." I wanted it both ways, to give them opportunities and experiences we did not have when we were young and to see them appreciate each and every moment as if it were unexpected. The fact that this was illogical was not lost on me. I knew my kids were usually grateful, but I still could do little to restrain my anger when I sensed a blithe indifference to the privileges they enjoyed.

THE ROLE OF FORGIVENESS

The parental virtues that we hold in esteem—patience, warmth, consistency, affection—can remain elusive when put to the test in heated moments with a challenging child. As Crown (2009) points out, the wish to maintain unqualified devotion and love inevitably leads to feelings of shame and guilt when parents fall short. This pattern of hope and despair can be overwhelming to many adults. In her view, "anger is the hardest to bear," especially anger at the child, "which many parents believe they are not allowed to feel."

Although she was reflecting on her own experience as the mother of a child with significant developmental disabilities, Crown's disclosures are relevant to parents of children who struggle to regulate their emotions and behavior for other reasons. Despite his provocations and intense outbursts at her, Sandy did not feel she had the right to be angry at her son. Instead, she felt she should be striving always to "be a better parent" who did not lose her cool with him. The absence of a clear diagnostic label for her son further compounded her guilt and frustration that she was unable to make things right with him. Recognizing that she was repeating some of her mother's tendencies to reject and criticize left Sandy feeling deeply disturbed. She believed that she was bound to inflict traumatic memories on her children if she did not eradicate all the anger in her interactions with them.

It was self-evident to both Sandy and to me that she was unduly hard on herself and that she had unreasonable expectations about what a mother could achieve. That understanding alone however, did little to appease her guilt. Sandy had remained locked in a vicious cycle with Teddy—his acting out, her reprisal, and subsequent self-reproach and despair. Until she was able to look more fully at her own mother's shortcomings, and at the rage and barrage of criticism she had experienced as a child, she could not escape the feeling that she, too, was becoming an abusive parent. Nor could she begin to forgive herself for her occasional missteps.

Sandy's sensitivity to expressions of anger in any form had been multiply determined. She was never allowed to be assertive or independent as a child, and to speak up or confront others now felt out of character for her. Reacting with anger was humiliating, even in the face of her son's occasionally outrageous behavior. Despite recognizing the necessity of disciplining him at times, she was deeply troubled by how frustrated she could become. Having been raised in an excessively punitive home, Sandy had vowed "to do it differently," and she had indeed been successful in doing so. But she was much quicker to point out her failings and the times she "lost it" than to recognize when she had remained patient and calm in the face of her son's outbursts, despite the fact that the latter responses were far more frequent than the former.

Gradually Sandy grew more receptive to my observations that she was a caring and engaged mother, and she became less shamed by her anger. We reviewed a variety of behavioral interventions that improved things at home, including previewing difficult situations with Teddy, building in breaks from high-intensity activities and not overscheduling him. Sandy learned to give warnings when his behavior was escalating, and to find ways to distract him by spending time alone together or working side by side on backyard projects. She spoke openly with Teddy about his sadness and frustration that his older sister was moving away from him, and his fear of being rejected by his friends. Sandy grew more confident as a mother, and more willing to pardon herself when she wished to be alone or be free of parenting responsibilities.

Not surprisingly, limit setting remained an issue for Sandy. She realized there was no way around it, that she had to step in when Teddy lost control, but she still wished she could find the secret phrase or action that could calmly de-escalate each heated moment. I offered that children inevitably will frustrate their parents, and that as long as we do not attack or humiliate them, expressing our own intense feelings is not likely to cause them undue harm. We discussed that it is necessary for kids to experience a range of feelings and impulses, and to see that their parents can manage them and set limits when necessary.

As Henry (2010) points out, children need to be able to "enjoy the range of their sadistic, sexual, jealous/envious and narcissistic urges" and these impulses should be tolerated within reason. But if left unbridled, the urges can become destructive and more deeply ingrained in a child's character. Limits by the parent help children feel more in control, but the goal of these limits should not be "to create some absolute purity from vice but rather to allow the manageable negotiation of impulses."

Engaging this range of impulses in her children caused Sandy significant anxiety, primarily because she herself wished for *purity from vice,* a freedom from her own anger and rage. But tolerating and helping children grapple with their impulses inevitably requires parents to struggle with the same urges. A flat, disaffected response or an unduly calm and patient one makes little sense in the most rageful moments with children. By setting equanimity as her goal, Sandy was not only raising the bar impossibly high for herself but also limiting opportunities for her children to bump up against limits and experience fierce resistance, so that she and they could find a negotiated truce in the middle.

Without adequate role models, it can be exceptionally difficult for parents to learn to switch gears effectively, and to integrate reasonable expressions of anger with more benign interactions with their children. Those of us who had fairly positive relationships with parents interspersed with dramatic loss of control or outbursts of anger may look to avoid those flashes within ourselves as dangerous and toxic to the relationships with our kids. Children like Sandy, who grew up in more punitive and controlling environments, often try their best to avoid all contact with these darker urges when they become mothers and fathers. It can help most parents to recall images of significant adults who were able to do it differently. I can picture a particularly gifted early childhood teacher I worked with early in my career. Although she had a chaotic, disruptive group of students, she exuded a calm and confident demeanor and rarely appeared ruffled. If a disturbance occurred, she would quickly turn and point at the perpetrators, firmly remind them of the rules, and then return to her work. I was astounded at how she could move between two feeling states so quickly and seamlessly. She became my role model when I took a clinical position not long after in a therapeutic nursery for severely traumatized children, where I was frequently called upon to manage angry outbursts in the classroom.

This visualizing of successful limit setting and negotiations of anger can be helpful, but in order for parents to feel more confident in managing their own and their children's impulses, they also have to recognize the probability of failure. Even the most secure adult is unlikely to feel that they manage every confrontation in their life without difficulty. Exchanges that involve anger or limit-setting with coworkers, spouses, friends, or family members are invariably muddled and at least somewhat painful. Words get said, looks get exchanged, frustration seeps out. If more than half of those turn out to be fruitful interventions, most of us would feel more than satisfied. With children, especially challenging ones, these confrontations can be far more frequent. My goal for most parents is to aim for an 80/20 ratio of well-negotiated interventions to angry or impulsive outbursts. This is an ambitious goal, and many of us miss the mark on a regular basis, but at least it allows us room to fail without as much self-criticism or excessive guilt. This is not meant, of course, to give license to parents to unleash their rage at their kids in an unduly harsh or physical manner. Rather, it is an attempt to recognize the inevitable struggles with control that many parents will confront with their children, especially the more challenging and provocative ones.

Sandy was skeptical of this suggestion of the 80/20 rule. It seemed a vast departure from her own wish for perfection and avoidance of all anger even in the face of the tantrums and increasingly unreasonable requests from her children. We worked closely to review the minute details of her angry moments with them, and despite a keen sense of what she could have done differently to prevent the more heated incidents, Sandy reported feeling "less haunted by her mistakes." She was able to maintain a more consistent identity as a good mother and recognized that her efforts to remain patient would not be foolproof. It was by no means a steady progression for Sandy, and she could still feel surges of guilt and self-loathing after aggressive exchanges with Teddy. These were counterbalanced, however, with recognition that her longing for a "fairy tale land" with no harsh words or bad feelings was not only unrealistic but also an unworthy ideal for either her or her children. Teddy needed to duke it out at times with her in order to feel more in control of his impulses and to manage his frustration. Sandy knew that she, too, needed to learn how to experience and tolerate his rage and her own anger if she was to be a more resilient and engaged mother.

TRANSCENDING LABELS

Recognizing the inevitability of our own shortcomings does not mean that we should avoid revisiting the times that tempers flare and heated arguments erupt. Rather than glossing over these moments, parents can try to learn from them and find ways to reconnect with their children in the wake of temporary ruptures. First, we have to be careful not to label them. I regularly hear a range of value-laden descriptions about children and have been guilty of using some of them with my own kids. They are "manipulative," "selfish," "mean," "disrespectful," "bratty," and "cruel." These labels serve to reify what are often impulsive behaviors and turn them into character assessments. This trend is particularly troubling when we overvalue their *intent* ("You are doing this to me"; "You're taking advantage of us") and *magnify* their behaviors ("This happens every single time") (McKay, Fanning, Paleg, and Landis, 1996). This insidious pattern can leave parents feeling defeated and hopeless, and pessimistic that substantive changes can occur in their relationships with their children.

Here the ratio metaphor can also be useful. If kids are extremely difficult 20 percent of the time (or 30 or 40 percent), that still means that the majority of their interactions with their parents are not unpleasant. Further, contrary evidence can be readily available from teachers, coaches, and other parents. More often than not, those same "house devils" are "street angels," respectful, kind, and well related to other adults. Knowing that their kids are capable of behaving and controlling their anger elsewhere can draw further ire from parents. Why can't they do this at home?

But reflecting on children's interpersonal strengths and their relatedness in other settings can allow parents to be more forgiving, and to consider other possible triggers for their aggressive behavior. Many of these kids have temperamental struggles. They may be moody and prone to irritability, demanding, and sensitive to overstimulation, and they may have difficulty adapting to new situations. Often they are easily frustrated and not particularly flexible. In a word, they are *intense.* I prefer this description as a more neutral assessment of many of the children I have treated and otherwise known, and some parents readily adopt its usage at home. For these children, it is just more difficult to contain themselves when their demands are not met and their needs are not satisfied.

Developmental challenges, particularly the critical points of separation in early childhood and adolescence, can also lower the threshold for frustration in children, even for those with less challenging temperaments. This can be extremely difficult for parents who see their "easy child" suddenly turn more ferocious and unyielding. This was the case for Sandy when her daughter Annie entered preadolescence and began to have an attitude with her mother and dismiss her younger brother.

Parents can also unwittingly model behaviors that increase the likelihood of their children reacting with anger. Being witness to impatience, haughtiness, or unwarranted criticism of others can limit children's motivation to restrain their own impulses when frustrated, and spur them to act in kind. If parents struggle with anger outside of the home, and children see them berate or lose control with fellow parents, coaches, or teachers, they may learn that such outbursts are justified, even against people in positions of authority.

Looking more closely at the root causes of children's anger can help parents feel more hopeful, and more in control of their own reactions in volatile situations. Although temperamental states can seem intransigent, most children can become better equipped to handle frustration if they understand their triggers and learn how to anticipate stressful situations. A developmental perspective can provide relief that the current crisis will likely resolve itself. Sandy's recognition that her daughter's quick metamorphosis was "just a phase" soothed her, allowing her to be more patient with wild gyrations between Annie's increased neediness and surges of independence. Rethinking the models we offer our kids for resolving conflict and managing anger can present another avenue for change that can potentially calm the waters at home.

Children are works in progress and our relationships with them are more dynamic than we might imagine. Logging the hits and misses, and the intensity, frequency, and duration of the outbursts at home, can give us a clearer sense of whether we are moving forward, even if progress seems painstakingly slow. Children and adolescents are inherently more capable of recognizing and feeling the transient nature of events, and less likely to hold on to the negative emotions associated with anger than their parents. As my daughter explained to my wife after she and I had one particularly combative episode, "Dad and I are just like that. We forget about it and move on." It was not quite so simple for me, but her breezy assessment that our relationship was intact, and her confidence that we could bounce back from anger and hostility, left me feeling buoyed and reassured. Her optimism also reminded me that although I did not relish our arguments, I always admired her feistiness. She was the one in the family who could speak the unvarnished truths and keep us all honest. That reframing has helped me to be less judgmental and to retain a sense of optimism regarding what the future would bring for her and us.

ACTIVE LISTENING

The second and equally difficult task for parents is to listen intently to the grievances and frustrations of their children that precede or follow the confrontations with them. In my clinical experience, there is almost always some justification, however minor it may appear, for children's provocative and outrageous behaviors. Parents can easily get caught up in their child's "overreaction" and de-legitimize the original trigger for their anger. Too often we can overlook their rationale and focus on the seemingly irrational behavior, ostensibly giving us license to come down hard on our kids with impunity. The goal is to try to appreciate the child's point of view, or, as Barish (2009) reminds us, "to acknowledge what is right about what the child is saying before we point out the wrong." If we can reflect on their complaints, and what may be done to resolve them, children are more likely to seek to negotiate with us rather than lash out in anger.

Early in our work together, Sandy was growing increasingly irritated at Teddy for his behavior at large holiday gatherings. After initially appearing fine, he would repeatedly storm off in the middle of dinner. This had become a source of frequent clashes between them and Sandy grew to dread these events, which occurred with some regularity. Only after slowing down and beginning a more active dialogue with Teddy did she realize how much he felt trapped in the tight quarters where the dinners were held. He also complained of feeling humiliated by the reprimanding looks of his grandmother and other older relatives when he began to squirm and become uncomfortable. Although his reaction appeared outsized and bizarre in context, Sandy realized that Teddy was being put in an untenable position. She worked with him to help him anticipate how long he could manage in the larger group, and how and where he could take breaks on his own. Both of them felt relieved that they had discovered ways to resolve his struggle, and the family events began to run more smoothly. In retrospect, Sandy realized how on edge she had been and how quick to blame her son.

Rarely does the source of children's anger present itself so readily or resolve so easily. But the notion that we can recognize our children's perspective in a conflict and seek to negotiate a solution together with them helps to build their sense of trust and motivate them to regulate their behavior. If words can get the job done, they may not always have to act out or protest so vociferously. With younger kids, this may involve access to electronics or a more active say in how to balance homework, play dates, and other activities. With older children, it may mean compromise over curfews or rights to the family car and other privileges. These efforts won't eliminate arguments with them or prevent times when they call us on our inconsistency or hypocrisy. But building a tradition of good faith negotiation can help prevent parents from lashing out in a more unrestrained manner, and from feeling helpless when their children do not listen to them.

REPARATIVE MOMENTS

In addition to their ability to move past negative emotion, children frequently look to reestablish connection with their parents after periods of open hostility. For parents, this transition can come too soon and in unexpected fashions. Sandy was often flabbergasted that her son could switch gears so easily: "We have a knock-down drag-out fight and then a few minutes later he wants a hug. . . . How am I going to survive? I just can't do it." For her, the anger and accompanying swells of emotion took a long time to subside. As a result, she would often retreat and avoid her son's entreaties to make up, and she felt exceptionally guilty about rebuffing him. Ordinarily Sandy was openly affectionate with both of her children, but the heat of these moments left her feeling depleted and frightened about her own potential to lose control. We discussed ways she could learn to sit with the anger and stay with these situations long enough to respond to his longing to be held.

Allowing for healing in the wake of intense conflict is critical to relationship building between children and parents, no less so than it is between adult partners. Talking things out can help, but, like Teddy, most kids appreciate small gestures of support or active opportunities to make amends. Sandy had those readily available to her, and she and her son would often reestablish warmer relations by working on crafts, bike riding, or playing board games. She especially appreciated Teddy's help in preparing for her work exhibits.

Those of us who have struggled with combative teenagers recognize how much small efforts at rapprochement can mean in the aftermath of frayed tempers and shouting matches. My daughter would sometimes clean the kitchen or spontaneously make meals for us after arguments, or ask to spend time together watching movies or planning trips. Though often still stung by her words and still feeling the intensity of my own response, I came to understand that her active attempts at reconciling were essential to our ongoing relationship. She would also design and address lengthy cards to me for my birthday or on Father's Day, acknowledging our struggles and reaffirming her wish to remain close with her mother and me. I was extremely touched by her words, and they helped me gain perspective and more control over my own anger. They also gave me confidence that we could overcome our disputes as long as we could tap into the reservoir of good feelings between us.

ACCEPTANCE

Holding on to moments of reconnection can help parents feel that the situation at home is not so dire. If the positive interactions in the family outweigh the negative by a considerable margin, there is reason to be hopeful. Accepting the notion that children and adolescents who struggle with intense emotions are not doomed to live a diminished life or to constantly struggle in relationships can help reduce the pressure to fix things immediately. It can also provide mothers and fathers with the breathing room to make their own mistakes. We will not masterfully handle every heated exchange with our kids. There inevitably will be times when we cross a line that leaves us feeling helpless and dejected. If we can recover, make up with them, do our best to learn from our missteps, and limit our fury the next time around, we are likely to demonstrate that even the most dangerous impulses can be managed and overcome. If our relationships emerge intact, chances are good that our children will respect that we did our best to handle the most difficult times together and fought through some painful moments to get to a better place with them.

This is not to say that all will be bread and roses going forward. The learning curve can be painfully slow. Many of us have children who were well into adolescence before we felt more in control of our anger and had an understanding of the patterns that we kept repeating. There are, however, some protective mechanisms we can access along the way. Using humor can be a powerful salve with our kids. Finding ways to mutually make light of our situation, and tolerating their gibes and mimicking of our behavior when we lose control, can further demonstrate that anger is not so toxic. As they got older, our kids enjoyed poking fun at my intense reactions and lectures. One of my daughters came up with a quick rejoinder to my warnings and reminders: "Thank you, Doctor Obvious!" Much to my chagrin at first, this nickname stuck for a while in the family, and later it became a source of amusement as we all looked back on some of our more heated (and sometimes petty) arguments. I learned to laugh at my children's jokes and dead-on impressions of me. Like my father before me, I came to appreciate the value of not taking every situation at home so seriously, and of giving them more space to make their own decisions and mistakes.

Feelings of intense rage can place a heavy burden on parents and children, but if we cultivate the resources to manage and recover from these urges, we can strengthen the bonds with our kids. By not avoiding conflict and finding mutual ground to resolve differences, parents can enhance their children's resilience and their ability to identify with strong but compassionate adult figures. In the process, families can develop a different legacy of anger management and expression. Weaving a new pattern that more readily includes moments of reflection and reconciliation, and an active commitment on both sides to anticipate and defuse volatile conflicts, can provide parents and children with a formidable defense against future high stress situations. This resolve can also allow us to appreciate and enjoy the times we have left together with our children, freed from the weight of shame, and the anxiety that lurking just beneath the surface is a dangerous and unconquerable foe.

REFERENCES

Axelman, M. (2009). On holding the situation: Parental affect tolerance, limit setting, and the transition to object usage. *Journal of Infant, Child and Adolescent Psychotherapy, 8*, 96–103.

Barish, K. (2009). *Emotions in child psychotherapy*. New York: Oxford University Press.

Crown, N. J. (2009). Parenting a child with disabilities: Personal reflections. *Journal of Infant, Child, and Adolescent Psychotherapy, 8*, 70–82.

Fosshage, J. L. (1998). On aggression: Its forms and functions. *Psychoanalytic Inquiry, 18*, 45–54.

Henry, C. (2010). Aggression, containment, and treatment enactments in the psychodynamics of limit setting. *Journal of the American Academy of Psychoanalysis, 38,* 341–56.

Kurcinka, M. S. (1991). *Raising your spirited child.* New York: William Morrow.

Lerner, H. E. (1980). Internal prohibitions against female anger. *American Journal of Psychoanalysis, 40,* 137–48.

Lichtenberg, J. D., and Shapard, B. (2000). Hatred and its rewards: A motivational systems view. *Psychoanalytic Inquiry, 20,* 374–88.

McKay, M., Fanning, P., Paleg, K., and Landis, D. (1996). *When anger hurts your kids: A parent's guide.* Oakland, CA: New Harbinger.

Nason, J. D. (1985). The psychotherapy of rage: Clinical and developmental perspectives. *Contemporary Psychoanalysis, 21,* 167–92.

Ornstein, A. (1997). A developmental perspective on the sense of power, self-esteem, and destructive aggression. *Annals of Psychoanalysis, 25,* 145–54.

Stern, D. (1977). *The first relationship, infant and mother.* Cambridge, MA: Harvard University Press.

Turkel, A. R. (2000). The "voice of self-respect": Women and anger. *Journal of the American Academy of Psychoanalysis, 28,* 527–39.

Winnicott, D. W. (1947). Hate in the countertransference. In *Through Paediatrics to Psycho-Analysis.* New York: Basic Books.

EIGHT

"I Can't Stand Her"

The Role of Hatred in Development

Marsha Levy-Warren

—

*This chapter provides a most compelling companion piece to Paul Donahue's chapter, as the present chapter by **Marsha Levy-Warren** also focuses on the role of rage in parent-child interaction. Levy-Warren speaks to the role of hate as a central aspect of all relationships and thus can draw on her experience with that affect as a parent to help guide her reactions to parents who enter treatment consumed by these feelings toward their clearly loved children. She makes the critical point that being essential in some primary way involves the acknowledgment of hate and that it is only in fact when this hate can be fully accepted that essential connections between parent and child can be fully realized.*

—◈◈◈—

There is so much obvious hatred in the world. There are countless, senseless murders and untoward violence to the body and soul in every corner of the earth. This violence is to people, to property, even to historical treasures. Perhaps this is one of the reasons why I sometimes find it so difficult to hear of hatred in my office. I already feel like I am on hatred overload.

Nonetheless, time after time, parents come in to see me to speak about their hatred toward their children and adolescents. They are most often deeply distressed about this hatred. They feel that it is unseemly, or it is displaced from somewhere else that they cannot trace. Sometimes they just feel like something is wrong with them for feeling it.

When I encounter this in my office, I—too often for my own comfort—find myself feeling a lack of sympathy for these parents. I also feel an overabundance of empathy for their (hated) child or adolescent. I know that I have to think deeply about my reactions or I probably will not be effective in helping them.

I realize that I once had had some of those feelings of hatred myself, many years ago, when my now grown-up children were still kids. I particularly remember some moments during adolescence. Despite the fact that I recall and accept that I had these feelings, I know that I still feel very uncomfortable about them. I remember my personal struggles with having the feelings back then. I also remember my self-condemnation for having them.

At times I would flash on some experiences that *I* had as a child and adolescent: the feeling of being the object of my mother's hatred, the dark look on her face as she expressed her rage, the feeling of seeing my siblings serving as the object of her hatred, and (probably the hardest of all to accept) my relief when it was a sibling rather than me that was the object of her hatred.

All of this contributes to my deep discomfort in listening to parents speaking of their hatred for their children and adolescents. These moments with parents create an internal cacophony of images and feelings that I need to sort through to be as fully present as I wish to be. It is reminiscent of moments of feeling that I heard my mother's voice in mine when I was a parent of young children and adolescents, or moments when I see my mother's image in my mind's eye as I listen to parents who speak of hating their children. These are uncomfortable images and feelings.

The discomfort of listening to parents has a particular quality to it: it is as though these parents are voicing something aloud that I feel should not be spoken about—something that should only be thought, never expressed. Then that—if they *had* to speak of it—it should not be with me, a perfect stranger!? It feels too intimate. I know that this is a rather strange notion for a psychoanalyst, but there it is.

In thinking about this discomfort, I was reminded of a talk that I gave many years ago. It was in the 1980s, it was at a women's college, and it was about the erotic aspects of breast-feeding. I spoke about how complex it is to breast-feed: how what one feels in the act of breast-feeding is related to what one feels in the act of love-making, but how breast-feeding requires creating a new category for that feeling. I spoke about how difficult it is for nursing mothers *and* their partners, and how for women it requires a reconfiguration in one's relationship to one's breasts.

The paper did not go over well. The women in the audience mostly were appalled. How could I think about the purity of breast-feeding in any kind of sexual way? What was *wrong* with me?

I suspect it was much like what happened to Freud when he talked about infantile sexuality. I also am sure that thinking this helped me deal with how disappointed I was at the reception the talk received.

But back to the present issue. What *is* it about hating one's children and adolescents that is so undoing for parents? And what makes parents hate their children? Why is it so ubiquitous? And why does it feel so terrible to the parents themselves and (sometimes) to the clinicians who work with them?

The experience of hating one's child requires a reconfiguration in one's sense of what it means to be a parent, much like the experience I wrote about in relation to the erotic aspects of breast-feeding. We usually make the decision to parent with the best of intentions. We want to love our little ones, nurture them, aid them in growing up to be as strong and healthy and loving as possible. So, how is it that we can come to feel hate?

Whereas we as clinicians often learn from our experiences as parents to work in the consulting room, in this instance, we also learn from our experiences as clinicians to guide parents through this developmental conundrum. The invaluable lesson that D. W. Winnicott (1949) taught us in his groundbreaking paper "Hate in the Countertransference" can embolden us in working through these difficult moments.

He makes it clear that it is part of normative development for mothers to hate their children and for children to hate their mothers. He also notes that hating is only possible once ego integration has taken place. This means that "mothers" (i.e., caregivers) probably hate their babies before babies are capable of hating them. Babies and very young children may *act* in ways that the caregiver experiences as hateful (e.g., biting the breast, hitting the caregiver, throwing food), but the children are not capable of knowing that they are acting hatefully until they have a clear sense of an "I" who *can* act this way. This "I" is what is meant by ego integration.

Christopher Bollas (1984) defines a concept of "loving hate" in his paper of the same title. He beautifully describes how some people engender hate so that they can feel closer to the other person. These are people who preserve relationships by sustaining what he calls a "passionate negative cathexis." When children and adolescents who are in need of differentiating themselves from their caregivers engender hate in those caregivers, it is because they simultaneously need to be separate and need to stay attached. They accomplish this by creating a situation in which the caregiver separates from them (because of the "hatred"), but they themselves stay attached (by not directly expressing or even consciously feeling the hatred).

Bollas cites Erikson's (1968) concept of "negative identity," in which the late adolescent becomes all of what is perceived as what the parents would least want their child to be. Erikson speaks of this as the identity that feels most real to these adolescents. In this situation, the adolescents demonstrate that they remain attached to the caregivers because the caregivers' ideas are central to their identity (even in their negative form). These adolescents have not yet established an identity that is independent of their caregivers' views, so what is most real to them is what their parents think they should be. Their at times almost caricatured rejection of their parents' views thus suggests that there is an appearance of a separate identity without the establishment of an authentic separate identity.

Particularly in thinking about what engenders hate during development, I think Winnicott , Bollas, and Erikson offer us important wisdom.

It is often the children and adolescents who feel most attached to their parents that engender the most hate. They have trouble disengaging (Levy-Warren, 1996/2004, 1999) and do not feel comfortable with the direct expression of antipathy toward their parents for fear of losing the connection they have, and stirring up hatred in their parents creates the space they need to be more autonomous. I think of these types of connections as "sticky" attachments: sometimes because of where they are in their own development, sometimes because the nature of their attachment is such that it is hard for them to leave people with whom they have felt close and situations with which they have become familiar.

As I will describe in a brief vignette later in this chapter, this issue seems to come up disproportionately in families in which there are adopted children. As Winnicott noted in his "Hate in the Countertransference" article:

> It is perhaps relevant to cite the case of the child of the broken home, or the child without parents. Such a child spends time unconsciously looking for his parents. It is notoriously inadequate to take such a child into the one's home and love him. What happens is that after awhile a child so adopted gains hope, and then he starts to test out the environment he has found, and to seek proof of his guardians' ability to hate objectively. It seems that he can believe in being loved only after reaching being hated. (p. 72)

There is so much that is complicated in the adoptive family system. Two relevant factors are whatever led the parental unit to make the choice to adopt, and whatever understanding was conveyed to the adopted child about what led to his or her being placed for adoption. Both of these have potential for engendering hatred.

If the parental unit was infertile, the adopted child can be a constant reminder of this disappointment. If the adopted child comes to feels that s(he) was rejected by the biological parent, that parent could be hated or could be seen as hating the child (Levy-Warren, 2001).

This potentially complicates attachment by infusing it with negative feeling, and a need for the subject of the hatred to find some other way of conceptualizing the relationship. I will return to this issue later.

Let me offer some clinical anecdotes to illustrate some of the family interactions in which hatred may be engendered in caregivers. This hatred often serves to facilitate the child or adolescent achieving a greater sense of autonomy, but often leaves caregivers feeling extremely unsettled. Clinicians may also find elements of hatred in *their* reactions to these situations.

IN A PERMANENT SNIT

"She just can't get over Edward being born. What is her problem? I had six brothers and sisters, and I never pulled this kind of stuff. I can't deal with it."

Martha was beyond frustrated with Amanda, her five-year-old daughter. Since Amanda's younger brother was born, eight months ago, she has been telling her mother that she "doesn't want him there," that "it isn't fair" that he is around, and that she "wants to leave this family and go to live with her friend Talia's family" or her maternal grandparents. She is demanding, competitive with baby Edward ("why does he always get to be held?"), and often absolutely contrary ("I will *not* take a bath now, I am not ready").

Martha came for a parent guidance consultation. She told me that she was repeatedly having images of smacking Amanda (though not acting on the impulse), that she was screaming at her "all the time," and that she "was at her wits' end."

"I can't stand her. I mean, I love her, of course . . . but I also really *hate* her. I just can't put up with her obsession with Edward getting something that she doesn't get. And why can't she just go with the program? He is here to stay. Is she ever going to get on with life? My husband has had it with me. He thinks I am crazy at this point. He says I have turned into a screaming maniac. He has no idea how much I just want to *slap* her."

I felt uncomfortable with Martha's recurrent wish to hit Amanda. Learning more about her upbringing tempered my reaction, but I still felt uneasy when she spoke about Amanda. She had no empathy for Amanda's struggle.

Martha had grown up in a very strict household. She was one of seven children, and her parents had run a tight ship. "Everybody had to share, no one complained. We did what we were supposed to do . . . especially at *her* age! Maybe we got into things when we were older, but *at five*? She's gotta be kidding!?"

She had been raised in a household in which order and obedience were highly valued. In Martha's upbringing, knowing and following the rules was extremely important—and doing so was guaranteed to gain the approval of her parents. Martha did not recognize that she and her husband were raising Amanda very differently. Rather than focusing on adhering to rules, there was a focus on the growth of individuality and creativity. Her intellectual commitment to this kind of childrearing was in stark contrast to the attitudes she had developed in response to her own childhood.

Amanda's need for her parents' attention intensified when Edward was born. She needed to feel that her place in her parents' hearts was secure. Her mother, Martha, the main focus of this need, had trouble mustering up the requisite sympathy for Amanda. What Amanda needed was exactly what Martha had been raised to suppress in her childhood. It created a real collision of past and present for Martha. Amanda expressed wishes and feelings that Martha had never dared to say aloud.

Martha found herself hating Amanda—and I found myself not really caring much for Martha. Hate was floating around in the family system.

It began with Amanda's hatred of Edward's presence, if not Edward himself. It was the indirect expression of this hatred (in her recalcitrant and whiny behavior) that Martha found unbearable. The indirectness of Amanda's expression involved a projective process in which Amanda's hatred found its manifestation in Martha's hatred toward Amanda. Amanda knew that hating her brother would not meet with her mother's approval, so she projected it, and Martha took it in and redirected it toward Amanda. My intolerance of Martha was another pathway in this projective process.

Without expressing it directly, Amada made clear that she hated Edward's presence. She blamed his presence on her parents, toward whom expression of direct hatred was not possible: she was too much in need of them. Her persistent unhappiness with Edward's presence was unbearable for Martha, whose reaction of hatred was because of both her own upbringing and her taking in of Amanda's hatred for Edward.

CAN'T GUYS JUST BE GUYS?

Beau came in to discuss his intense discomfort with (his thirteen-year-old son) Jesse's lack of interest in bodybuilding and sports. He was vehement: "He has to build himself up. He can't just play with fabrics and paints. He won't survive if he is such a pansy."

I cringed.

Jesse is a very different kind of sixteen-year-old boy/guy than Beau is as a man. Jesse is much more into fashion and the arts. Beau hates it. Jesse makes him uncomfortable. His husband, Greg, thinks Beau is way out of line. He feels that Beau should just let Jesse be whom he is, even if he is different from his parents.

Beau is afraid that Jesse will be the object of teasing and/or bullying if he is "this kind" of boy. Beau certainly had had his share of this kind of torment as a child in the farm country of Iowa. Greg grew up very differently. He lived in San Francisco in a very diverse neighborhood, where he could be any way he wanted to be. Beau grew up "in the boonies," where "men had to be men—or they were crushed."

As a boy and adolescent, Beau described himself as "a good kid" in a religious family that encouraged him and his four siblings to be responsible at home, respectful of others, and modest. He was not especially athletic and tended to enjoy wandering in the meadows, musing about life, and writing songs and poetry. He was seen as "faggy" by the other boys and, as a result, was bullied.

He felt ashamed to call attention to himself by speaking to his parents, but he did seek counsel from his minister. Father John encouraged him to stand up for himself—even if it meant devoting himself to getting bigger and stronger so that he could literally fight back when provoked. He told Beau that he should keep his other interests to himself. What Beau gleaned was that he had to be a "man's man" to survive. There was no room for him to be otherwise, and he could not bear for his son to be otherwise.

When he first came in, all that he could address was how much he hated who his son was becoming: "I tell him he should put his paints away and go outside and get some exercise like a normal kid, and he looks at me and his eyes water up. He doesn't *say* anything. He just looks at me. Makes me want to shove my fist through the wall. I hate him. He is such a weakling. It's pathetic. I know I am not supposed to feel this way, but I do. I really do."

His complete lack of empathy for Jesse, despite his own early experience, was hard to address with Beau. I found myself getting very frustrated. Beau was fixed on the idea that Jesse was purposely enraging him by being so passive: "He is just trying to get me pissed off. He could get off his butt and run around, get stronger. Instead, he just looks at me with those eyes and sits there until I blow up at him."

I found myself wanting to do battle with Beau. I couldn't stand his intolerance of who Jesse was and wanted to be. I also found it hard to believe that he could not see how much he was crushing Jesse.

It was difficult to find a way to describe to him how Beau himself had been crushed, and thus—though he was probably trying to protect Jesse—he might also resent that Jesse could have the freedom to be who he wanted to be. Beau had not felt free because of the way he was bullied by his peers and because of his minister's implicit acceptance of hiding his more artistic bent. Beau had suppressed his rage at the implicit demand that he could not be the musing, literary young man he had started to become, but it was emerging in his relationship with his son.

Jesse's hatred of his father for Beau's attempt to make him be someone he did not want to be was getting expressed passively. Beau's reaction was to be enraged, both because Jesse was projecting his rage (into Beau) and because it was touching a raw nerve inside of Beau with regard to the suppression of his own artistic nature. I felt discomfort with Beau because I was holding some of Jesse's hatred, and also because I was having so much trouble conveying to Beau that he had to expand his own sense of what had happened to him as a child and young man in order to be able to accept that Jesse was being raised in a different time and place, and thus might well be able just to be who he wanted to be.

With time, we were able to get there. I had to be somewhat forceful in my communication to Beau about the importance of his revisiting his own story *and* some willingness on Beau's part to be open to reforming his own narrative. He *had* to be able to include his upset at the early suppression of important aspects of who he was to be able to revise his reaction to Jesse.

PROVOCATION

They were an attractive couple—Serena, with her big smile, bright blue eyes and blonde, curly hair, and George, tall, thin, bespectacled, and warm faced. They came into my office holding hands, sat on the couch together, and then—nervously—looked at me and at each other. I asked what brought them in.

"I don't know how to deal with her," said Serena. "She is surly, impertinent, self-involved, and demanding."

"It gets really bad," said her husband, George. "She and my wife really get into it."

"And you?"

"Seems like it is more difficult between *them*. Samantha really pushes Serena's buttons. I don't understand why our daughter gets so provocative, but we are at our wits' end in dealing with it."

"I can't stand her. Sometimes I wish I could get rid of her," Serena blurted out. "You cannot imagine what it is like to feel like this toward your own child. I really *hate* her."

George looked stricken. I could empathize with his reaction. I, too, felt a wave of feeling overwhelmed by the intensity of Serena's hatred.

Serena and George had adopted Samantha at birth. Serena was at the hospital at the time that Samantha's birth mother went into labor. Serena and George had met Samantha's birth mother beforehand, and they had exchanged calls and letters and photos over the course of the pregnancy.

Samantha is the daughter of a teenage mother in another part of the country who gave her up for adoption. This was an accidental pregnancy, and Samantha's birth mother was against abortion. She also knew that she was not ready to raise a child. She wanted to continue in school. It was a private adoption arranged through an attorney and an adoption agency.

Serena and George have no other children. They were unable to conceive because each parent had fertility issues. They both very much wanted to be parents and decided that they wanted to be available to a child who needed to be placed for adoption.

The years of Samantha's childhood were happy ones for the family. They did a great deal together, and each parent enjoyed a good relationship with Samantha. She was a strong student in school and popular with her schoolmates. There were a number of families with whom the family spent time, both at home and on vacations.

Samantha was told from an early age that she was adopted, though she and Serena resembled each other, so their telling of her adoption was always a choice—not one prompted by an obvious difference in appearance between Samantha and her parents. What Samantha was told about her early life was that her birth mother was not able to care for her—that she was too young and did not have the means to take adequate care of Samantha. Her birth mother had looked for a couple like Serena and George, just as Serena and George had looked for a child like Samantha. Samantha knew that Serena had been present at her birth.

When Samantha began to go through puberty at age twelve, she became more moody and distant. Her body also began to change in ways that accentuated the differences between her and mother. She outgrew Serena in height, her breasts became larger than her mother's, and her curly light hair began to darken and straighten.

It seemed that these changes brought into bold relief that Samantha was from a different biological background. "We are *completely* different," "You're not my real mother," and "You don't even really know me" were near-daily refrains from Samantha to Serena.

Serena could not believe what she was hearing from Samantha. She felt that Samantha was turning into a stranger—that, in fact, Samantha was right: she *didn't* know her own daughter. They had been *so* close, and now they were engaged in daily battles. Serena did not like what Samantha wanted to wear, she was furious that Samantha would not let her know where she went after school, and she did not like the older boy with whom Samantha was spending a good deal of time.

"I don't recognize her. And the person I see is not someone I like," Serena reported. "It is like she up and left and this monster replaced her. I can't stand her. I really can't. She is torturing me."

Serena's mother had died when she was an early adolescent. She had no direct experience of mother/daughter relations during adolescence to draw upon. She felt rejected by Samantha, fed up with her, and blindsided by the change in their relationship.

George was mystified as well. He had grown up with two brothers and no sisters. He did not know what to make of what was happening at home. When he tried to intervene, both Samantha and Serena dismissed his efforts, saying that he did not understand. He readily agreed.

"What am I supposed to do? They are like screaming banshees, one louder than the next. I am not used to this and I find it extremely unsettling." George looked upset. He could not look at Serena when he said this during our session.

I talked with George and Serena about adolescent development, especially the separation/individuation process.

"That's all fine—but she can't say these things to me and she can't hang out with that boy. I am sick of it," responded Serena.

It was hard to normalize what was happening in their home to George and Serena. Serena especially felt that Samantha was heading down a path from which she would never return.

"Sometimes I think that blood is thicker . . . well, you know . . . that she is just going to turn into her birth mother . . . that her true colors are not going to be like ours."

It was not easy to persuade Serena that what Samantha was doing was within normative limits for adolescents in a differentiation process with their parents, especially adolescent girls with their mothers. She was convinced that Samantha was going to get pregnant and would be lost to them forever. I felt frustrated with her apparent unwillingness to give Samantha any bandwidth to experiment with other ways of being in the world and her conviction that she and Samantha would never be close again. It began to feel like it could become a self-fulfilling prophecy.

I was finally able to make some headway in calming the situation by meeting with Serena alone for a few sessions to speak with her about her own adolescence. She had apparently been a very controlled and responsible teenager, called upon by her father to help raise her younger siblings. The self-restraint she had to exercise at the time made her that much more resentful of Samantha's outbursts and "lack of gratitude."

The particular issues presented by adoption during adolescence, with its developmental focus on identity formation (Levy-Warren, 1996/2004; Levy-Warren, 1999), were part of our conversation as well. Serena needed to understand how pressed adolescents feel about figuring out who they are, how they came to be who they are, and who they are becoming, and how these concerns, at times, are heightened for adopted adolescents and may lead to challenges at home that are even more intense than might be the case in non-adoptive families.

We also talked about Serena's terrible disappointment in not being able to conceive. She felt that her femininity, her "woman-ness," was compromised—and seeing Samantha developing into a young woman, with this older boyfriend, made her felt envious and competitive in a way that she had not previously experienced. These were painful sessions but illuminating for both of us.

Ultimately, Serena and George were able to set appropriate limits with Samantha, in terms of both her outbursts with Serena and her comings and goings. Things settled down substantially.

HATRED AT HOME AND IN THE CONSULTING ROOM

It is hard to talk about hate. It is hard to feel hate, especially when you know that you also love the person you hate—which is the case in most parent/child situations. Having said that, I think that feeling hate toward one's child or adolescent is normative—especially during particular times and in particular situations in development.

These times in development are often times during which struggles for autonomy are prominent. Toddlers, four- to six-year-olds, and early adolescents are good candidates for evoking hatred in parents. Sometimes people at the end of their lives can similarly evoke hatred in their (adult) children.

When these struggles occur, parents often feel as though their children simply do not need them. The children appear to reject them and parents feel impotent. Unessential. This is an illusion. The evoking of hatred is because the caregivers *do* feel essential to the children and adolescents. Indeed, it is because they feel *so* essential that the children and adolescents evoke this hatred. Because of this hatred, the parents distance themselves from their children and adolescents. Their progeny thus are able to stay attached while simultaneously becoming more autonomous.

In each instance in development, the child or adolescent evoking the hatred needs and wants to be independent, but also fears being independent and losing the person from whom there is a wish for independence. They may well hate that they are dependent upon the caregiver, even hate the caregiver, but, for fear of losing them, be unable to express that hatred directly. In such instances, hate is projected—thus, evoked in the caregiver.

When the feeling of hatred cannot be metabolized, either because the child is too young to frame and contain the feeling or because the dyad with the caregiver makes it too fraught to fully see and express, there is a high likelihood that such a projective process will ensue. This happened in each of the case anecdotes described earlier.

For five-year-old Amanda, the hatred probably was projected and evoked in Martha because Amanda sensed that the direct expression of hatred—toward Edward, or her mother for having him—was completely unacceptable to her mother. There certainly are many five-year-olds who tell their parents that they hate them or that they hate their newborn siblings. In this instance, Amanda did not feel she could say this directly aloud—she could only speak of the ways that she felt she was being treated unfairly because of his presence and her wish for things to be as they were before he was born—so it was projected and evoked in Martha.

Jesse wanted his father's love and approval too much to directly express his hatred about Beau's demands upon him to be a different kind of guy. He acted in ways that expressed his rejection of this demand, but he could not directly fight with Beau about it. The hatred he felt was projected and evoked in his father.

Samantha really had to test her mother's love for her. She was very attached to Serena during childhood but needed to forcibly push her mother away to establish herself as an autonomous young woman once puberty began. She could not love her the same way and still feel that she was a separate person. She had to leave behind the mother of childhood and find a new way to be with her as a mother of an adolescent, but she did not know how to get from there to here without evoking a need in her mother to take a step back. She could not let herself be in the position of directly pushing Serena away from her, because she also felt such a strong need for Serena.

In each of these instances, the caregiver had historical issues that made the direct expression of hatred especially unsafe for the child or adolescent. These issues furthered the need to project the hatred onto (or into) the caregiver. The caregivers' earlier needs to repress hatred, which they could not identify and accept, clearly played a role in the projective processes in the families.

The feeling of hatred toward loved ones is, by nature, held ambivalently. There is a readiness to suppress or project the feeling. Clinicians are also prone to be part of the process when these families are encountered in our consulting rooms. We all have our own charged histories with hatred, which contribute to the discomfort we feel, but there is also a projective process into which we become ensconced when we work with families in which the volume of the hatred is turned up.

There are also situations in which hatred is more likely to be part of the family system's dynamics. They tend to be situations in which intensely ambivalent attachments are expectable: foster care and adoption, chronic illness in a caregiver, or a sudden change in the abilities of a caregiver are all examples of such situations.

In any case, we need to reframe our ideas about hatred in development. We need to see it as normative. We certainly need to see it as a possible (perhaps probable) step in the process through which our children and adolescents become autonomous people. We, as clinicians and parents, aid them in doing so through having transient feelings of hatred. This reconfiguration in the conceptualization of the relationship between parents and children is critical for all of us. It especially makes it clear that we must redefine our sense of what it means to remain essential in the lives of our children, adolescents, and patients.

REFERENCES

Bollas, C. (1984). Loving hate. *Annual of Psychoanalysis, 12,* 221–37.
Erikson, E. H. (1968). *Identity.* London: Faber & Faber.

Levy-Warren, M. H. (2001). A clinical look at knowing and telling: Secrets, lies, and disillusionments. In Vivian B. Shapiro, Janet Shapiro, and Isabel H. Paret, *Complex adoption and assisted reproductive technology: A developmental approach to clinical practice* (251–75). New York: Guilford Press.

Levy-Warren, M. H. (1999). I am, you are, and so are we: A current perspective on adolescent separation/individuation theory. *Adolescent Psychiatry, 24,* 3–24.

Levy-Warren, M. H. (1996/2004). *The adolescent journey: Development, identity formation, and psychotherapy.* Hillsdale, NJ: Jason Aronson.

Winnicott, D. W. (1949). Hate in the countertransference. *International Journal of Psycho-Analysis, 30,* 69–74.

Part III

The Impact of Clinical Work
on Parenting

NINE

Transformative Aspects of a Personal Analysis

Impasse and Resonance Across Multiple Relational Realms

Lauren Levine

*In this chapter, **Lauren Levine** describes how our own relational stories, our "wounds that must serve as tools" (Harris, 2009), represent both our greatest liabilities and deepest resources for change, at times facilitating and at times impeding our capacity to engage deeply with our children and our patients. She describes how a transformative piece of work in her own analysis in relation to her young son resonated in her work with a patient, enabling the patient to reach out to her vulnerable teenage son in new, reparative ways. As her own analyst helped Levine get to know and give voice to buried, shameful parts of herself, she began to see the path to reaching her son, to understanding the disavowed pain fueling his provocative behavior. Feeling deeply known and recognized by her analyst, she discovered new places within herself that she could draw upon to meet her son's underlying emotional needs. Transformative aspects of our personal analysis, often unconsciously or preconsciously, can thus provide a potential source of creative change in our selves, our parenting, and our work with our patients.*

―◦◉◦―

In this chapter, I will explore ways in which our patients' growth and the healing of old wounds are intimately connected to the analyst's openness to her own vulnerabilities and ungrieved losses (Harris, 2009; Levine,

155

2016). I will describe how a powerful piece of work in my own analysis around the struggle to connect with my young son in the face of his impulsivity and aggression resonated in my work with a patient, Susan, and subsequently created new possibilities in her relationship with her teenage son. Though I had never talked with Susan about my son, I believe that on an implicit relational level (Stern et al., 1998) the experiences in my own analysis and healing in my relationship with my son opened potential space with my patient, enlivening and deepening the treatment. In the process, Susan discovered new places within herself, which enabled her to "join" her son in ways she had never thought possible.

While psychoanalysis has embraced relational notions of intersubjectivity and mutuality in the realm of countertransference, little is known about what Harris (2009) calls "the analyst's wounds that must serve as tools, aspects of the analyst's capacities that are simultaneously brakes and potentials for change." Our own relational history at times facilitates, and at other times hinders our capacity to engage deeply in the analytic process. Transformative aspects of our personal analysis reside, often unconsciously or preconsciously, in our analytic work with others, creating unexpected obstacles and opportunities in our work with our patients.

Years ago, the mother of a young child patient told me the following story. Tired and cranky after a wonderful but very long day in the park, her little boy's behavior escalated into a full-blown tantrum. Kicking and screaming, at some point he picked up a belt and hit her—with the metal end. After taking a deep breath, the mother gently put her arms around him; they sank down to the floor together, and he began to cry, finally allowing her to comfort him. Moved by her capacity to respond lovingly in the face of her son's aggression, I asked her, "How were you able to do that?" She responded, "Someone very wise once told me that when your kid is at his *worst*, he needs you the *most*."

That story has stayed with me for fifteen years. It still brings tears to my eyes. I find it deceptively simple and surprisingly profound, because in reality, when your kid is at his worst, particularly in an ongoing, challenging way, it can bring out the worst in you as a parent. To have the grace and fortitude to take a step back and reflect, to take a deep breath and allow your rage to dissipate, to be able to tune into your out-of-control child's underlying need for holding and soothing rather than reacting to his bad behavior—that is an inspired act, and something to aspire to. The story also highlights how much we learn from our patients, and the ways in which our patients' fault lines and vulnerabilities can, at times, collide with our own in surprising, unpredictable ways (Levine, 2015). But I'm getting ahead of myself.

At age four, my younger son was hyperactive and impulsive, with expressive and receptive language processing issues. Frustrated by his difficulty communicating and being understood, he was often aggressive at home and in trouble at school. This was many years ago, but I can still remember him standing in the schoolyard, fists clenched, tears streaming down his face, yelling at another child who was running away from him, "You're not listening to me!" It broke my heart. I was desperate to help him. I was his staunch advocate and supporter. But privately I also felt frustrated, angry, and helpless, as we were frequently stuck in polarizing power struggles.

In her paper "'Betwixt the Dark and the Daylight' of Maternal Subjectivity," Kraemer (1996) deconstructs romanticized, idealized notions of the "good-enough" mother and explores the complexity and anguish of maternal anger, shame, and helplessness. I would argue that the idealization of motherhood in our culture creates an even greater burden for mothers in our profession. It felt particularly painful to me that I seemed to be able to help other families in my practice wrestling with similar issues, and yet I could not unlock the secret of how to reach my own son. What would my patients think if they knew how much I was struggling with my son? I felt enormous shame in "not knowing" how to calm him, heal him. It wasn't that I did not see the sweetness in him, the passion and exuberance; we had many affectionate, loving moments. It just felt so hard to "hold" him in a Winnicottian sense, to stay connected in an ongoing way in the face of his provocative behavior.

Although he was receiving a range of therapies, I believe it was a challenging piece of work in my own analysis that had the greatest impact. Having grown up in a family of girls, the oldest, responsible "together" child, I experienced this intense boy as "unknowable" on some level, hard to identify with. Feeling overwhelmed and exhausted, it was difficult for me to acknowledge that what he might need was *more* of me but *something different* that I had not been able to give him before. My son was struggling mightily at school and at home, acting aggressively in ways that frightened other children, and as much I was trying to help him, it was not making enough of a difference, and things were escalating. So I struggled with my analyst to own my part in it, determined to be there for my son in the ways in which he needed me to be. My analyst challenged me to see what I had been missing, to understand my son's aggression not only as biologically driven but also as a protest, a response to being misunderstood. I began to see how difficult it was for me to feel "in sync" with him when he was agitated or acting out—that I was responding more "from the outside" by trying to contain him. I began to realize the importance of not just reacting to his behavior, which was making me anxious or angry, or both, but also trying to stay calm, to join him from the inside. Gradually, his agitated states began to feel less foreign to me, and he began to feel less "bad" and more understood.

How did this happen? It took time for me to recognize the degree of anguish that my son and I were both experiencing and to acknowledge that we needed help. It felt shameful to reveal to my analyst the extent of the difficulties in my relationship with my son. I worried that she would be critical, see me as a bad mother. Although we had never talked directly about her grown children, I had the idealized fantasy that she was a wonderful mother, deeply committed to her children; that she had weathered challenging moments herself; and that she drew on her experiences of mothering in our work together. Unconsciously, I think I was terrified of recognizing and owning my own aggression and destructiveness. But it was through my beginning to acknowledge the extent of my frustration and anger at my son that I became more able to empathize with him. As my analyst helped me get to know and give voice to those buried, shameful parts of myself, I began to see the path to reaching my son.

Without ever meeting him, somehow my analyst had faith in him and, I suppose, in me as well. She saw his sensitivity and vulnerability, his capacity to be healed and held, through me. Even when I couldn't, even when I felt desperate, frustrated, not "getting" him, she believed he would be all right, and she helped me to believe it, to feel that whoever he was, was "good enough." She helped me to see the disavowed pain that lay underneath, fueling his provocative behavior, the pain of rejection by other children, the pain of not feeling understood on multiple levels. And when he felt known, recognized and loved for all of him, he settled down, his aggression *fell away*. My son's attentional and language difficulties had clearly compromised his ability to regulate his emotional experience, but as I became more able to join him and help him put his experience into words, he began to calm down. I could feel and see the impact it was having on him, on his sense of self as well as on his behavior. It became apparent over time just how sensitive and articulate he could be about his own emotional experience and attuned to the affective experiences of others.

I want to convey what a unique perspective this was, what a revelation. Almost everyone was relating to him as a difficult, demanding child. The feedback he was getting all around him, from many family, friends, and teachers was that his behavior was unacceptable, that *he* needed to change. So, not surprisingly, he had begun to feel like a "bad boy." Of course, the parallel message to me, as his mother, was to set more limits, to *control* his behavior. We both felt the shame of not being good enough. But what I began to discover was that he needed me to be different from everyone else, to not react to him based solely on his behavior and other peoples' expectations. Like the mother who was able to wrap her arms around her son after he hit her with the belt buckle, to soothe him and help him regulate his distress, to connect to his shame in feeling out of control, I discovered new places within myself that I could draw upon to meet his underlying emotional needs.

There was something initially frightening but ultimately liberating about letting go in the presence of my analyst, helping me break out of a state of aloneness and collapse, which allowed me to fall apart, to be a mess, to acknowledge the depths of my own pain, anger, and helplessness. Not surprisingly, I began to feel freer to express aggressive feelings toward my analyst as well, to provoke and challenge her directly, and over time I developed an increasing capacity to play with aggression within the context of the analytic relationship. This led to a greater sense of emotional freedom, authenticity, and aliveness, which in turn enabled me to provide that "safe enough" environment for my son, so that I could embrace *all of him*. When it goes well, psychoanalysis gives one the experience of being in a relationship that feels safe enough that one can begin to feel less ashamed and humiliated by, and more aware of, those split-off, unacceptable parts of oneself. There was something so powerful for me about my analyst's acceptance and faith in me and my son, her embracing of our vulnerabilities, and her belief in our resilience and capacity for change.

One Monday morning on the way to school, my son was agitated, distressed, *not* listening. Momentarily exasperated, I felt something shift in me as I saw him with fresh eyes. I asked, "Is it hard to go back to school on Monday when we've been together all weekend?" He stopped moving and looked me directly in the eye. "Because it's hard for me to go back to work. I miss you when I'm at work." His *whole body calmed down,* and he took my hand and we walked to school together.

Years later, my son, the little boy in the schoolyard who cried out "You're not listening to me!" has become a serious musician: guitar player, singer, composer of original music. He has found his voice—and it's passionate and soulful.

Solow Glennon (2007) describes how singing was a source of healing for her in the mourning process after the death of her first husband. She suggests that "access to genuine, heartfelt emotion can be facilitated by artistic expression as well as by the immediate experience of an authentic affective engagement with another." Drawing on Ogden's work, she then proposes that at its heart, psychoanalysis seeks to foster authenticity, aliveness, and creativity—which leads me to the second part of my story.

Having never been in therapy, fearful of the ghosts and unbearable affects that would emerge if we delved too deeply into her past, Susan asked in the first session whether we could focus exclusively on helping her leave her emotionally abusive husband and on her tremendous fears about the impact of divorce on her son. Once I gave her permission to define the boundaries and determine the pace of our work together, Susan felt safe enough to begin treatment. I soon understood that Susan was a woman who had experienced significant trauma, much of it dissociated, and that it would take us a while to get to those darker places.

Over the years, Susan made remarkable strides. She began to separate from and make peace with her domineering father, mobilized herself to leave her marriage, survived breast cancer, and began the process of mourning her mother, who had committed suicide when Susan was only four years old. But even with all the growth and change, there was still a subtle affective flatness, a constriction and caution, and difficulty taking action. Susan periodically asked me whether I thought she was making progress, wondering if I was "pushing her enough." Though we explored questions about what blocked her from feeling more spontaneous and empowered, this didn't enliven the treatment in any sustained, meaningful way.

Susan grew up with her father and younger sister in Chicago. As I mentioned, her mother committed suicide when Susan was four. There had been no room for mourning in her family. It was clear that her father, a lawyer, traumatized by the death of his own mother in childhood, could not tolerate the pain of mourning his wife's death or help his young children do so, particularly given the unbearable trauma and guilt of suicide. Thus, there were at least two generations of maternal loss and abandonment, unmetabolized, unprocessed. Rather than helping his children keep memories of their mother alive, he tried to bury all traces of her.

Not surprisingly, Susan had few memories of her mother, and it took time for her to develop a real curiosity about who her mother was, as well as an appreciation of the impact of the loss. Not wanting to anger her volatile father or cause him more pain, Susan had refrained from asking questions about her mother or the exact circumstances of her death, which had been shrouded in mystery. We explored questions about knowing and not knowing, wanting and not wanting to know. Eventually, it dawned on Susan that her mother had never recovered from a severe postpartum depression, or possibly postpartum psychosis, after her birth.

Susan had been a good girl, a superior student, eager for her critical father's approval. Susan's grandmother (her mother's mother) was also a significant parental figure—a gentle, loving presence, the only person who provided unconditional love. She died when Susan was in her early twenties, and Susan married soon afterward. Though she had doubts about her husband, she deferred to his pressure to get married, anxious for the security of a relationship. He was familiar: critical, controlling, and ultimately emotionally abusive. They had one child, a son with significant learning and attentional issues as well as emotional vulnerabilities.

When Susan entered treatment, then in her early forties, she was terrified of the impact that divorce would have on her son, as he was already vulnerable. However, her husband was also emotionally abusive toward her son, and Susan ultimately realized that she needed to move out for her son's sake as well as her own. After a number of years of therapy, and with great trepidation, she left the marriage, only to be diagnosed with breast cancer soon afterward.

After bravely enduring a mastectomy and chemotherapy, facing her own mortality at age forty-eight, and the fear of abandoning her son by dying, Susan fell into an agitated depression. Having always been high functioning and self-sufficient, it was terrifying to her to feel such help-lessness and despair. During this period, sessions never felt long enough; it was uncharacteristically difficult for her to leave each one. I felt her maternal longing and hunger in a way I had never experienced before.

Enormously relieved as she was beginning to come out of the depres-sion, she came in one day and told me, out of the blue, that she was planning to move to Chicago to be close to her father, leaving her son to live with her ex-husband in New York City. She rationalized that her son would be able to manage with his father in New York. It so took me by surprise that I almost fell off my chair! Or, more accurately, I felt the urge to jump out of my chair and shake her, to cry out, "Are you kidding me?!"

How to understand this enactment after all the concerns she had had about the impact of divorce on her son, and her anguish about the pos-sibility of abandoning him to his abusive father if she had not survived the cancer? What was she trying to communicate that "was not yet other-wise expressible . . . a signal of what was stirring just beneath the surface of the waters" (Jacobs, 1991, p. 49)?

I was powerfully aware of the risk of intergenerational repetition of abandonment: her father's mother had died when her father was a child, her own mother had committed suicide when Susan was four, and now Susan was on the verge of abandoning her son to the care of his unstable father. Of course, there was another level of the threat of abandonment lurking just below the surface of our mutual awareness: we were still right in the thick of our work together. Where did she think she was *going*? Suddenly, I was thrust into the position of the little girl being left without warning. What was Susan trying to help me understand about her experience that I had not been aware of before? Bass (2003) has sug-gested that in enactments, "the analyst is especially challenged to locate in herself personal forms of creative responsiveness to the complex sub-tleties of an analytic moment, and the fate of the analytic process itself often hinges on the patient's and the analyst's both coming to new, ex-panded modes of self-awareness" (p. 661).

While offering Susan my interpretation about the repetition of inter-generational abandonment was critical, I think that what really allowed us to begin to think, to reflect together on this enactment, was that it resonated powerfully for me, and I drew on my experience, as a mother who had had to reckon with the ways in which I had abandoned my own son, perhaps in more subtle but still powerful ways. I struggled to lean into my own experience with my son, to tap into the challenges of embracing a child who has hit you with a belt, without shaming him. Shifting back and forth between the positions of mother and child, trying to hold *the relationship in mind*, I felt the urgency of breaking through Susan's denial of the devastating impact this would have on her son while being mindful of not shaming her. As I wrote in a previous paper, "shame can travel insidiously across relational realms, passed back and forth, alternately projected and introjected, from analyst to patient" and back again (Levine, 2012). Susan, like me, had been a very different child from her son, and she, too, found it difficult to identify and join with her son. Initially, I had not seen the degree to which she was emotionally abandoning him, due to my own identification with her as a good mother doing the best she could, a good girl with a challenging boy. Clearly, identifications with patients, overlaps in our lives and histories, can present potential blind spots as well as "bright spots," or opportunities for resonance (Goldberger, 1993). But the threat of this multigenerational abandonment broke through our mutual dissociation so that we could begin to understand how her unconscious identification with her mother had led to the threat of this intergenerational repetition of abandonment.

For the first time, Susan began to grapple directly with her mother's death as a suicide and the treatment took on an affective urgency that we had never experienced together. As we processed this enactment together, Susan gained access to deep layers of unconscious identification with her mother, and we began to understand her depression and the repetition of abandonment as an unconscious attempt to *get to know* her mother, to *feel* her through this experience, from the inside out. Having hit bottom in this depression, she began to understand for the first time the depths of her mother's anguish before she killed herself by jumping off a building. She could finally empathize with how excruciating it had been for her mother to feel so hopeless. This allowed her to become conscious of her anger at her mother for abandoning her, of the rage and guilt underlying the sadness of the loss. Susan had looked down into the abyss but hadn't jumped. Why had her mother?

Months later, Susan came in one day feeling depressed without knowing why. She spent the session talking about work-related issues. Near the end of the session, Susan told me that we were approaching the fiftieth anniversary of her mother's death and wondered if that could be related to her vague sense of depression. Even after months of mourning, working through the layers of dissociation around her mother's suicide, the impact of this profound loss was difficult to hold onto, echoing Stern's (1983) notion of "rescuing unformulated experience from the oblivion of the familiar." Susan looked so lost at that moment, so alone, like a sad, little girl. Having survived divorce, breast cancer, and depression, this motherless child stood stricken before me as she got up to leave.

Spontaneously, we reached out and hugged each other and she burst into tears, letting me hold her for a few moments.

In the next session, Susan reported that she had cried for two days after our last session. She had gone for a walk that night and sat on a park bench weeping inconsolably and cried out, "I lost my mother! I lost my mother!" We talked about what it meant to Susan that I had hugged her at that moment, a spontaneous gesture perhaps evoking unconscious, somatic body memories of being held by her mother. This, in turn, unleashed both tremendous longing and heartbreaking loss. Unlike her mother, Susan had had the experience of hitting bottom and surviving, walking around in the world of intolerable pain while being held, letting go in a safe enough environment in the presence of another. Unlike her experience as a little girl (and earlier in the treatment), this time she was able to mourn her mother more freely with another who could now tolerate the depths of her rage and pain, so that Susan could begin to forgive her. Having gotten more deeply in touch with both love and loss, Susan poignantly reflected, "If my mother felt as bad as I did, or worse, she didn't kill herself because she didn't love me—I think she *did* love me—but she couldn't stand the pain. It was just too much to bear."

Interestingly, Susan's announcement to me that she wanted to move to Chicago opened up the lens to the emotional abandonments that had already occurred that we had not seen clearly until now. While we had talked about her son and his struggles, we had not focused as much on aspects of their relationship that were problematic, the power struggles, the intense fighting. She was so invested in being a good mother, and ashamed about her struggles with her child, that she had successfully kept this raw material out of the room, and largely out of awareness. In my unconscious identification with her, I had colluded with her in her perception that it was her toxic husband who was damaging to her son, his rage, his pathology. This was true, but not the whole story, as it also obfuscated the degree to which Susan had not sufficiently protected her son from his father's abusiveness.

On his sixteenth birthday, Susan gave her son a card that said, "No matter where you go, remember you'll always be loved." Her son's response was "That's nice, but where were you all those years that Dad was being abusive to me?" Susan was speechless, hurt, and angry. Not wanting to be defensive or retaliatory, she said nothing. We talked about her son's sense of having been neglected, how Susan wished she could "erase" the past.

"What would you erase?" I asked.

"His hurt," she responded.

We discussed how excruciating it felt to bear witness to her son's anger and blame, to take responsibility and apologize for not being there when he had needed her protection, familiar territory for me. Perhaps Susan had been blind to the extent of her husband's abusiveness toward herself and her son because allowing herself to experience this horror would have meant opening up access to intolerable pain in her past which she had not yet been ready to face. I have enormous admiration for Susan's efforts to come to terms with the anguish she has suffered as well as the pain she has caused. In her genuine efforts to reconnect with her son, Susan has had to reckon with the tragedy of repetition while creating space for reparation and forgiveness.

The treatment continued to open up into a more flexible, affectively vibrant place as we explored themes of aliveness and deadness, presence and absence. In the transference, there was a noticeable shift from seeking approval to a search for recognition of her true self, a desire to be seen in all her complexity. With much sadness, Susan wistfully mourned the passage of time, the years she wasted in her unhappy marriage and less than fulfilling career. This led to an opening up of creativity, and a desire to take meaningful action.

Susan had a dream that she was on an island that was burning, a wasteland. It was terrifying. Suddenly a giant horse with wings (and brown hair!) flew down out of the sky. She climbed on its back, and they soared off over the island, finally at a safe distance from the danger, as they surveyed the horrors below.

As we analyzed the dream, Susan began to smile, then cry, and was able to articulate with intense feeling, how much her relationship to her brown-haired analyst meant to her. She talked about the relief of being able to look at her life, past and present together, with open eyes and greater perspective. She told me that what was most striking to her about the dream was that although we were soaring miles above the earth, she was not afraid. While neither Susan nor I realized it at the time, I think Susan's dream of flying poetically captures the transmutation of her unconscious identification with her mother and her mother's suicide (by jumping off a building) to a less dissociated, more painful, but more authentic affective experience, flying *up* as opposed to *down* (Neil Altman, personal communication). It felt palpably clear to both of us that flying up instead of falling down like her mother was a remarkable transformation.

Susan decided to take a memoir writing class, and we had many conversations about how the process of writing both facilitated her access to painful memories and helped contain them, echoing Solow Glennon's (2007) notions of how the creation of "an aesthetic container is a way of channeling the chaos of pain into a potentially healing beauty and form." Interestingly, it was around this time that I began to consciously make links between my own experiences in analysis and my relationship with my son and the ways in which it resonated in the work with Susan, and I was first inspired to write this paper. Clearly there was an opening up of creativity and a capacity to play in the treatment that reverberated deeply for both of us.

A year later, Susan began taking acting classes. Acting had been a passion of hers as a child, and she had shown promise, but she had been discouraged by her father from pursuing an acting career. She discovered, to her delight, that she was inspired by acting and received recognition from teachers, leading to an invitation to join a master class for talented actors. We discussed the importance of rediscovering acting after thirty years, realizing that she had not pursued it earlier not only because her father had disapproved but also out of her own fear of tapping into terrifying feelings: the fear of falling apart, the fear of going crazy like her mother. She said, "I never could have articulated that years ago, but that's what it was. Acting requires me to dig deep into painful emotional territory. Therapy has freed me to go to those deeper places within myself with less fear."

When I talked with Susan about my paper and asked her permission to write about our work together, I was revealing a great deal about myself, my relationship with my son, and my own vulnerabilities. And yet. After twelve years of work together, we knew each other on multiple levels, both conscious and unconscious. It resonated for her that I knew something about the exquisite pain of mothering a struggling child. She told me that she had always felt my empathy for her son as well as for her, and that I had always kept him in mind in a way that mattered to her, just as my own analyst had kept *my* son in mind. This paper was complicated to write for many reasons, including concerns about exposing my son's privacy, my patient's, my own. I worried that Susan, a private person, wouldn't give me permission to write about our work. When I asked her, she felt moved and, more important, trusting of me with this delicate task in the context of a deepened therapeutic relationship. We discussed how she might not have felt comfortable earlier in the treatment, before the mutual opening up of creativity I described. When the paper was done, she wanted to read it in its entirety but felt anxious about reading it on her own, so we came up with the idea of reading the paper together in our sessions.

Susan pored over it slowly over several months, asking questions, wanting to understand the theory as well as the clinical material. She read it twice. Sometimes the paper would evoke intense feelings or memories that she wanted to pursue, and we would follow those associations. Sometimes she would put the paper aside when she had other things on her mind. What I never anticipated was the degree to which Susan, whose mother had committed suicide when she was four, would feel found and recognized seeing herself reflected through my eyes. Reading about my parental angst led to both a de-idealization of me and a stronger identification and intimacy. Reading the paper also evoked envy, competition, and a yearning to know me more deeply, along with some frustration and sadness about the limits and boundaries of our therapeutic relationship. All this we continue to process, with many unanswered questions about the meaning and impact this will have on the treatment over time.

Not surprisingly, the paper reopened old wounds: her mother's suicide, unresolved issues with her critical father, her abandonment of her son. With her aging father, it increased her sense of what remained unspoken between them. On a recent visit, her father went on a tirade about how disappointed he was in her, how he had given her everything. Tempted to either yell at him or cry, something shifted in Susan, allowing her access to love and anger. She said, "Dad, I love you." Taken aback, he responded, "Well, I love you too." "Well, it doesn't always feel that way," Susan retorted. Afraid of killing him with her anger for fifty years, Susan now opened a new dialogue, disarming him with love. Reading about neglecting her son was agonizing, and yet it resonated for her, renewing her resolve to be there for him.

Ehrenberg (1992) describes the "intimate edge" as "not simply at the boundary between self and other; it is also at the boundary of self-awareness. . . . It is a point of expanding self-discovery, at which one can become more intimate with one's own experience through the evolving relationship with the other, and then more intimate with the other as one becomes more attuned to oneself" (pp. 34–35).

My son challenged me in ways I had never been challenged before. He put me in touch with my most vulnerable selves. He, together with my analyst, gave me a gift for which I'm enormously grateful, pushing me to stretch myself beyond my limits, to embrace previously disowned anger and pain, permitting access to deeper love and connection. This allowed me to be more responsive to my son's pain as well as the anguish of my patients. I believe that the transformative experiences in my own analysis and, subsequently, in my relationship with my son opened new possibilities in my work with Susan, helping us both free ourselves from old identifications and constraints, thus making possible a deeper level of vulnerability, intimacy, and mutual recognition.

REFERENCES

Bass, A. (2003). "E" enactments in psychoanalysis: Another medium, another message. *Psychoanalytic Dialogues, 13,* 657–75.

Ehrenberg, D. (1992). *The intimate edge.* New York: Norton.

Goldberger, M. (1993). "Bright spot," a variant of "blind spot." *Psychoanalytic Quarterly, 62,* 270–73.

Harris, A. (2009). You must remember this. *Psychoanalytic Dialogues, 19,* 2–21.

Jacobs, T. (1991). *The use of the self.* New York: International Universities Press.

Kraemer, S. (1996). "Betwixt the dark and the daylight" of maternal subjectivity: Meditations on the threshold. *Psychoanalytic Dialogues, 6,* 765–91.

Levine, L. (2016). A mutual survival of destructiveness and its creative potential for agency and desire. *Psychoanalytic Dialogues, 26,* 36–49.

Levine, L. (2015). Mutual vulnerability: Intimacy, violation, and the shards of trauma. Paper presented at the International Association of Relational Psychoanalysis and Psychotherapy Conference. Toronto, June 2015.

Levine, L. (2012). Into thin air: The co-construction of shame, recognition and creativity in an analytic process. *Psychoanalytic Dialogues, 22*, 456–71.

Ogden, T. (2005). *This art of psychoanalysis*. London: Routledge.

Solow Glennon, S. (2007). Affective authenticity: Crossovers between artistic expression and the therapeutic action of psychoanalysis. Paper presented at the International Association of Relational Psychoanalysis and Psychotherapy Conference, Athens, June 2007.

Stern, D. (1983). Unformulated experience: From familiar chaos to creative disorder. *Contemporary Psychoanalysis, 19*, 71–99.

Stern, D., Sander, L., Nahum, J., Harrison, A., Lyons-Ruth, K., Morgan, A., Bruschweilerstern, N., and Tronick, E. (1998). Non-interpretive mechanisms in psychoanalytic therapy: The "something more" than interpretation. *International Journal of Psychoanalysis, 79*, 903–21.

TEN

Why Did You Choose Me?

Some Thoughts on the Wish to Have a Child
and the Child's Wished-For Parent

Banu Seckin-Erkal

*This chapter, written by **Banu Seckin-Erkal**, will explore some aspects of parenthood that have to do with the wish to be a parent, the child's thoughts and fantasies regarding why he/she was wished for, and finally the child's efforts to create his/her wished for parent. Psychoanalytic concepts of unconscious wish/ fantasy, interpenetration of affects, introjective/projective mechanisms, and projective identification will be utilized to think about this fascinating process of discovery and creation of the other in daily parent-child interactions by providing personal anecdotes and clinical examples. The writer argues that this process is ubiquitous in all child-parent relationships, and when it is primarily positive/ libidinal, as it is in most cases, it markedly strengthens and enriches the primary bond of parenthood, making the process of becoming essential and staying valuable far easier.*

He was born on an island far away where imaginary friends were created. Here, they lived and played, each eagerly waiting to be imagined by a real child. Every night he stood under the stars, hoping for his turn to be picked by a child and given a special name. He waited for many nights. But his turn never came. His mind filled with thoughts of all the amazing things that were keeping his friend from imagining him. So rather than waiting . . . he did the unimaginable.

—*The Adventures of Beekle, the Unimaginary Friend,* by Dan Santat

A BEDTIME STORY

It was just like any other night. We read our book. Talked and laughed. I tucked him in and reached out to turn off the light. He said, "Mom, why did you choose me?" "What do you mean?" I asked. "Why *me*; why did you want *me* among all my friends as your baby?"

I did not know what to say. Where was this coming from? I wanted to go with something like "Honey, *you* came our way, boy or girl, did not matter for us, we just wanted a healthy baby and it turned out to be the wonderful you!" But I just couldn't say it. It did not feel right when he was looking into my eyes in such a way, clearly expecting something less mundane and much more interesting from me, but I did not know what. I am embarrassed to admit it, but I fell into the therapist mode with my own six-year-old son and asked, "Love, can you say more about what you are thinking?"

Oblivious to my therapeutic address, he eagerly went right ahead and, Valentine's Day imagery aside (yes, we were in February when this exchange happened), I heard a better story than the one I read that night. He said, "Mommy, listen to this. Me and my bow-and-arrow friends were sitting on the clouds. I saw you guys walking around on the ground. I first stuck you and then Daddy with my arrows because I knew *you* wanted *me,* and then I got down on my cloud to your stomach when you kissed Daddy, and voilà, you had a baby in your tummy!"

At that point I was so amused that I just went along with it and asked gleefully, "And exactly why we wanted *you*?"

He said, "Because *you* knew I was the son *you* always wanted."

"OK, then, what about you, why did *you* choose us?"

"Because *you* were the mommy and daddy *I* always wanted." And then he said, "It is a perfect match, isn't it?"

I said, "Yes, it is, so happy to have *you,*" and turned off the light.

A perfect match . . . What is the wish to be a parent really about, if not creating not any but *that* child who is . . . and you can fill in this blank with a myriad of things. What about the child's efforts to understand why *he/she* was wished for, but not any other child? Moreover, can the child also create his/her own parents in the ways he/she wishes them to be? This fascinating process of "the match," the co-creation and co-discovery of the self and the other was present in my son's story in such a simple, yet powerful, way. It is a ubiquitous process in the creation of all relationships, the core of which is formed at the place where it all begins—the parent-child relationship. This process, if it mostly goes well, not only strengthens and enriches that primary bond but also further shapes that particular match that leaves its irremovable positive mark on all subsequent relationships.

In this chapter, I will have a chance to explore some details as to how this process works in parent-child relationships, as well as why and how, at times, it can go off track, and also try to comment on its parallels in treatment between the therapist and the patient.

> He sailed through unknown waters and faced many scary things. But thinking about his friend gave him the courage to journey on . . . until he reached the real world.
>
> —*The Adventures of Beekle*

THE PERFECT MATCH IN THE REAL WORLD

Offerman-Zuckerberg (1992) affirms that parenthood is not only a biological but also a psychological milestone in people's lives. It is one of the most enriching, but at the same time depleting, life experiences. Parents make themselves available to their children as an emotional center to mirror, contain, and regulate their affective expressions and to be cherished, used, and battered in multiple daily interactions toward the child's internalization of these important affective relational capacities from their parents.

Marlin (1988) aptly names this process as the "emotional strain of optimal presence" where the parent is busy on a daily basis with containing and processing affects to facilitate growth. Parents' innate and learned sensitivity to their children's developmental needs and vulnerabilities guide this path of growth that starts with an essential union which moves in time toward increasing degrees of separation that enable individuation and autonomy.

Parents and children adapt to one another and grow together not only within the family but also in the community where they live. Anna Freud (1947) states that within the environment the child lives in, be it family or the larger community, the child's instinctual life is always subject to an evaluation that is based on the normal and ethical standards of that adult community. She gives examples such as children's oral wishes being seen as greediness, anal ones as dirtiness, aggressive and destructive urges as naughtiness, and exhibitionism as shameless.

Anna Freud adds that parents and children are often at cross-purposes during this maturation, adaptation and growth route, where parents are concerned with adaptation to the expected standards and children can be preoccupied with wish fulfillment. Freud says children understand these standards; yet they keep doing the not-to-be-done because the wish is too powerful to govern action (still picking up broken glass from the floor, leaving a parent's hand to dash across the street, or screaming and throwing a tantrum for a toy), and she adds that the sense of time is also vastly different as five minutes feels like eternity, which makes delay of gratification (waiting, being patient) very difficult. Hence, on this arduous road to growth, children exhibit various fears and anxieties as they fear parental punishment and loss of parental love, and their expected parental retributions often take cruel and fantastic forms like their hands or penis cut off, arms paralyzed, fears of being sent away, and so forth.

Anna Freud states that the child in time gives in and manages to keep in the unacceptable and learns to display the expected behaviors. So, what happens to what is kept in? How does it shape the child's sense of self and his/her interactions with parents? How do the parents further shape what's kept in and how are they impacted by it in their daily interactions with their children?

Kennedy et al. (1985) state that fantasy brings together diverse mental contents in the service of wish fulfillment in unique combinations, which do not correspond to either the past or the present reality. Fantasies are distinguished from memories and percepts, although memories and percepts, in literal and/or distorted form, are used as material for fantasy formation. Affects, percepts, memories, and all other mental contents provide the psychic bricks with which fantasies are constructed, as they foster a kind of adaptation to the reality as stressed by Hartmann in 1939. Or one can say that fantasies are that mental phenomena that are kept in as one of the most powerful ways to put up with the constraints and disappointments the real world bears.

Fantasies are internal regulators bringing together conflicting wishes and they can change form and function over the course of one's development. One can easily think of the reversal of the feeding situation in serving pretend food to dolls and plush toys, or my son's fantasy of specialness, control, mastery, and turning passive into active that we, his parents, did not create him, but he created us and himself. Further examples include mastering separation in games ranging from peek-a-boo to hide and seek, to fantasies of heroic adventures or going on long journeys to different escape fantasies of adults. As fantasies increase in complexity throughout development, feelings of helplessness and insignificance warded off by carrying Mommy's bag or her car keys graduate toward having the latest technological gadgets and wearing brand-name clothing. Hence, wish and defense work hand in hand in fantasies toward an internal adaptation together with the help of the real world for its reinforcement. Opposite wishes also get reconciled, as exemplified by the child who in make-believe alternates between being himself and taking the persona of the naughtiest boy in his class and thus, by alternating identities, disowns responsibility for "bad behaviors," while at the same time continuing to express them.

One can say that fantasy formation involves healthy use of imagination to solve problems and fantasies ensure gratification and a certain mental equilibrium. Thus, as Kennedy et al. (1985) put it, fantasies and make-believe play should not become a source of disapproval, danger, and/or shame. Parents who just expect children to play with toys, or just by themselves and rarely engage with their play when invited, or parents who always mandate stillness and quiet, or who constantly intrude, interrupt, or impose and direct the child's play, are not really allowing children's wishes to come into play in a spontaneous way, or are denigrating and ridiculing them as childish in overt or covert ways. Usually children react to the above parental impingements by trying to obliterate the parental voice by shouting or singing over that voice, or covering their ears, or with passivity and withdrawal, and at times even with a total resignation.

Yorke (1996a) points out that most parents can indeed reach back to their child selves, and most of them know how to play with their children appropriate to that age and actually enjoy this involvement. It is as if somehow they remember through the various activities their children are engaged in just what it was like to be a child with wants and needs that they themselves have put behind a long time ago. This capacity to play, as noted by Kennedy et al. (1985), remains essential for future imagination and creativity in children, and also to internalize a sense of playfulness in their personal outlook to themselves, others, and the world. They state that children who exhibit an excessive impermeability of their defenses against their wishes/needs can display "a mental woodenness, excessive personal constraint and an intolerance of id derivatives in self and others" (p. 282).

THE PERFECT MATCH OF THE MINDS

In his paper "The Unconcious," Freud (1915) writes, "It is a very remarkable thing that the Unconcious of one human being can react on that of another, without passing through the Consciousness." Kafka (1992) states that parents can engage in a conscious communication of their affectionate desires in their discourse, behaviors, and play; however, children are influenced not only by this communication but also by the covert messages transmitted by the parents of which they themselves are unaware. So there is a shared mental space where children and parents both respond to one another's conscious and unconscious communication in order to secure the survival of their relationship and keep its internalization intact in their minds.

Examples of such communication can be found in the covertly guilt-inducing parent ("I am perfectly fine with leftover food for a few days until you can visit and cook for me") or in messages regarding valued interests and preferences ("Grandpa was a great artist, but nobody seems to take after him in this family"), in sought-after or denigrated character traits and behaviors ("I am glad you just took after Grandma's ears, not those stubborn eyes"), in slips and symptoms (every time a mother comes to help her daughter with her new baby she has a gastrointestinal issue), and in parental mood states (as one patient put it, "This is Dad, no matter what you do, and no matter that wonderful things he says about what you do, there is that drop in his face and it gets dark in the end without fail that I never understood, and frankly I never paid much mind to").

Such parental communications shape the child, while the child in turn molds his/her parent in a very particular way. Upon reflection in treatment, a mother may learn that her child's fear of separation, as she unconsciously wishes the child to remain a docile companion, is indeed fostered by herself and her own behaviors. This child can be clingy, but in her clinginess exhibited in her school phobia, there is a defiance against going along with what the mother wishes (for the child to go and be successful at school) and turning her into an angry resentful mother by putting her own rage at her mother's whims (mother keeping her close or sending her away as she wishes) into her. A father may learn that his son's behavioral problems at school may have something to do with him unconsciously encouraging his child to act out his own conflicted antisocial desires, thus being mad at his son but at the same time gratified by the bravado that his son displays that he could never have expressed himself. His son in return puts this father, over and over, into that position of ineffectiveness and humiliation, essentially depositing much of what he feels about himself into his father.

Freud (1914), in his paper "On Narcissism," classified parental love as love according to the narcissistic type, that is the parent loves what he himself is or what he himself was, or what he would like to be, or someone who was once part of him. Freud says in this paper that if we look at the attitude of affectionate parents toward their children, we have to recognize that it is a revival and reproduction of their own narcissism, which they have long since abandoned. The child will fulfill those wishful dreams of the parents, which they never carried out. He goes on to explain the motive behind this quest for renewal. Freud writes, "At the most touchy point in the narcissistic system, the immortality of the ego, which is so hard pressed by reality, security is achieved by taking refuge in the child commenting on not a biological continuity of the family lineage, but also an emotional continuity."

For expecting parents, the knowledge of a baby on the way leads to a cascade of wishes, both conscious and unconscious, coming to full bloom, the seeds of which were sown when the wish to have a baby first occurred. What we wish to see our children become, and what we need and want as parents, as Freud said, has little to do with ensuring a biological heritage, but a lot do with an emotional one. First, we are set to re-create aspects of our child selves we cherished, never to repeat its detested aspects. Next, we want to embellish it more with the child we wished we were but who never existed. Then we are set to accomplish this in the context of the parenting we wished we had but did not.

Parenthood constitutes this ultimate opportunity provided by our children to work this all through with different degrees of success. Parents can wish for children's independence but make them hostage to their affective whims; they can wish for a powerhouse son but emasculate him at every chance. Children idealize their parents in their discourse only to brutalize them in their dreams, or they identify with parents' intelligence and accomplishments but can't partake of their success. We impart ourselves consciously and unconsciously toward these aims of renewal and re-creation, often oblivious to the overcast of repetition and reenactment in life of that which is not remembered but gets automatically executed, causing significant psychic pain.

The following case example is presented to illustrate this kind of an unconscious overcast despite overt conscious efforts for renewal and re-creation. At this point it is also good to remember what Anna Freud pointed out in 1960 in her discussion of Bowlby's paper on attachment—that what we really deal with in our efforts to understand a person is their mental representations, not what is happening or has happened in the external world, but with the repercussions in the mind regarding how they were registered by them.

"My mom wants me to be happy. She doesn't want me to have a marriage like hers. She wants me to find that great guy, you know, kind, giving, loving and she is so supportive, always there for me. And I want that, too, so very much, but I just can't, what is wrong with me?" says a young female patient, sobbing after enduring another dream about having to use a soiled men's bathroom. She starts her session in her usual manner of listing her worries and fears, ranging from being unable to successfully date to failing to realize her career aspirations, to not being recognized and appreciated at her workplace and by her friends, to her racing, "irrational thoughts" that occur mostly at nighttime, regarding burglars or home invasion scenarios.

Among other aspects of her history and family dynamics, this patient's experience of growing up with a father who was mostly explosive, unpredictable, and self-centered and a mother who tolerated his affective storms, so as not to lose his devotion/obsession with her and her beauty, to the point of disavowing any impact of this environment on her daughter, is noteworthy. Additionally, in the patient's stories about her sister, one gets the sense that her sister seems to keep fostering a similar bond/devotion with her three-year-old son at the expense of excusing his violent tantrums and destructiveness, quite similar to the relationship between her own parents.

This patient's concomitant denial, as she joins her mother in this respect, of any impact of growing up in such an affectively charged environment gets manifested in another dream of hers about taking photographs of exploding mountains unfazed and with eerie calmness, typical of her usual apathy toward her frequent dream content of graphic sexuality and violence. This stance is at odds with the patient's everyday frenzy regarding her grim romantic and career prospects, about finding mice in her apartment, and fears of rape, theft, and home invasion to the point of being unable to sleep alone. How is one to understand this?

As Oppenheim (2013) mentions, meaning is constructed from events in the world and from the actuality of relationships whose representation is shaped by imagination, fueled by a blend of memories and fantasies, toward trying to achieve a gratifying, pleasurable equilibrium in the mind. Children and parents identify with selected aspects of one another through repetition of their relationship that establishes a pattern over the years. Both parties can put idealized/wished-for aspects into one another and rid themselves of what is experienced as intolerable by emptying it into the other during their interpersonal exchanges, and then come to identify with and internalize these affective exchanges that we call the cycle of projections and introjections, leading to projective identifications. Oppenheim further claims that there is the transmission of not just conscious expectations in these exchanges but also unconscious fantasies, anxieties, and defensive mechanisms, which extends across generations through the fluidity of psychic borders between the parent and the child using this very process of projective identification. The above clinical segment aims to illustrate such transmission as this patient who so does not want to repeat the life of her mother ends up trapped like her in her identification with the defensive stance of her mother's focus on the trivial, in denial of the real problems/trauma, and in how she feels emotionally miles away from her father, yet hostage to him in her dreams and her failing dating life.

Rucker and Mermelstein (1979) state that an individual is unique precisely because he or she is the particular child of a particular set of parents, at a particular point in time, under particular circumstances. Each parent creates a unique child, just as each child creates a unique parent. The creation of the child's psyche begins many generations before the birth, an heir to that family, being born into that family with its specific needs and history. They state that the innumerable potentialities for character development inherent in every human thus is limited and refined by this process. The needs and desires of parents shape certain styles of parenting creating a particular psychological environment for the children. This may fluctuate and vary in time with different circumstances, but it establishes a mold for certain personality characteristics.

As such, parents express their unconscious wishes, fantasies, and conflicts in a myriad of ways that tend to encourage some tendencies and discourage others in their children without being aware of what they are doing/creating. Similarly, children are also unaware consciously of what they are adapting to, and they are unaware of the purpose of their manifest behavior, including its covert aspects, toward their parents, further shaping/creating their own parents. Issues around acceptance, trust, idealization, criticism, rejection, aggression, gender identity, sexual orientation, fears of abandonment, and engulfment get worked through numerous times for both parties in multiple conversations and in being and living with one another.

What are parents to do with this all-too-dangerous gap between the wished for baby and the real baby is rarely discussed, and different efforts to undo this gap even less so. The rupture and loss of oneness is always attempted to be undone with some rationalization. There is as much ambivalence, and even at times hate (see Levy-Warren, this volume), as there is love and devotion, engendered by the relational repercussions of this gap, which both binds and unwinds the parent-child relational matrix in its own ebb and flow.

Parents who can make internal adjustments according to the child's needs and strengths and allow her/him to grow in a less restricted and more separate manner, while receiving gratification from acts of parenting, are what a child benefits from the most. The child who communicates with such parents can have more enriching and fulfilling relationships. One can then say that the capacity to allow and accept the gap between who the child is and who he/she should be seems to be the mutative factor in parenting, and, to borrow Winnicott's term, this capacity is one of the essential elements of "good-enough" parenting to create a "good-enough" childhood experience. In such a scenario, the child attempts to master and integrate the parents needs and wants, and parents do the same in return, and it ends up being more than a repetition but a novel integration and a creative synthesis.

Growth is a path of ongoing change, where earlier stages of life reverberate toward renewal with its concomitant losses within oneself and in the relationship with one's parents. If the gaps in respective wishes, fantasies, and expectations are tolerated and worked through, both the child and the parent end up enlivened, empowered, and re-created by one another in their mutual discoveries along this road.

A FEW WORDS ABOUT THE PERFECT MATCH IN TREATMENT

Harris (1960) states that one can think of two important relationships in which emotional growth occurs. One is that of the parent-child and the other is the therapist-patient relationship. There are obvious differences between these two emotionally significant relationships that have been much discussed and debated in the literature for years (Gitelson, 1952; Harris, 1960; Sandler, 1976; Marlin, 1988; Offerman-Zuckerberg, 1992) that go beyond the scope of this chapter. However, one of the main points of these discussions and debates is that the therapist should be aware of the pitfalls of assuming the position of a parental substitute or attempt to be a better parent than the one the patient had or has, or be the one that the patient never had, no matter how much the patient consciously or unconsciously pulls the therapist to fall into one of these positions. As enticing as this idea of a perfect match is in therapy, its inherent impossibility sooner or later surfaces in enactments, impasses, and foreclosure of exploration or premature or explosive terminations.

However, an important similarity between the parent-child and the therapist-patient relationship is the fact that the patient and the therapist also make a unique pair, and discover and co-create one another in their affectively charged relationship to ensure the psychological survival of both parties, in a way very similar to that of the parent and the child. How patients evoke responses in their therapists and how therapists respond to what has been evoked by the patient have been discussed in the vast literature on transference-countertransference and on enactments in treatment (Heinman, 1950; Benedek, 1953; Kernberg, 1965; Racker, 1968; Brenner, 1983; Joseph, 1985; Chused, 1991; Ellman and Moskowitz, 1998).

Patients evoke wished for responses consciously and unconsciously by their discourse and behaviors, for instance in their neediness, withholding, seduction, and attacks, making the therapist affectively engage in different ways, like passivity, rage, envy, desire, guilt, or retaliation. As patients stimulate certain parent-like reactions in the therapist, the job of the therapist becomes, with the aid of his/her work ego (a composite of years of training, experience, and self-treatment), that of handling these reactions so that they are sublimated toward expanding self-understanding and furthering curiosity and exploration of how the patient's mind works.

A prime source of the power of the psychoanalytically informed treatment is that this network is discovered and gets unfolded in the transference and countertransference matrix to repair and overcome what has gone astray and to create a new perspective, the discovery of that possibility which was never entertained before, as the vignette below aims to illustrate.

A male patient with a congenital musculoskeletal disability and severe social anxiety, "dragged around like a ragged doll," to use the patient's words, for years to specialists, physical therapists, and other therapists by his mother, sums up his life experiences and relationship to his mother as follows: "In short, I am my mom's fixer-upper project."

After some years into treatment, this patient starts to insist on knowing whether I will ever write about him to publish his case or present him at a conference. As we inquired more into his growing need/demand to know, we discover how he wants to feel he is special for me and share this specialness with me in making me the special therapist of a special patient that deserve a clinical discussion, but at the same time he fears my exposure of him/his defects and my using him for my own purposes to gain recognition in being able to handle and treat such a difficult patient. In this constellation of ideas about a grandiose symbiosis between the two of us and its macabre undertones, which we both felt at times in the sessions, what made a difference was not really talking about this dynamic but being able to think together about this demand to hear a concrete answer.

In this preoccupation with the binary of the "yes" or a "no," there was the idea of a lack of any genuine interest and concern on my part for the patient, as I was felt to be only preoccupied by my own clinical advancement and pursuits. This idea of another's interest in or concern for the patient never figured into his experiences and understanding of his relationships.

This novel understanding culminated in its significance when the patient said in subsequent sessions, "You know what's funny, and shameful at the same time, we just discovered that I was really thinking you have no concern for me, but actually I have no concern for you, never had it all along, never considered for a minute what it is like for you all these years being with me in this room. I question you like am I a person for you, but really are you a person for me other than my therapist? I was always preoccupied with did I matter to anyone but really did anyone matter to me, no. I know this all sounds terrible and very hopeless about me, but it is good and a relief to finally know these things about myself and how I choose to see other people, or really not see them at all."

Loewald (1960) points out the essence of the "new object" tie provided by the therapist being really the opportunity to rediscover and rework old pathways of connection, enabling a rediscovery and renewal through transferential relinking and interpenetration of the past and the present. It is the reanimation and reshaping of the old experience within a new relationship. Goldberg (2007) emphasizes the repressed, disavowed, buried "good-enough" aspects of old objects of patients, as in the case of my patient's discovery of his denial of interest in, and concern about, his parents, others in his life, including me for him and what that denial cost him. Goldberg further states that "to go productively to the darkest inner places one needs one's familiar good old object there; no one would go alone, or with a stranger" (p. 266), which also underlines the fact that we were able to have the depth of discussion we had because he had his good old objects, like most of us do, and they were ready to be unearthed.

Parents and therapists both engage in empathic identifications and facilitate growth in different ways. The therapist holds hope and good will, and faith in the process as well as in the patient, which seems to be the bedrock of the therapeutic relationship, from which mutative interventions can spring. In this intimacy of the therapeutic relationship, the felt closeness and support decreases the patient's fears, anxieties, and inhibitions, allowing them to get to a place where they can self-reflect, feel enlightened, and utilize the gains of treatment in a more autonomous way without being dependent on the therapist for his/her psychic survival in a way similar to the healthy growth pattern in a parent-child relationship.

The emotional investment of the therapist in treatment also has a similar motive to that of the parent, the perpetuation of oneself in the patient's mind in memory (see Samstag and Samstag, as well as Bowen, both in this volume), but also, as exemplified in the clinical segment above, as a vital function of regulation and understanding, which now the patient has made his or her own.

There is also an affective feedback component, not much talked about in the literature, that when all goes well, similar to that of what parents experience, the therapist feels that gratitude, affection, admiration of the patient, sometimes expressed in words, but mostly felt in the sessions, that the therapist embraces with happiness, satisfaction, and pride in return for the patient and for him or herself. Ultimately, there is always the excitement about the new discoveries in the sessions and the joy of growth for both parties.

FROM THE PERFECT MATCH TO PERFECT TOGETHER

A perfect match . . . What makes the match perfect in both the parent-child and the therapist-patient relationships, or what works, is not about either of them being a perfect fit, but maybe more of their perfect togetherness. As opposed to the ideas of a perfect match or a perfect fit, in togetherness, if and when it is achieved, there is a proximate, an almost-there quality. It is that inescapable but so valuable gap between the parties that gives the opportunity for a simultaneous surrender and revolt. It is the experiencing self that is being shaped by the other and at the same time resisting a complete surrender, thus furthering its agency. It is almost like saying, "I will have pieces of you in me, but I will not be you." As a young male patient of mine said, "I always got the sense from my mom that I failed her, but you know what, I failed in my own way, not the way she thought, so it is sad that I cannot save myself from what she set me out for me to feel and be, but still I am me, if that makes any sense." In the context of this present volume, what I am describing here is that the "perfect" essentialness of the parent in their child's early infancy inevitably shifts to an experience of "good-enough" mothering that provides the essential gap under discussion. As the parent and child move over time to an experience of ongoing valued relevance on the part of the parent (see Tuber, this volume) and an internalized essential object on the part of the child (see Samstag and Samstag, this volume), the experience of being perfect together comes into fuller relief. In the endearing refrain of my six-year-old, being "good enough" and being "perfect together" are the same, indicative of the all-or-nothing cognitive frame of the early-school-age child. This idealization, regrettably, doesn't last, but the shift to being good enough can be more than tolerable if done gracefully by both parent and child.

In relation to this important idea of the child's simultaneous surrender and revolt, one is reminded of Winnicott's 1963 article, "Communicating and Not Communicating Leading to a Study of Certain Opposites." In this work, Winnicott posits that feeling real, which he links to what he calls the true self, only occurs in the context of a deep sense of existential aloneness, which is never communicated or influenced by external reality. For him, at the center of each human being is an incommunicado element that, in his words, "is sacred and most worthy of preservation" (p. 187). He refers to this phenomena also in his writings about the capacity to be alone (Winnicott, 1958). Both this level of authenticity and the capacity to be alone thus arise from paradox: the gap between surrender and revolt, between being perfect together versus being good enough together, develops from the shift from a perfect essentialness to a valued relevance in the ongoing development of the parent-child relationship.

Ogden (1989) makes a similar claim when talking about the protective function of a degree of personal isolation against the ongoing strain of the unpredictable matrix of relationships. In his work as well, one sees the central role of privacy, a necessity of a temporary suspension of relatedness where this to and fro from privacy to communication preserves a sense of reality and vitality on a phenomenological level.

In *Playing and Reality* (1971), Winnicott talks about the overlap of two areas of playing between the parties involved, a ubiquitous tension between privacy and relatedness. One can say that there is always a degree of battle of wills in a good mutuality. Winnicott, in his usual profound and poetic way, states this dialectic in a 1963 article as follows: "It is a joy to be hidden and a disaster not to be found" (p. 186).

As opposed to the perfect match, in being perfect together, the space in between, allows for a mutuality that involves finding and creating one another, establishing the ability to *be* with another. That is why admitting limits in understanding and being with one another, in both the parental and the therapeutic relationship, is crucial to sustain each person's agency and creativity.

In writing this chapter, two stories inspired my thoughts. One of them is my son's, which I shared at the beginning, and the other is Dan Santat's 2015 Caldecott-winning magical story *The Adventures of Beekle, the Unimaginary Friend*. It is a beautifully illustrated children's picture book from which I sprinkled a couple of selections throughout.

Freud always admired and mentioned in his writings artists'/writers' powers as seers, their ability to intuitively grasp truths about human nature that requires extensive study of psychology for others. In this vein, Santat does intuit and exactly capture what I have been trying to say in this chapter with many more words and still less well than he. In this charming story about doing the unimaginable, a snow-white marshmallow-like magical creature with a golden crown sets off on an adventure to find/create/own another and to be created/named/owned by that other, in the most unlikely match between him and a girl. Their meeting is awkward, tentative, gradual, and even confusing in their attempt at a handshake.

I would like to conclude this chapter with the ending of this story:

> He climbed to the top of a tree and looked out, wishing and hoping his friend would come. But no one came. He thought about how far he'd come and how long he'd waited, and felt very sad. Then he heard a noise below. Hello! Her face was friendly and familiar and there was something about her that felt just right. At first, they weren't sure what to do. Neither of them had made a friend before. But . . . after a little while they realized they were perfect together.

REFERENCES

Benedek, T. (1953). Dynamics of countertransference. *Bulletin of Menninger Clinic, 17,* 201–8.

Brenner, C. (1983). Transference and countertransference. In *The mind in conflict.* New York: International Universities Press.

Chused, J. (1991). The evocative power of enactments. *Journal of American Psychoanalytic Association, 31,* 617–39.

Ellman, S., and Moskowitz, M. (Eds.). (1998). *Enactment: Towards a new approach to the therapeutic relationship.* Hillsdale, NJ: Jason Aronson.

Freud, A. (1947). Emotional and instinctual development. In *The Writings of Anna Freud* 4, 458–88.

Freud, A. (1960). Discussion of Dr. John Bowlby's paper. *Psychoanalytic Study of the Child, 15,* 53–62.

Freud, S. (1914). On narcissism: An introduction. *Standard Edition,* Vol. XIV.

Freud, S. (1915). The unconscious. *Standard Edition,* Vol. XIV.

Gitelson, M. (1952). The emotional position of the analyst in the psychoanalytic situation. *International Journal of Psychoanalysis, 33,* 1–10.

Goldberg, J. (2007). Refinding the good old object: Beyond the good analyst/bad parent. *Contemporary Psychoanalysis, 43,* 261–87.

Harris, I. (1960). Unconscious factors common to parents and analysts. *International Journal of Psychoanalysis, 41,* 123–29.

Hartmann, H. (1939). *Ego psychology and the problem of adaptation.* New York: International Universities Press.

Heinman, P. (1950). On countertransference. *International Journal of Psychoanalysis, 31,* 81–84.

Joseph, B. (1985). Transference: The total situation. *International Journal of Psychoanalysis, 66,* 447–54.

Kafka, E. (1992). The influence of parents' unconscious fantasies on children's adaptation as illustrated by transsexuality. *Journal of Clinical Psychoanalysis, 1,* 547–59.

Kennedy, H., Moran, G., Wiseberg, S., and Yorke, C. (1985). Both sides of the barrier: Some reflections on childhood fantasy. *Psychoanalytic Study of the Child, 40,* 275–83.

Kernberg, O. (1965). Notes on countertransference. *Journal of American Psychoanalytic Association, 13,* 38–56.

Loewald, H. (1960). The therapeutic action of psychoanalysis. *International Journal of Psychoanalysis, 41*, 16–33.

Marlin, O. (1988). Parenthood in the life of the analyst. *Contemporary Psychoanalysis, 24*, 470–77.

Offerman-Zuckerberg, J. (1992). The parenting process: A psychoanalytic perspective. *Journal of American Academy of Psychoanalysis, 20*, 205–14.

Ogden, T. (1989). *The primitive edge of experience*. Northvale, NJ: Jason Aronson.

Oppenheim, L. (2013). *Imagination from fantasy to delusion*. New York: Routledge.

Racker, H. (1968). *Transference and countertransference*. New York: International Universities Press.

Rucker, N. G., and Mermelstein, C. B. (1979). Unconscious communication in the mother-child dyad. *American Journal of Psychoanalysis, 39*, 147–51.

Sandler, J. (1976). Countertransference and role-responsiveness. *International Review of Psychoanalysis, 3*, 43–47.

Santat, D. (2014). *The Adventures of Beekle, the Unimaginary Friend*. New York: Little, Brown Books for Young Readers.

Winnicott, D. (1958). The capacity to be alone. *International Journal of Psychoanalysis, 39*, 416–20.

Winnicott, D. (1965). Communicating and not communicating leading to a study of certain opposites (1963). In *Maturational processes and the facilitating environment*. New York: International Universities Press.

Winnicott, D. (1971). *Playing and reality*. New York: Basic Books.

Yorke, C. (1996a). Childhood and the unconscious. *American Imago, 53*, 227–56.

Yorke, C. (1996b). Anna Freud's contributions to our knowledge of child development: An overview. *Psychoanalytic Study of the Child, 51*, 7–24.

ELEVEN

Becoming a Grandparent

Identifications, Memories, Reenactments, and Reworking

Jerry Meyer

*In this eleventh chapter, artist and psychoanalyst **Jerry Meyer** provides a compelling narrative on the vicissitudes of being a grandparent. He begins by noting the "half empty" glass that conveys the very clear, painful message that being a grandparent can often mean one's own life is on the wane. He then shifts to the many identifications that become alive in the context of grandparenting: an identification with one's own grandparents and memories of one's own childhood; an identification with one's own children as they teach you improved ways to parent; and an identification with one's own grandchildren, seeing in their vitality and spontaneity a renewed reason to cherish life. He also contrasts the anxiety and vulnerability of being a parent with the more relaxed perspective of the grandparent, especially when they only take on the role of parent on a transient basis. Being a grandparent therefore provides an avenue for grace that parenting itself often provides only with far greater angst and trepidation.*

———◦◦◦———

> But at my back I always hear
> Time's wingèd chariot hurrying near.
> —Andrew Marvell

There are two certainties about becoming a grandparent:[1] earlier we were parents ourselves and now many of us older grandparents are in the final stages of our own lives. Writing that sentence makes me feel terrible. I become aware of a nagging sense of mourning and sadness that didn't occur when I became a parent. I try to focus on the joys of being with my two grandchildren. Such powerful and opposing experiences: the narcissistic wounds of aging versus the sweet optimism I feel just thinking about my grandchildren. I am reminded of Erik Erikson's eight stages of psychosocial development.[2] As we know, Erikson calls the eighth and final stage, where I am now, *maturity* or *old age*, and the conflict at this stage is between ego integrity (*wisdom*), and despair. Wisdom that derives from a self-examined life helps the individual overcome the regressive pull of the challenges of aging. Faced with the tendency to despair, *wisdom* allows us to think "perhaps the glass is half-full."

While I've had to confront the reality that being a grandfather is a sign that I am entering the final psychosocial phase of my life, I continue to reassure myself that this final phase might last a very long time. Better than comforting myself with the wish that I can avoid despair by denying mortality, I've discovered that having grandchildren can be a profound reparative emotional experience. Interacting with our grandchildren offers the possibility of reworking the way we see ourselves as parental figures, caring for and interacting with our young progeny. And it simultaneously strengthens a global sense of ourselves as competent in a world beyond how we are as grandparents.

But for now, it's back to the half-empty glass (which is getting emptier by the hour). During the several years between when our first child married and the news that a grandchild would be born, I thought to myself and expressed to friends that I wasn't particularly eager to become a grandparent. I've always thought of grandfathers as old men. When I learned that our daughter was pregnant, at first my reluctance to be a grandfather was cast aside, as I reexperienced the same delight and happy anticipation that I remembered when we learned that my wife and I were going to have a child. But this time I wasn't about to become a father; I was going to be a grandfather. Both of my grandfathers had died when they were about the same age that I am now. I wasn't prepared for the inevitable narcissistic blow to my wishful sense of myself as youthful.

While there is a plethora of information available about parenting (mostly advice on "how to parent" in the mass popular literature and psychodynamic studies of parenthood in the scientific literature), there is a paucity of information about the experience of being a grandparent. When grandparents are mentioned in a psychological or psychoanalytic context, they appear as object, not subject (as in *my grandfather . . .* or *her grandmother . . .*). Very little has been written about becoming a grandparent save the mundane, cheery platitudes found in drugstores in the *grandparent/grandchild* section of the greeting card aisle. There is much more to be learned. For example, what are the psychodynamics that shape ones identity as a grandparent? What experiences trigger sadness or joy in a grandparent? Are there narcissistic and oedipal issues specific to being a grandparent that differ from being a parent?

A fruitful arena to learn how some of us feel about becoming grandparents is to examine what we choose to be called as grandparents. Although sometimes the name that we go by as a grandparent is determined by what our first grandchild calls us as they learn to speak, many grandparents-to-be choose what to be called before the grandchild is born. Usually, it is the first time that a person has the opportunity to pick their own name from a wide variety of possibilities. Most of us have an idea of why our parents chose our given name. Although familial, religious, and cultural factors sometimes play a significant role, the name that parents give their children (their *given* name) may tell us of the parents' hopes for what that child will become. They wish that the child would have the same positive qualities as the person they are named for.

The psychodynamics of what we decide to be called as a grandparent are similar to a parent picking a name for their child. The choice betrays a wish. We may have in mind qualities that we admire in some other grandparent, perhaps our own grandparent or what our parents called themselves when they became grandparents. If we pick a name that another grandparent uses, we can think about what it is that we admire in that particular grandparent. Whatever name is chosen, it tells us something about how we wish to be seen. I chose to be called *Papa* when our granddaughter was born. Neither of my grandfathers or any other grandfathers whom I knew were called *Papa*. When I picked that name I was already aware of my concern about growing old, and I already knew more than one father whose children call him *Papa*. My wish is evident.

I suspect the same resistance to growing old and conflicts about assuming the role of *paterfamilias* exists when parents and some grandparents choose to be called by their first name. I remember visiting a colleague, an involved and encouraging father, and hearing his ten-year-old son call him by his first name. My first take was "What a liberated kid this is. He and his father must have none of the difficulties that I experience with my sons." Only later did it occur to me that of course it was the father's choice to be called by his first name. Was this a manifestation of my colleague's competitive struggles with his own father that had so often inhibited my colleague in his life? Was he once again sidestepping an awareness of his deep-seated competition with his own father, known by his children as *Grandpa*? Was his opting to be called by his first name an example of one more man conflicted about aging?

As I experienced myself, this is not unusual: A woman I know chose the name "GG" when her first grandchild was born. I asked her where the name came from and she answered, "I know someone who calls herself 'GG' and it stands for *Gorgeous Grandmother*, and that's me!" I was told of another grandmother who is addressed as *Maman* by her grandchildren. *Maman* is French for *mother*. As far as I know, neither she nor her grandchildren speak French. Whatever it takes to avoid being reminded that grandparents are old.

Trying to deny the sorry realities of aging and mortality by choosing a particular name for ourselves as a grandparent is magical thinking. As I mentioned earlier, the experience of being a grandparent by itself, without magical thinking and reassuring wishes, can serve as a reparative emotional experience and foster positive adult development. Before understanding how being a grandparent can serve as a reparative emotional experience, we need to investigate some aspects of the parent-child relationship.

—◦◦◦—

I can't believe what I just said to my child! What came out of my mouth is something I haven't heard in thirty years.

Of course, I am the one who spoke these words. I was troubled to hear myself repeating to my children critical, guilt-provoking comments spoken to me long ago by my mother and father. This is similar to observing friends treating their children in precisely the way they complained about being treated by their own parents. What would lead me to make remarks to my children that were once so disagreeable to me? Is chalking it up to identification with my parents sufficient to explain my behavior? There must be more than simple identification operating here. I knew I could do better than that with my children. Although I was frustrated and angry when I admonished them with guilt-provoking words, I was aware at the same time of feeling ashamed of myself.

My sense of shame and the thought that I could do better provides an insight into my behavior. I could hear my mother saying, "You should be ashamed of yourself! You know better than that, Jerome!" "Jerome" is how my parents addressed me when they were angry and disapproving. They meant business. Calling me by my formal name telegraphed their threat of abandoning me, of withdrawing affection. This was my mother's ultimate warning and frightened me enough to try as hard as I could to control whatever I was doing that was upsetting her: "Do what you want Jerome, I don't care." Perhaps I was forever replaying my own early dysphoric experiences with my children in an attempt to master them. When my mother was angry and despairing with me, she said, more than once, "I only hope I live to see the day when you have children like yourself so you know what you put me through." Maybe I was enacting her prophecy. As we learn to function as parents ourselves, are troublesome as well as positive identifications irrevocably linked? Was I *remembering, repeating*, and hopefully *working through*? I need to mention my certainty that I never have and never will make these critical remarks to my grandchildren (more about this later).

All of us are familiar with the experience of a teacher or parent proclaiming, "Do as I say, not as I do." Invariably we place much more weight on what they do rather than what they say. How we act in the world, our behavior and the way we portray our social roles, is predominantly determined by modeling, by simulating other's actions. We are evolutionarily programmed to identify with significant early figures in our lives. The expression "monkey see, monkey do" applies to higher primates as well.

Conscious and unconscious identifications with one's parents and early caretakers play a vital role in how we behave when we become a parent. We can justifiably say that the survival of our species depends on learned parenting behavior. Of course, parents can struggle to modify bedrock identifications and develop their own style of raising children, especially once they become aware of their discomfort with the negative identifications. As a patient once said, "I hate the way my father treated me and I don't want to treat my children that way, but I can't seem to help it."

Of course, it is not possible to know how much of one's character is genetically programmed or learned from experience. Whether our individual identities are derived from *nature* or *nurture*, we can agree that humans are a highly socialized species, especially if we consider language and the ability to communicate and modify our behavior as a measure of socialization. For example, parents will often attempt to adjust their parenting style as they observe and try to emulate their spouses and other parents. Some adamantly struggle to raise their children with the opposite approach from the way they remember being treated by their parents. Consider the example of a young mother who as a child was rigidly controlled by her own mother, who consistently set firm rules determining what her young daughter was permitted to say and how she should act (including wearing a crib harness marketed as a "soothing device" that was nothing more than a set of restraints designed to prevent her from standing up in her crib). In reaction to how she was raised, this mother encouraged her daughter to openly express her feelings and proudly championed her independence.

Our propensity to identify with or away from our own parents as we begin to parent ourselves should not obscure the more basic fact that we look to our children/grandchildren from their earliest moments for indicators that we *matter* to them. Thus we are drawn to that important landmark in an infant's socialization that begins when the very young child first recognizes the pattern of a human face and smiles. It is called the *social smile* because it signals a social connection with other humans. The baby's smile is positively reinforced when the other face smiles back, especially when it is returned with great enthusiasm accompanied by excited, approving vocalizations. The social smile originates with the infant's recognizing the pattern of a human face in the chaos of visual images (or, for blind children, the sound of an important caretaker's voice) and exists throughout life. We all smile when we greet a friend. We smile at someone we admire, even if they don't recognize us: stand outside of a stage door and observe the faces of audience members when they recognize an actor leaving the theater.

Often parents vividly remember their child's first social smile and record their second social smile if they've run to get a camera or pull out their iPhone to document the event. For the parent or important caretaker experiencing the infant's social smile, it is a robust validation of self and strengthens their bond with the infant. While the infant doesn't initially recognize that the face they are smiling at belongs to their parent, they know that it is a human face. It is a significant milestone marking a new level of parent-child attachment. Although grandparents are sometimes not present to witness their grandchild's first social smile, they intuitively understand that it is a commanding event based on their experiences with their own infants.

I saw both of my grandchildren on the day that they were born. Because our daughter and grandchildren live in another state, weeks would pass between visits. We observed their social smiles by the time each of them was two months old. Soon afterward, their social smiles evolved into *special smiles* reserved for familiar caretakers and confirmed the durability of our relationship with them. We were now "members in good standing" of their social universe.

The responsibilities and required vigilance of a grandparent are not the same as they are for a parent immersed in the necessities of family life. When I am with my grandchildren, I can attend to them without other responsibilities. It is always a special time when we are together. I pay attention to their developmental growth and observe how they interact with their parents and with my wife and myself. When playing with them I am more able to follow their lead than I was with my own children at the same age, when I was distracted by other responsibilities that required my attention. My memory of that time is that I tried to merge my time with them with other obligations: "OK, now we are going to do this" or "Get into the car. We are going to the grocery store and one of you can sit in the cart and the other one will help me push it." Or worse, "All three of you are coming with me to the grocery store and you can all pick a treat for yourself." This was a recipe for mayhem. I was attempting to "multitask" when I've now discovered the gratification that comes with "monotasking."

I've learned from our granddaughter that she has her own supply of ideas for how to spend our time together and I have the mental space to follow her lead. "Papa, read this book with me," or "Let's make a fort with the cushions." I watch her play and am curious about her in a way that was not always available to me when our children were her age.

I've been happily surprised to discover that I can learn how to be a better grandparent by watching our daughter and son-in-law play with our grandchildren. For example, when our grandchildren were rapidly developing language skills in the second year of life, their parents would play the game of intentionally using the wrong word and they would laugh together heartily. It is the perfect pedagogic game to play with verbally adept two-year-olds. I see how this has augmented their well-developed sense of humor. I enjoy writing illustrated letters to them. Each letter ends with a "joke section." Perhaps from playing the "wrong word" game, they've learned to appreciate puns. My letters to them usually include a continuation of a game we play when we are together—inventing outrageously silly recipes for inedible meals. Additionally, writing to them helps me deal with how much I miss them.

Besides the well-recognized developmental significance of the social smile, there are other significant moments in a child's social maturation that may not be as apparent. For example, stranger anxiety first occurs when a baby is about eight months old. They feel uncomfortable or frightened when approached by someone they do not know even in the presence of a trusted caregiver. Stranger anxiety signifies the child's ability to recognize who is a stranger. A corollary, especially meaningful to me, is that it's a sure sign that the child knows who is not a stranger, who is a familiar member of their trusted circle. It's comforting to know that our grandchildren have a durable internal representation of us that endures when we are not with them.

When our grandson was eight months old and his sister nearly three, our son-in-law continued his yearly summer ritual of spending four days with a few of his closest friends from high school and college. I was invited to spend those four days helping to care for our grandchildren. During the day, while our daughter worked, a mother's helper was present, although she spent most of her time playing with our granddaughter. I focused on our grandson. At the end of each day our daughter returned home to spend time with her children and put them to bed. By then I was exhausted. I'm sure that I never spent as much protracted one-on-one time with any of my own children.

My parenting style has always been to engage children actively with the world. For instance, when we would read a book together, our granddaughter and grandson were in charge of turning the pages, even if I sometimes had to pull the page slightly away from the ones below so they could get a firm grip. In the course of these four days with our grandson, I believe I could see his developmental progress every morning and even between naps. He and I were both thrilled with his fine motor skills and his growing mastery of receptive speech. Our grandson and I explored the world inside the house, and with the good weather we spent much of the time outside. "See the big tree. Do you want to touch the tree? See the red flower? Let's smell the flower. Doesn't it smell good? See the children playing with a ball? Soon you will be able to throw and catch a ball. See the puddle left by the rain? Here, let's take our shoes off and step in the puddle."

Changing his diaper was a challenge. Like many eight-month-olds, he resisted lying still, and unlike his parents, I was out of practice changing a diaper in mid-air. His dresser doubled as a changing table and was situated next to a window where the blinds had been closed to facilitate his taking a nap or sleeping later in the morning. When it was time for me to change his diaper, I opened the blinds and continued the activity that we had been playing: "Can you see the tree? Look at how tall the tree is. Is there a bird in the tree? Do you think a bird will fly onto one of the branches?"[3] He would lie still, looking out the window and searching for what I was pointing out to him. For four days this worked every time.

When I left to return home I was relieved to have some time to myself. But I missed them terribly and was eager to see them as soon as possible. Five weeks later my wife and I visited them again. We arrived at their house midafternoon, just as our grandson was waking from a nap and our daughter was entering his room. I suspected that she probably wanted to be alone with him for a few minutes before he saw us. Not letting that stop me, I opened the door to his room and my wife and I stood in the doorway just as our daughter was lifting him out of his crib. Immediately he saw me, leaned in my direction, and reached his arms out toward me. I picked him up and he pressed his head into my chest below my left shoulder and reached his right hand around to my back and held me tightly. It was as vivid an experience of pure love as I've experienced as an adult. It represented a powerful, durable connection between us, so compelling and reassuring in the context of my concerns about aging. Sometimes the cup is overflowing.

I've heard other grandparents describe their relationship with their grandchildren as "special," and I've used the same word. What exactly is so special? Obviously it is special because we are not with them every day and our time together is a special time. But there is another, less obvious, and more poignant explanation of why a grandfather's relationship with his grandchildren is "special," and it has nothing to do with the character or personality of his children or grandchildren.

When my wife was in her third trimester of pregnancy with our first child, I was a first-year student in training to become a psychoanalyst. I wrote a paper for a course I was taking and titled it "The Laius Complex." We did not know the sex of our unborn child, but I fantasized that it was probably a boy, and simultaneously I began to worry that this baby would take my wife's attention away from me. We had been together for over five years before making the decision to have a child. In my classes at the Psychoanalytic Institute, we were studying *The Interpretation of Dreams*, where Freud mentions the Oedipus complex for the first time. According to Sophocles's *Oedipus Rex*, Laius, the father of Oedipus, heard the Delphic Oracle prophesy that his future son will kill him. "The Laius Complex" examined Sophocles's drama from the perspective of Laius. My choice of this subject was surely motivated and informed by my experience as an expectant father concerned that my unborn son would take my wife's attention away from me. And, as universally experienced by all parents, the demands of their children (certainly very young children) take energy and attention away from the primacy of the parents' relationship. I was already jealous of my children who were yet unborn.

Yet, crucially, I have never been envious of our grandchildren. Clearly I was not jealous of their taking our daughter's attention away from me. On the contrary, I am proud of her as a mother. My wife and I spend more time with her now that she has children of her own. What's more, being grandparents brings my wife and me closer to each other. It is a major experience that we share together. For me, being a grandparent is "special" because it does not invoke oedipal dynamics, so different from my experience of being a parent.

—=◉/◉/◉=—

What's the matter, Jerry, there were no other faces available?

This was spoken to me thirty years ago by a cousin whom I hadn't seen since I became a father as I entered a family gathering proudly holding one son in my arm and the other by his hand. My sons look like me, and now my grandson looks like me. When our first son was born, the first thing I recall my wife saying was "Jesus Christ, it's Al [my father] at ninety." This brings me to the topic of grandparents' narcissism. I think now of how many times I have the urge to show photos of my grandchildren, even to people I have just met. I've even had the thought while writing this chapter of including pictures of my grandchildren in the text. I've seen others eagerly show pictures of their grandchildren to one another and boast about how smart and talented they are. It has been described as *competitive grandparenting*. Whether accurate or not, my sense is that it is more common for grandparents to openly brag about their grandchildren than for parents to do the same about their children. Why is this?

Do we become less inhibited as we age? Certainly it is a manifestation of narcissism. When I walked into a family reunion with my two sons many years ago, I was aware that I was showing them off, although actually I was showing off myself; I was exhibiting my children as a sign of my potency. Adding my grandson to the list of "who looks like me" is an extension of the same exhibitionistic impulse. Perhaps the ubiquitous showing off of one's grandchildren has become so prevalent and socially acceptable because it attempts to disguise the fact that the grandparents are also bragging about themselves. Although there are those individuals who do openly brag about themselves, most adults have learned to control their public narcissistic displays. Bragging about one's grandchildren may be further augmented because grandparents are frequently worried about their diminished mental acuity and loss of youthful looks, and they displace these narcissistic features onto their brilliant, beautiful grand-children.

Identification with one's own grandparents also contributes to the bragging. I spent a lot of time with my paternal grandfather who lived nearby and died suddenly of a coronary occlusion at the age of sixty-five, a few months before my ninth birthday. Many years later, near the time when our daughter first told us that she was pregnant, I began to think about him more frequently. I was aware of wanting to tell everyone that my daughter was pregnant, but this paled in comparison with my subse-quent urge to brag about my grandchildren and is linked with tales of how proud my grandfather was of me. I have many memories of going for rides in his car, but only later did I make the connection between these memories and being told by relatives how he would "show me off" to his friends.[4]

My grandfather owned a jewelry story in our town, and every morn-ing before I went to school my father would remind me to telephone him to ask what time it was. My father knew how much pleasure it gave his father to hear my voice on the phone. "What time is it, Grandpa?" "It's half-past eight," he'd say, an unusual locution for "8:30." And come to think of it, I've used that expression a few times lately with a comforting awareness that I'm talking like my grandpa. In effect my father used me to please his father and reinforce their bond with each other. I was a gift my father could give to his father. And I've often observed myself ex-pounding my children's virtues in a similar manner with my father and father-in-law. I wonder whether I am describing a moment in the endless, evolving resolution of the Oedipus complex?

Now that I have my own grandchildren, the quality of my memories of my grandfather has changed dramatically. Once static visual memo-ries are now often enriched and reconnected with missing affect. For example, I saw my father crying on the morning when my grandfather had died. I remember thinking to myself that I, too, was supposed to cry, but I didn't feel like crying. Mostly I was curious about death and the rituals that accompanied a family member dying. I found it all a bit spooky. I suppose that is a common experience for a child of that age whose grandfather dies. To tell the truth, I don't remember feeling a longing for him.[5] Now when I think of his dying I feel sad for him and can get teary-eyed thinking of all that he missed. My visual memories are now flooded with sadness (although the affect is sorrow, not happiness, it is not unlike experiencing the movie *The Wizard of Oz* when the film transitions from black and white to Technicolor once Dorothy has arrived in Oz).

Sadness isn't the only affect that had been absent from my memories. When I play a simple game with my grandchildren and remember my grandfather playing the same game with me, the memory is a joyous one.

I fondly recall how happy I was with him, and I feel a warm connection to him and wish that he were here to see me, now a grandfather myself, playing our game with his great-great-grandchildren. These are visceral connections with him, and I miss him. It's fascinating that I am finally more fully mourning him sixty years after his death. And along with mourning him, I realize that there are other possibilities available to me than being a doddering old grandfather. Being a grandfather is a gift, an extension of time, time back to my own grandfather and time ahead to the lives of my grandchildren.

NOTES

1. There are many grandparents (and some great-grandparents) who assume the role of the primary caregiver for their grandchildren. Here, I use the term *grandparent* in the traditional sense as the parent of the parent of the grandchild, as is the situation in my family.

2. Erik Erikson. (1950). *Childhood and society*. New York: Norton.

3. There was no bird in the tree. As I write this, I remember an interaction with my grandfather. I must have been seven or eight and we were looking out the window together. He said to me, "See the bird in the backyard?" I didn't see a bird, and I asked him where it was. He replied, "April Fools." It was April 1 and probably the first time I had experienced an April Fools' joke. My choice of a mentioning a bird was both an identification with my grandfather and a reenactment of a pleasant forgotten memory of spending time with him.

4. Writing of my grandfather's bragging just brought to mind his telling me the story of what he did when both the First World War and the Second World War ended. He paraded around the town carrying the loudest alarm clocks from his store all chiming at once. My memories are habitually visual and I can see him walking with a wooden billboard hanging over his shoulders filled with ringing alarm clocks. I probably invented this image as I listened to him recount the story.

5. I had a different experience when my beloved paternal grandmother died when I was fifteen. I profoundly mourned her death.

TWELVE

Thinking Like a Parent

An Essential Aspect of Psychotherapy with Adults, Children, and Their Families

Monique S. Bowen

*In this twelfth chapter, **Monique S. Bowen** adds further nuance to the overlapping feelings of essentialness that are created by both the parent-child and the therapist-patient dyads. She delves especially into the role countertransference plays in the therapist-patient relationship and how, under certain spelled-out conditions, the use of self-disclosure can be a crucial linchpin in the creation of feelings of mutual essentialness in the patient and therapist. She describes the role brief, but telling, reveries within the therapist may play in furthering her understanding of her patients. These reveries can also play a key role in furthering the internalization of the therapist as an authentic, benign person increasingly made real over the course of the treatment. Last, she speaks of the parallel processes by which our experiences as a child with our own parents may be conjured up in our work with both child and adult patients, leading to how "thinking like a parent" may prove to be a useful paradigm in clinical work.*

―᷈ல்ல―

We work in tandem with our patients to acknowledge internal struggles, to recognize unresolved conflicts, to respect self-doubts, and to accept ambiguities. To become effective in these tasks of psychotherapy, therapists must learn to be light enough on their feet to know when to expand and when to contract our collaboration and independence as we, and the evolving therapeutic relationship, become more significant to our patients. Like parents, even when maintaining our role as models and our function as participant-observers, we as therapists are often in the tricky situation of experiencing and being experienced as both captain and companion on the same journey. In either position, we can become engaged in an essential, yet tripartite, conflict: being empowered by our patients/ children to offer them guidance, being denied that opportunity even if we believe such denial is maladaptive, and yet equipped to choose whether and when to give this guidance, whether wanted or unwanted.

Managing the influence of "thinking like a parent" has been a significant and evolving aspect in my roles both as a therapist and as a mother. Some of what I have learned about being a parent has come about from the "working play" that is child therapy, and some of what I have learned by being a mother has also guided me during periods of conducting therapy. In this chapter, I will explore becoming essential to our therapy patients, alongside an exploration of countertransference themes, and how consideration of these unique by-products of the therapeutic relationship have been of service to me as a therapist, even as I think like a parent.

ABOUT COOKIES AND JUICE

My child supervisor for my first clinical case was a petite woman who packed a wallop of clinical know-how and commonsense talk about working with children and supporting their parents. But, in that moment, she had grown weary of my doubts about the process of giving snacks to child patients when they first arrived at our clinic. Though she maintained a level of calm, she was steadfast in her disappointment, and her expression belied something else: Was it anger or, worse, disgust? With a deeply furrowed brow, she replied, "What exactly is wrong with giving them a snack? It doesn't make any sense not to feed children after school. Surely you get that." She launched into a treatise on the vagaries of upper-class idealism and that the only misguided thing was to believe we were sending the wrong message by offering children cookies and juice after school: "When you are a mother, you will understand. I instituted the snack at the clinic based on my experience with children. Yes, families are coming for therapy. But what you all seem not to understand is that you can't treat a child when they are hungry. It's basic."

Within the framework of this book, the snack can be understood as an institutionalized mechanism for helping transform the therapist into someone *essential* to the child, and indeed I *was* trying to become that valuable to a nine-year-old girl who struggled with expressive language and reading difficulties. Psychological testing noted her restricted affect and behavior throughout the testing, and that she became tearful and acknowledged feeling sad during the feedback session with her mother and father. From my earliest observations of Christina,[1] her father, and her older brother in the waiting room, I also saw lots of laughter. Over the course of my initial meetings with Mr. P, her father, and later with her mother, they gave me a sense both of the potential for levity in her life and also of her great sadness. Ms. P confirmed details provided by Mr. P regarding the length of their relationship (twelve years), and that she and Mr. P married shortly before Christina was born. She reported that they were married for six years before they separated. Both parents indicated that continuing to live together before the divorce became final caused significant tension, but they made efforts never to argue in front of their young daughter. Ms. P tearfully relayed that Christina often painted scenes involving her and her parents, depicting herself in tears or actively crying while drawing or painting.

My lasting memories of Christina are of a caring and energetic child, with a capacity for great warmth and affection. However, at our first meeting she presented as shy and withdrawn, initially slow to leave her father and requesting that he stay nearby as she hesitantly entered the playroom. In subsequent sessions, she was able to walk down the hall to the room without him, and after a couple of weeks, she began to run down the hall toward the room, hopping from one foot to the other, asking me to come faster to open the door. Her paucity of language was apparent early, and most of the dialogue in the early sessions consisted of very simple phrases. There were few, if any, conversational exchanges, and the work of the therapy seemed to be tracking her inconsistent interest in the activities on hand and surviving the lengthy silences between us. Her engagement with the playroom was stilted, especially with card and board games, which were played without rules and with no organizing structure imposed by either Christina or me. Though Christina offered no comment on the fact that rules were not in use, she would become inevitably frustrated, looking at me sheepishly and speaking quietly to herself in Creole.

Christina's difficulty with spontaneous play became more pronounced. No longer was I seeing her as mostly shy and hesitant; I began to perceive her monosyllabic responses, lack of eye contact, motor retardation, and difficulty attending to tasks in our play as indicative of a depressed mood. Though her difficulties with receptive and expressive language were significant factors in her ability to listen and receive information, as well as to recall and express what she had learned, her underlying depression made having more than a very basic bidirectional exchange with Christina laborious for us both. The possibility of making myself essential to her seemed daunting and exhausting.

After one month of therapy, I grew concerned that she might not return. She was able to show me through our sessions how painfully difficult it was for her to have a conversation with much complexity, to retain new information, to follow directions of more than a few, short words, to initiate play (concrete or symbolic), to focus on a game or activity long enough for any mastery, or to experience these activities as in any way approaching "fun." In retrospect, I think I may have secretly hoped she might beg her parents to stop this "*not* having fun." So, I chose to double-down: I became increasingly vocal about how hard it was sometimes to know what to do or to know whether others maybe knew the rules to the games we had and therefore were enjoying them: "It's not fair, you know. I wish I knew if these games were hard for you or just hard for me." I became direct, feeding lines to her, but she resisted my advances, or any suggestions to follow a set of rules that I later offered in hopes that our combined misery would end. She shook her head "no" and would continue to mix cards and game pieces together on the table, keeping her hands busy and her eyes looking toward a distant corner of the room. Games or activities that required any reading or decoding of words quickly brought on a depressive haze, wherein Christina retreated from games, gave up during her turn, looked away from the activity, and sounded out nonsense words in a singsong way. Her frequent retreats from the play, though short-lived, brought to life for me the feelings of isolation and sadness common to children with learning problems and, in Christina's situation, feelings also common to children from divorced families.

We continued in this way for another month before the clinic closed for four weeks in the summer. I was thankful for the reprieve and for the opportunity to gather my thoughts and begin anew. And then a joyous thing happened: the institutional bureaucracy interfered with the one thing that kept our delicate equilibrium intact. *The snack.*

Christina enjoyed the snack at our clinic. I daresay she loved the snack—two oatmeal cookies and container of juice. Few children ever refused it, and sometimes children became enraged (or excited) if the cookies became graham crackers. The point is that the snack was part of the agreement. A steady stream of us picked up our toy kits and the snack on our way to gather our charges from the waiting room. Others would set up the snack at a table in the therapy room so that it was there along with a few napkins, waiting for the child. For the child therapist, the snack was an integral feature of establishing rapport with the patient. It was during snack time that I was able to gather a subjective sense of how Christina was doing that day. What few words there were between us occurred across the table where she crunched happily on her cookies, wondering aloud why there were not three cookies instead of two, and lustfully drinking her juice from the cup, licking the mouth of the container so as to get every last drop. The snack was how I showed I cared for her and—save an occasional cookie or juice shortage when one or the other was unavailable for days or a week—how the clinic satiated the dozens of children in therapy at our clinic. The snack had come to concretize the essential, the fundamental feeling that the therapy experience involved *being given to,* and that this feeding either re-created or, for some children, created for the first time the feeling that their basic needs were worthy of being addressed first, without them having to give something in return. In that sense it harkened back to an early requisite of infancy, perhaps the greatest luxury we are granted in our lives: the expectation that care was forthcoming and that it could be taken for granted.

Then the clinic reopened, with no more snacks for the children. What had been a consideration—children come to us for therapy, not a sugary snack—was now a real decision to no longer offer it at the clinic. Senior therapists balked and bought their own stash for their clients, while others engaged parents who were enraged about the sudden change in routine. Snacks became the topic in the waiting room, in the therapy rooms, in supervisions, and in clinic meetings.

For Christina, the absence of cookies and juice changed things. *No good now.* Where once she ran ahead of me to our room, she walked slowly, stopping first by the room where I had always gone to get the snack. Looking at me with pleading eyes, she would only walk away after seeing another child go by empty-handed, confirmation that I was not depriving her alone of nourishment. My first supervisor had been right: snacks seemed the foundation on which all of our treatments were erected. And yet, without the snack, Christina's orientation to the therapy room changed. Her priority shifted from one primarily built around the established snack routine to one that included the room, the toys, and me. Without the snack, she started sessions with "Now what?" She openly sighed and would tell me she was bored. She walked around the room each session without much intention, still not knowing where to start with a game or a toy; however, she was looking for something, and I was there as both participant in and observer of the frustration.

One afternoon, we walked by the open door to another therapy room, and Christina responded excitedly about seeing into another room and viewing other kids' toys. But her curiosity quickly turned to annoyance because that room was bigger than ours. When the child rushed by us holding a special, forbidden snack given to him by his therapist, Christina looked at once wistful and enraged. "I want that," she said as we continued down the hall. I wondered aloud if things seemed better next door. At the end of our session that day, Christina noticed three broken toys in our room. After pointing at what was wrong with each one, she lined them up by the door so that "they can fix them." When I wondered aloud whom they were and how they would know if the toys needed to be fixed, she sat quietly for a while and then suggested that someone could leave a note for them so they would know to do something. It took another week for her to ask me to write the note with her, but we did it. Getting to the note meant that she had to open my toy kit, something she had not done since our very first session. Seeing the paper and markers and clay stored inside brought on spontaneous giggles and moved us for a time away from the rule-bound games that limited our interactions. For the first time, imaginative play emerged and engaging other items in the room seemed less fraught with danger and more inviting to us both.

Christina further came to life in the room once the clay and paints were introduced. With painting, drawing, and molding clay, she enjoyed herself and looked upon her work in the room as successful, so much so that she often wanted to share her creations with her family even though I often hoped she would leave a few behind for me to ponder. Her drawings—some crude, in that she almost exclusively used expressionless stick figures to represent herself and others—often told a story of some importance to her and spoke to a relevant theme in the treatment. One early drawing was that of a figure positioned between two squares. Christina said little about the drawing other than she was on her way home. Though no insight was offered or interpretation made, Christina represented one of her greatest struggles—her reality of having two homes and two parents who want her to choose which home and which parent she most wanted to be with. This stark drawing communicated the solitude of her reality, along with the great sadness that came with shuttling between two homes and two parents who seemed at times to be competing for their daughter's loyalty and love. In the context of this volume, her drawing spoke so poignantly to the need for a child not to have to split apart what had become essential to her: two parents, bound to one another and to her. Her next drawing she described as her "walking home in the rain. It's raining really hard." She made large, dark raindrops covering the figure such that it was barely able to find cover under a too-small umbrella.

Christina's growing capacity to express herself through art and to depict her feeling states had become exceeding useful in our work, and it allowed me an entry point to her internal life. Here, without many words, Christina was able to focus the session on her sense of loss of comfort, reassurance, and attention when her parents separated and later divorced. Once she opened this window into her inner life, I was able to acknowledge in words, her struggle over "having to choose Mama or Papa but not feeling there was an option of choosing them both." Though she had redirected her anger and rage about the divorce by being a good girl and an obedient student who avoided conflict by doing what she was supposed to (according to Christina, her parents, and her teachers), she had also exhibited some preoccupation with the cleanliness and orderliness of the room, the chalkboard, and our work space, and she showed increased investment in the cleanliness being in her domain of control. Some of the work in the treatment room and in my work with her parents came to be increasing the opportunities for Christina not to be "a good girl" all the time, and for that to be okay with her and the caregiving adults in her life.

Aside from normal breaks and an extended leave of four months after the birth of my first child, I saw Christina for nearly four years. I often arrived at the waiting area to find her working on homework assignments, leafing through books on her own, or chatting with her father and brother animatedly before sessions. She had come to own her routines of the Psychological Center, noting for the first time whether someone was present at the screening area to greet her when she arrived for sessions, sharing her displeasure about the absence of cookies and juice for a snack, and commenting on the conditions in the therapy room. Her level of attention and observation, though possibly present in the past, had broadened widely and this change seemed remarkable.

Our work together began to focus more on Christina's feelings of loss and separation as related to her parents' divorce. We played and discussed how sad she was about the end of her parents' marriage and her hope and daily dream for their reconciliation. Her parents' lack of communication about anything other than who was to drop her off and pick her up from school greatly saddened Christina and made her wishes for repair even more painful and frustrating. Her father reported that she would tell him, "You don't even try to love Mama." In the therapy room, her queries were then turned on me: Why could she not have the things she most wanted, even if it was against the rules, such as writing on the table with indelible ink, having more cookies than the "allowable" limit, and, eventually, not having to clean up cookie crumbs in preparation to leave the room? "What will happen? Will you be mad? Will you tell me you're mad? Can I have it this way just one time?" It seemed these were such important questions for a child trying to determine how much of what had happened in her family was her responsibility.

Through these challenges, Christina began to laugh more, often finding humor in her actions, as well as in others, and had even begun to use sarcasm in her communications with me. It had been a joy to discover that she now laughed easily and robustly about her day, the game we were engaged in, or the accidental expression of some bodily function. In an age-appropriate manner, she also grew to share when she was displeased and disappointed, and she could be very direct about perceived offenses. Given that most of her early experiences in therapy went on with next to no observable response, it was refreshing for Christina to inhabit the therapy room in a more alive way. As part of that enlivening process, where once she was almost always early for her appointments, I grew to appreciate her occasional lateness or absence as she approached adolescence and trusted that our "working play" had made it possible for her to test our treatment relationship in this way.

WHAT CAN I SAY? HOW NOT CONCEALING TOO MUCH
OR SHARING TOO LITTLE HELPS US ALL

At the midway point in our work, I formally presented my treatment with Christina. Though the case presentation was supposed to focus primarily on the transference and countertransference themes that arose in the treatment, because the professor was also my clinical supervisor, I had already begun to think like a parent, and I was not eager to plumb some of the problems I had in negotiating the case. Yet the presentation, along with its tacit questions about mothering a child while myself being new to motherhood (I was six months pregnant at the time with my first child), brought to the surface some things I had not fully processed about the treatment relationship.

Christina's mother became pregnant with her second child at this same time. After a very difficult first and second trimester, her labor was induced and the child was born, only living for one day. Christina knew of the newborn's death immediately, and it was difficult for her to talk about her own feelings about the loss. She spoke mostly of her mother's experiences throughout the pregnancy and during her hospital stay, following the emergency birth. These issues were made more complicated by my developing pregnancy, both in my role as therapist and in Christina's position as one who was curious about my unborn child, its health, sex, and due date, as well as its impact on our work.

My pregnancy also coincided with a burst of expressive language from Christina. It was interesting to observe her reaction to my expecting a child given her knowledge of her mother's simultaneous pregnancy. However, it was heartbreaking to sit with her as she talked about the death of her little sister as I sat there with my child still growing steadily. I shared with her my thoughts that it must be hard for her to talk to me about her mom and sister. "Yeah. You still have your baby and my mother doesn't." When she talked about taking care of her sister when she arrived, Christina also began to speak to me about taking care of my child: "When will you bring him or her here? Do you know if it is a boy or girl yet for me to take care of? If I don't still come to therapy, can I still hold the baby for you? Why won't you bring the baby here for me to take care of now?" There were so many fundamental questions about her role and where she would fit within this new life of mine, of ours. It highlighted for me the complex structure of revelations and self-disclosures in psychotherapy and their role in maintaining or creating the experience of therapy as an essential process to both patient and therapist in a way that went well beyond my work with Christina and on to other work with children as well as adults.

WHEN *KNOWING* SEEMS ESSENTIAL TO
BOTH PATIENT AND THERAPIST

Many years after my work with Christina ended and six months into a recent treatment, an adult patient called me one evening to confirm an upcoming appointment. I received this message but thought it strange that he, not me, was checking in this way. We had experienced some flux in our appointment times to accommodate his schedule, so it was not unusual for me to call or e-mail him to confirm our next session's day and time. After first querying about the appointment time, he said that he heard a DJ on a popular radio broadcast send condolences to me following the recent and unexpected death of my mother. For my patient, it was clear that this news must be about me, given my uncommon name and the suddenness of the death. "After hearing that, I knew immediately that it must be you, so feel free to cancel this week's appointment. You probably need to make arrangements. I understand." My initial reaction was one of concern for my patient who sounded quite worried about me and how I might be doing. How unnerving to receive such news out of the blue and not to have any way to confirm it! Next, my focus shifted to the impossible worry that accompanies such a discovery and I wondered what responsibility I had to assuage his concerns as quickly as possible. However, for a therapist disclosure to become essential to the patient, it is key that it be formed with its usefulness to the course of treatment foremost in mind. In the weeks leading up to my patient's phone message, our sessions revolved around three interrelated topics: the absence of "alone" time in the patient's life; the long-standing challenge of limit-setting the patient had vis-à-vis his school-aged child; and the consideration of a career change that would likely result in a relocation for the patient and his family.

After a few more moments of reflection, my thoughts shifted from the words and toward my patient's anxiety, to his worry about loss—perhaps due to my possible retreat to mourn or, worse still, to concerns about my own sudden demise. Had I already become a valued someone, so much so that he imagined me in a vulnerable state and in need of comfort and reassurance? Or might this also reflect a confession of sorts, where I had not acknowledged the extent of my patient's vulnerabilities and his concern that I might not be there for him when he needed me most? Conversely, was his message meant to reassure me that his own self-mothering function remained intact should I not be able to fulfill my substitute role? Well, I thought, here we were together, both tortured by our thoughts of my dead mother and what it meant for the immediate future of our therapy relationship.

Going into that next session, I was clear in my mind that I would not speak directly about my mother with him, but I also had imagined the possibility of his question(s) and whether I might disclose something:

"No, she wasn't sick. She just never woke up from an afternoon nap." But it took some time for the topic to come into focus during that next session, and as I sat with him, waiting for the inevitable question—"Well, is she dead?"—I could hear the soothing lilt of my mother's voice. Along with an overwhelming wish to make out her words came the feeling of wanting to be alone and yet realizing that there was no place for me to hide. Here is the first of two reveries that followed in quick succession in the few seconds I had in the company of my patient as we started that session:

I was six years old when my mother and I moved into a tiny apartment in a three-story brick house. I could bring next to nothing familiar, and I felt deeply the separation from my father, my private elementary school, my friends, my clothes, and my toys. I would ask for this or that shirt, a favorite woolen hat, and her wedding veil, which had become a preferred dress-up clothing item. My mother reminded me of the movers who had come "to put our things away for us until we had enough space for them again." "When will that be?" I asked, and she replied, "Soon, you'll see. . . . When we're all together again. Until then, it'll just be you and me. And, of course, Ping, George, and the Cat!" The stories of Ping (and the Yangtze River), (Curious) George, and Dr. Seuss's Cat in the Hat were the only three books we were able to take with us. My mother and I would curl up side by side, she with her hardcover and me with mine. The books served as reminders that despite the many unexpected changes there were constants.

This shift in attention briefly spurred another:

I was attending my first international conference, an excellent, convivial gathering of mostly family therapists, cementing my sense that a systems perspective was key to clinical work, no matter the client. I was thinking about how happy my choice of career made me feel. A few weeks later, I learned that I was again pregnant. Though it was not meticulously orchestrated with charts and diagrams, it was not unplanned. And yet something was just different. Not right, somehow. Next, I was lying across an examination table cradling myself, wishing I had never known I was pregnant because the pain would be less. Lacking restraint, the technician said to us, "You're young. You'll try again. It wasn't meant to be, but you'll be fine." The little manifestation of anxious hope and endless preoccupation had gone still inside me during a span of six weeks, and I was left with not meant to be.

I have shared these two very intimate moments with some concern about possible interpretations by the lay reader and therapist alike. I know that few of us would readily divulge this level of intimacy to just anyone outside of a therapeutic relationship, and certainly it would not occur to us to tell our patients directly about them during the course of treatment except under exceptional circumstances. And yet this was where my mind went as I considered what my response to my patient might be about my mother. To me, that these were the two life fragments rattled loose by his anxious call and the moments leading up to his questions in the treatment room that day seemed deserving of further study. My very specific reverie about my mother, mothering, and parenthood seemed too potentially constructive to be minimized as self-indulgent. For such difficult and painful memories to be stirred up both abruptly and distinctly felt to me to be a kind of internal communication that had present implications (Reik, 1948). I believed then, as I do now, that his was as much a question about the woman who cared for me, and about the woman, or women, who mothered him, as it was about my capacity to care for, even parent, him.

Some self-disclosure seemed necessary—indeed, essential—to my ability to meet him at an authentic place, and yet I feared that I might lose my professional stance if I became too absorbed with gratifying his need to know by satiating him with my actual narrative. Determining whether to disclose a significant aspect of the therapist's lived experience, without burdening the patient, was at the heart of this psychotherapeutic dilemma. The choice in direction here was not unlike the clinical moment in my treatment with Christina when not being able to provide her with a snack compelled us to focus less on the distraction that "real" nourishment had come to represent for us, thus allowing us to deepen and extend our working play.

In the years since my mother's death, my reveries about her have passed closely over the surface of both my first-person image of her, my real mother, and an idealized version of her (my mother "phantom") into an unfinished work that I imagine and reimagine all the time. My ensuing self-talk has been about my mother and her peer group, and the women around me that have grappled with similar realities, helped by the budding awareness that we do not grieve alone. In recalling my wish to be left alone to mourn her and my miscarried hope, I remembered that I also had my breakdowns, metabolisms of both hurts, which helped me to accept the permanence of these losses without retreating too far from my life then and to stay in the moment with my patient now.

THE COMPLEX, ESSENTIAL NATURE OF
COMMUNICATION *FROM WITHIN*

"Our patients come to us with the hope that we will listen with an open mind, that we will have educated thoughts and opinions about what is going on with them, and that we will, at moments, share our point of view with them" (Bowen, 2013). Within the therapeutic interplay of each psychotherapy session, the patient and the therapist co-create the language and communication of the treatment. Here, the transference and

countertransference relationship serve as the source material for exploring the patient's experience of self and others. My interest in patients'
subjective experiences and therapists' interpretations of those experiences emanates from an interest in the attempt on both parts to co-create
a space for this exploration of the self—through words and associations,
but also in the form of unconscious, un-metabolized material, which has
also been referred to as "unbidden" (Wilner, 1999) experience. Although
many who have written about countertransference acknowledge the
interrelationship of several phenomena that comprise this important aspect of the treatment, I have been particularly interested in moments
when therapists disclose certain countertransferential reactions to their
patients and the impact these reactions may have on the feeling of being
essential.

Aron (1996) places an unmistakable emphasis on the reciprocal contributions that both the patient and the therapist bring to the therapeutic
relationship, contributions that inform their own internal monologues as
well as their conscious and unconscious communications with one another. Typically, it is our patients' emotional responses, perceptions, conscious awareness, and unconscious processes that are the ready material
for our observations, analyses and interpretations. In contrast, our own
experience of the clinical milieu as it may seem to relate—or even appear
unrelated—to the relationships with patients have until late in the last
century been largely written about as countertransferential reactions that
should be limited, or to be understood as indicative of some unexplored
pathology in the patient or with the therapist herself.

Aron (1996) presents a simple challenge to these perspectives, inas-
much as he and others challenge the false dichotomy between patient
and therapist. Surely, dichotomies do exist in the relationship between
patient and therapist; however, the notion that there are basic processes
occurring within the patient that are not also occurring within the therapist is becoming myth. Instead, he speaks to a mutuality that exists within the dyad. With this empathic connection, based in a shared humanity
and in the hope of the patient that the therapist can be of help to him,
comes the possibility of being understood by another. It is here that my
moment with my patient acknowledging my mother's death comes into
stark relief. Hoffman (1994, 1998) observes that clinical work "requires an
underlying tolerance of uncertainty and with it a radical, yet critical kind
of openness that is conveyed over time in various ways, including a
readiness to soul-search, to negotiate, and to change" (1994, p. 215). The
therapist is ideally able to hold her patient's past experiences in mind
while making space available for images formed from their mutually
imagined hopes for what is possible for the patient. Could I place my
patient's fears and concern about me simultaneously in the context of his
past relationships (transference) and my past relationships (countertrans-

ference)? Could I do it, moreover, in a graceful way such that our sense of authenticity was able to stay present?

In *Reverie and Interpretation*, Ogden describes his use of transference-countertransference during analytic sessions, and he acknowledges that his descriptions of unbidden experiences (Wilner, 1999) will seem unusual to those unfamiliar with sharing these kinds of ruminations. Rather than leaving him concerned or feeling guilty, Ogden (1994, 1997) describes the shift in his attention as an opportunity to reflect on the feelings that get stirred, so that he might better understand what his patient might be experiencing but has not yet been able to grasp. My going into the split-second reveries about my mother's last day and our traumatic move years earlier are vivid examples of the value of studying one's shifts in attention. Furthermore, Ogden also points to the use of reverie as a countertransferential experience that is part of the process of what is created in the interplay between analyst and patient (Bion, 1970; Ogden, 1997).

Some clinicians are able to comfortably use themselves and certain of their experiences consistent with the needs of their patients at a given moment in the treatment (Bloomgarden and Menutti, 2009; Hirsch and Roth, 1995; Jacobs, 1991; Knafo and Feiner, 1996; Ogden, 1986, 1994, 1997; Tansey and Burke, 1989; Wachtel, 1993, 2008). However, whether to disclose one's private thoughts remains a complex decision even for the most experienced therapist, including those who find value in its clinical application (Bromberg, 1998; Davies, 2004; Ehrenberg, 1992; Hirsch, 2008; Hirsch and Roth, 1995; Maroda, 1991, 2005; Renik, 2006; Searles, 1975; Wachtel, 2008). Despite the desire to share something with a patient, we often struggle along with our patients to make ourselves understood, even as we endeavor to understand them. And yet there remains a dilemma about therapist self-disclosure and its value to the treatment and to the therapeutic relationship. Often viewed as a self-gratifying act on the part of the therapist, there is also an overwhelming sense that self-disclosure to a patient is a declaration of the therapist's own humanity—a potential acknowledgement of the vulnerability that also gets stirred for the therapist when faced with the transactional burdens of reciprocity in the clinical situation (Jacobs, 1991).

The prevailing clinical wisdom regarding technique is that self-disclosures, like interpretations, be offered first and foremost with regard to their usefulness for the patient (Maroda, 1991; Ogden, 1986). It is here that I have found the most comfort about considering the disclosure to my patient about my mother, for I do believe that our subsequent discussions about our therapy relationship were of use to him. Whether the context be a dream, the therapist's reverie, or some other manner of "intersubjective analytic event" (Ogden, 1997), it is the exploration of the patient's associations to the material that remains at the core of understanding the patient's unconscious anxiety, defense, or resistance. Indeed, even my affirming young Christina's reaction to the lack of a snack provided an avenue for self-exploration that was of significant use to her. Not unlike Freud, for Ogden (1989, 1994, 1997), to analyze the unconscious processes—or better-termed "preconscious" formulations (Freud, 1912; Tauber and Green, 1959)—of the therapist and his patient, it is essential to look at the reveries of the patient and the analyst.

In terms of contemporary theorists writing on the use of countertransference, Maroda stands apart as one of the rare few to write about therapists' disclosures of countertransference as an important aspect of analytic technique. Maroda (1991, 2003) offers the student and the experienced therapist basic reasons for revealing countertransferences to patients; moreover, she provides her readers with tools toward the incorporation of some of their own experiences into the treatment milieu without delegitimizing the analytic process. As an advocate for the expression and disclosure of countertransferential experiences, she delineates disclosures of information at the request of the patient from disclosures of what gets stirred up in the therapist when the patient requests information. In the case of Christina, speaking directly to her questions about the lack of a snack fit the first category, while my musings about disclosure to my adult patient about my mother's death fit the second category. Despite their demands, few patients are ready for the latter early on in treatment (Maroda, 1991). Ordinarily, I do not think first to disclose a reverie to my patients; however, some circumstances provide an all-too-present reminder that what makes the most sense theoretically often must be discarded when we face the "real" spasms of everyday life. The power of the well-timed countertransference intervention comes when the disclosure is done to support the patient and the treatment, not to relieve the therapist of her reactions to the patient.

Maroda (1991) also provides several recommendations to help guide psychoanalysts and psychotherapists alike through the myriad of questions from patients that may require one to respond. As the therapeutic relationship matures, the patient develops a greater curiosity about the layered communication with the analyst and a particular awareness of the analyst as a separate person (Maroda, 1991). She writes that most patients will inform their analysts when they are ready to explore the therapist's thoughts or feelings. Typically, patients will begin with the standard questions about the therapist and will take note of the therapist's reactions, looking for ease or discomfort, and, when ready, move toward questions that plumb for understanding of the analyst. It is important to recognize that the patient is querying the therapist so as to know whether she has made an impact—to feel she is important to the therapist. In the vernacular of this volume, the patient is looking for validation that they are *essential* to the therapist. In this context I am reminded of one of the last pages in the *Child's First Book about Play Therapy* (Nemiroff and Annunziata, 1990). The book, geared to young children, gives the last question a child may have after they have ended therapy: "Will my therapist remember me?" It is a universal question in life, not just therapy: Are we memorable; do we continue to exist in some essential way in the mind of those with whom we have connected? To the degree to which the therapeutic relationship provided value to the patient, their wish to feel that they would be remembered becomes more essential. As Samstag and Samstag discuss in this volume, the therapist has become an internalized *essential object* to the patient, and, as such, the wish on the patient's part is that the therapist will, likewise, internalize her. Self-disclosures as "countertransferential" moments in the treatment may thus be critical to the internalization process for both patient and therapist.

Maroda (1991, 2003) deftly offers clear signposts for the disclosure of countertransference. If a direct answer to their question is what is required, the patient will return to the question until an answer is given. If the therapist senses the request for a disclosure is coming from a deeply genuine place, then a disclosure in acknowledgment of the relationship with the patient is appropriate. If the therapist feels uncomfortable about not answering—as though she is doing it to protect her own feelings— then a disclosure rather than a withholding of information is indicated. However, Maroda is clear that if the discomfort is significant and not related to the therapist's own acknowledged fears, the therapist should wait, because if it is important to the patient, an opportunity will present itself again (Maroda, 1991). In retrospect, as I considered self-disclosing to the aforementioned patients, I had an emerging sense to follow these all-important principles when accepting these messages from within.

Wachtel (2008) also strikes an important note about the ordinariness and even inevitability of therapist disclosure, and he questions the viewpoint of self-disclosures as an infringement on the therapeutic frame: "Rather, self-disclosure is a feature of *all* therapeutic work." Wachtel discusses the inevitable trade-offs clinicians make as they treat their patients, and the impact that therapist disclosures have on the therapy and on the therapeutic relationship. The therapist is simultaneously observing and experiencing something with the patient throughout any given treatment. But it is the continuing choices that the therapist makes to do one thing or another (or not to do it) that Wachtel (2008) sees as the real challenge. For him, there may be positive or negative implications regardless of the choice that is made, and certainly consequences that lie in either direction. He therefore urges therapists to attend to their patients' and their own levels of comfort and discomfort with unexplored feelings, difficult topics, and the transference and countertransference. He details how even "errors" of self-disclosure can become opportunities for repairing ruptures. The therapist needs to appreciate his own participation in therapeutic misattunements and to acknowledge that there may be costs and benefits in the choice to withhold or to disclose information, advice, feelings, and so forth (Wachtel, 2008).

The internal conflicts about therapist self-disclosures are natural ones and not easily resolved by a simple, consistent strategy of choosing to disclose or choosing not to disclose. Is it the case that if the therapist feels comfortable with a line of inquiry from the patient, or an issue or a feeling that comes to the fore in the therapy, he is more likely to answer a direct question from, interpret the mutual meanings with, or disclose something intentional or unintentional to his patient (Frank, 1997, 1999)? Conversely, if the therapist feels uncomfortable or self-indulgent, or wrong in his understanding of his reaction to the patient or the material, will he be more inclined to ignore his reactions so as to avoid exploring the thoughts and feelings that have been stirred in him? Thus, if the therapist feels uncomfortable disclosing his reactions to his patient, is it because he fears exposure, and if the therapist is comfortable with self-disclosure, are the feelings evoked more likely to have a positive valence and the intervention viewed as having therapeutic value?

The extent to which a therapist can effectively and ethically uses oneself is one of many thorny questions in this arena. To push therapeutic practice into an optimal zone, therapists must work to understand what makes them comfortable and uncomfortable clinically, as it is the scientific practice coupled with an instinctual know-how that light the path toward therapeutic action (Maroda, 1991, 2003). This does require that therapists attend more to their own experiences along with those of their patients. The therapist, in paying greater attention to that which seems irrelevant or not pertinent to the patient's own reflections, may be able to glean so much more data from the dyad. Therefore, it stands to reason that in paying attention to the therapist's own explorations of the seemingly unimportant and random that one might learn something about his patient and their mutual therapeutic interactions. The theoretical implications for using therapists' disclosures are explored by Wachtel (1993, 2008) and other relational theorists (Bromberg, 1998; Davies, 2004; Ehrenberg, 1992; Frank, 1997, 1999; Hirsch, 2008; Hirsch and Roth, 1995; Maroda, 1991, 2005; Jacobs, 1991; Knafo and Feiner, 1996; Ogden, 1986, 1994, 1997; Renik, 2006; Searles, 1975; Tansey and Burke, 1989), but the impact of the relational theories on technique is lean in comparison to the hundred years of prohibition on therapist reactions and self-disclosures from the more traditional end of the spectrum of psychoanalytic thought. Keeping in mind the all-too-human need to feel essential as an experience that is at the core of the therapeutic process for both patient and therapist may allow us to be of greater use to our patients and to ourselves.

As I considered where to begin with my adult patient given the themes from the treatment, I first sought to link what there was in common between his reality and my reveries: grief and mourning; the simultaneous gratification and anxiety evoked by the dynamics of parenting;

and the paralyzing fear that accompanies phase-of-life-related change, which can evoke emotional and behavioral parallels to earlier separation-individuation struggles. We were approaching these matters in an indirect way, and I had begun as if not only the content of the reverie but also the shift in attention itself exemplified something important. Had I been minimizing the extent to which my patient was growing to count on our sessions as a steadying force, or relying upon me so greatly that his sense of himself as possessing the means to effect positive results in his life and career was threatened?

The dawning of this awareness was not unveiled with precision but came as single phrases — "only three books; we'll all be together again . . . until then, it'll just be you and me; feeling happy in career but something does not feel right, not meant to be, but you'll be fine" — and imagistic representations — a child looking to her mother for answers and for comfort; a parent overwhelmed by their child's anxiety and yet clear that their presence and reassuring words might suffice; a tearful mother lying on an exam table clutching herself. These words and images were the source material that inspired the following reflections I provided my patient over three subsequent sessions:

1. I think you had a moment of realizing how important therapy has become, and how much it means to be in this room with someone who cares about your experience and your feelings.
2. I felt very cared for when you left that message this weekend. And I hope you know I care about you. In our last session you told me you may take that job, which would mean you'd need to leave the treatment as it is now, and the nature of our work together would change. I am not prepared for that change yet myself.
3. I wonder if you have begun to tell yourself that you'll be fine if we have to stop our work, so much so that you would be okay if I said we had to stop abruptly, without any notice. But when you left your message saying I could cancel today, you also made me aware of feeling that this might be a way for it not to feel as hard for you if you were the one delivering that news to me.
4. This is not unlike when D [patient's child] has felt anger and frustration and you felt those same feelings when your hugs and words of comfort don't seem to match what he needed in that moment. So, rather than tell you that it will be okay or that you'll be fine, I want you to know that though I want for you to have success in your work, it will be hard for me too if we have to end abruptly. I hope that we can be thoughtful about how best to use our time together to honor the work we've done and to begin to grieve together what we will both certainly miss.

This honoring of what was essential to us both, maintaining connection and yet preserving our authenticity, permitted us to continue our work with a vivid and heartfelt sense of what we all strive for in treatment and in life: a sense of grace.

NOTE

1. The patient's name and other identifying details have been changed to conceal identity and to maintain privacy.

REFERENCES

Aron, L. (1996). *A meeting of minds: Mutuality in psychoanalysis*. Hillsdale, NJ: Analytic Press.

Bion, W. R. (1970). *Attention and interpretation*. London: Heinemann.

Bloomgarden, A., and Mennuti, R., Eds. (2009). *Therapists speak about self-disclosure in psychotherapy*. New York: Routledge.

Bowen, M. S. (2013). Through the looking-glass: Exploring identity development for a beginning therapist and her late adolescent patient. *Journal of Infant, Child and Adolescent Psychotherapy, 12*(4), 286–300.

Bromberg, P. M. (1998). *Standing in the spaces: Essays on clinical process, trauma, and dissociation*. Hillsdale, NJ: Analytic Press.

Cohen, M. (1952). Countertransference and anxiety. *Psychiatry, 15,* 231–43.

Davies, J. M. (2004). Whose bad objects are we anyway? Repetition and our elusive love affair with evil. *Psychoanalytic Dialogues, 14,* 711–32.

Ehrenberg, D. B. (1992). *The intimate edge*. New York: Norton.

Frank, K. A. (1997). The role of the analyst's inadvertent self-revelations. *Psychoanalytic Dialogues, 7,* 281–314.

Frank, K. A. (1999). *Psychoanalytic participation: Action, interaction, and integration*. New York: Analytic Press.

Freud, S. (1912). *Recommendations to physicians practicing psychoanalysis*. Standard Edition 12. London: Hogarth Press.

Hirsch, I. (2008). *Coasting in the countertransference: Conflicts of self-interest between analyst and patient*. New York: Routledge.

Hirsch, I., and Roth, J. (1995). Changing conceptions of unconscious. *Contemporary Psychoanalysis, 31*(2), 263–76.

Hoffman, I. Z. (1994). Dialectical thinking and therapeutic action in the psychoanalytic process. *Psychoanalytic Quarterly, 63,* 187–218.

Hoffman, I. Z. (1998). *Ritual and spontaneity in the psychoanalytic process: A dialectical-constructivist view*. New York: Analytic Press.

Jacobs, T. J. (1991). *The use of the self: Countertransference and communication in the analytic situation*. New York: International Universities Press.

Knafo, D., and Feiner, K. (1996). The primal scene: Variations on a theme. *Journal of the American Psychoanalytic Association, 44*(2), 2001–21.

Maroda, K. (1991). *The power of countertransference*. Chichester: Wiley. Reprinted in paperback (1995), Northvale, NJ: Jason Aronson.

Maroda, K. (2003). Self-disclosure and vulnerability: Countertransference in psychoanalytic treatment and supervision, *Psychoanalytic Social Work, 10,* 43–52.

Nemiroff, M. A., and Annunziata, J. (1990). *A child's first book about play therapy*. Washington, DC: American Psychological Association.

Ogden, T. H. (1986). *The matrix of the mind: Object relations and the psychoanalytic dialogue*. Northvale, NJ, and London: Jason Aronson.

Ogden, T. H. (1989). *The primitive edge of experience*. Northvale, NJ: Jason Aronson.

Ogden, T. (1994). *Subjects of analysis*. Northvale, NJ: Jason Aronson.

Ogden, T. H. (1997). *Reverie and interpretation: Sensing something human*. Northvale, NJ: Jason Aronson.

Reik, T. (1948). *Listening with the third ear: The inner experience of a psychoanalyst*. New York: Farrar, Straus.

Renik, O. (2006). *Practical psychoanalysis for therapists and patients*. New York: Other Press.

Searles, H. F. (1975). The patient as therapist to his analyst. In *Countertransference and related subjects* (380–459). New York: International Universities Press.

Tansey, M., and Burke, W. (1989). *Understanding countertransference: From projective identification to empathy*. Hillsdale, NJ: Analytic Press.

Tauber, E. S., and Green, M. R. (1959). *Prelogical experience*. New York: Basic Books.

Wachtel, P. L. (1993). *Therapeutic communication: Knowing what to say when*. New York: Guilford.

Wachtel, P. (2008). *Relational theory and the practice of psychotherapy*. New York: Guilford Press.

Wilner, W. (1999). The un-consciousing of awareness in psychoanalytic therapy. *Contemporary Psychoanalysis, 35*(4), 617–28.

THIRTEEN

Gardening in the Softball League

How Teachers Parent

Benjamin Harris

*Chapter 13, written by **Benjamin Harris**, examines the ways in which non-parents—specifically, teachers and other educators—provide parenting functions. The author describes the similarity between parent/child and teacher/student dyads. Further, using the examples of a summer camp and a clinical psychology graduate program, the author argues that when the culture of an institution allows for it, the culture itself can participate in and embolden the parenting. Last, when cultures participate in parenting, they often do so by enlisting elders from the "student/child" side of the dyad to partake in the parenting. The implications for these cultural and non-parental relationships on the feeling of being essential are highlighted.*

———❦———

In 2014, the San Antonio Spurs, widely thought to be the finest organization in the NBA, if not in all of U.S. professional sports, won the NBA championship. In assessing the success of the team over this period of time, current and former players have continually pointed to the *culture* of the team. What exactly does that mean?

Widely credited as essential to the creation of the Spurs culture, the president, general manager, and the coach of the Spurs, Gregg Popovich, is a figure revered by nearly all who have played for him (McCallum, 2013). During the seventeen years he has led the Spurs, they have won five titles, and the aptly named "Pop" provides a sense of stability, nurture, continuity, and guidance to the entire Spurs organization or, as

217

Winnicott (1960) would say, a going-on being. While he is not a literal parent to his players, my contention here is that in his capacity as a coach, mentor, and teacher, he is providing an essential parent-like function. He has created an environment in which players have the space to succeed, a culture of excellence.

I am a parent; however, I am writing this chapter as a teacher. I officially began teaching over twenty years ago, though as I will write here, I think my teaching began well before I stepped foot into a classroom. My core belief is that good teaching—whether it be in kindergarten, graduate school, or the NBA—involves so much more than the dissemination of knowledge. Good teaching involves the creation of the conditions under which optimal learning and development can occur. It requires the creation of space for learning.

The notion of a psychological space for learning is a derivative of Winnicott's ideas of transitional space (1971) and holding environments (1960). Just as Winnicott (1960) posited that good-enough parents create holding environments that provide the conditions under which infant development can thrive, as well as allow for the development of transitional space between the parent and the child, so too do countless teachers create these holding environments in their work with their students. A holding environment provides the literal and figurative cushioning that permits the child a sense of safety and connectedness; the parent's provision of this holding without suffocating the child creates the psychological space for the child to begin to transition away from her parents and toward a sense of privacy and individuality. In this conception, teachers do not replace parents. Rather, by creating these additional holding environments, good-enough teachers provide an essential function to their students, above and beyond what is created by a parent: the creation of learning space.

What I call learning space can also be thought of as the culture of a classroom. When entering a classroom or teaching situation, take a look around at what is happening between and among the teachers and students. What is said and not said? What kind of questions are tolerated? What kinds of mistakes are allowed? How much room is there for ambiguity and messiness? What do the other students say? How do they react? All of these factors take place in the context of the classroom culture, the culture that is set by the teacher. Just as Pop sets the culture of the Spurs, the teacher sets the culture of the classroom environment. In turn, classroom environments or classroom cultures provide learning space. The more this type of space is provided, the greater the capacity for learning and development, well beyond the curriculum.

I am proposing that a phenomenon akin to parenting takes place in non-parent/child dyads, specifically, dyads that relate to teaching, and that this phenomenon exists alongside and outside of a simple transferring of parental authority to the teacher.

The thesis of this chapter then rests on three related points and assumptions. The first assumption is that a teacher/student dyad can find *companion* in the parent/child dyad. I am using companion here to mean something *akin to*, rather than something *identical to*. For the purposes of this chapter, I am focusing on the teacher/student dyad. I use this dyad broadly to include its offshoots, the player/coach and (as I will turn to shortly) the camp director/camper dyad, as well as others that mirror it.

The second assumption is that just as a patient may shift or expand his or her transference from the therapist to the treatment or even to the entire helping profession, similar shifts can occur in other types of dyads. The student can shift and expand his or her transference from the teacher to the school to the entire learning process, the player to include the coach and the organization. This assumption further rests on the notion that the nature of certain organizations, and the cultures that shape and come to define them, can permeate the participants in the dyad. This in turn can expand the dyad to include other mentors from the culture.

The third and largest assumption is that something akin to parenting and the parenting process *over time* can take place in other non-parent/child dyads. When one is lucky enough to be a participant in either side of a strong teacher/student dyad, the process of the arc of development of that relationship also finds companion in Tuber's notion (this volume) of moving gracefully from being essential to remaining relevant. Just as the nature of parenting involves moving gracefully from being essential to being relevant, so, too, does the nature of teaching in teacher/student dyads.

This is not a zero sum game; rather, it is additive. To be sure, there are transferential elements woven into the roles of teacher and student, both having to do with early internal working models of parents, as well as of earlier teachers. But, like many modern conceptions of transference (cf. Bonovitz, 2009), I am arguing here that these relationships are their own reality-based phenomena, infused with transferential meaning, rather than simply being composed of projections. Thus, to the extent that a patient experiences something akin to parenting from the treatment and the therapist, the player can experience something akin to parenting from the coach and from the culture of the organization. This is the way in which, just as one's therapist can come to represent treatment, Pop has come to represent the Spurs and all that is thought and wished to be part and parcel of that culture. Rather than the teacher necessarily being a stand-in for the parent, or the student necessarily being a stand-in for the child, the teacher/student dyad is its own unique dyad, one that is informed from both sides by early representations of parenting and being parented, but also one that continues to inform (and in many instances rework, revise, or build upon) previous internal working models.

Further, my contention is that when these dyads are explicitly allowed to permeate the culture, they can pull related participants into fulfilling some of the parenting role. In the context of a learning culture, other students can play a crucial role in the continued development of learning space as well.

I am going to briefly describe two of my own experiences, one from each side of a teacher/student dyad. The first experience takes place at a summer camp and traces the course of a dyad from when I was a child; the second is an experience teaching, which follows a dyad I am in as adult. No matter which role I inhabit, something generative takes place that often involves more than just the two participants of the dyad. In each instance, I describe the process of development of the learning space. Additionally, I map out a path from the parental figure and/or institution being essential to being relevant, as well as the ways in which this process brings others into the dyad. In doing so, I hope to describe how the ways in which I was cared for at camp, and then in turn was a caregiver at camp, affected the ways in which I parent outside of the parent/child relationship now. Finally, I will discuss how this current experience of teaching has helped me to understand how my earlier experiences of being on the other end of this dyad have informed choices I've made in the present dyad and helped me to place myself along the essential/relevant continuum.

I did not plan to go to summer camp, but I did, and that decision decidedly shifted the course of my life. The camp I attended was eight weeks long. It is "old school" in that way, and is purposefully set up to allow time for the arc of an individual summer, as well as time for the arc of the five years that kids generally attend camp, to unfold. Kids generally start at age ten and continue until they are fourteen. There are about a hundred campers, evenly split between boys and girls.

The camp was run by two teachers, a husband and wife who had met as camp counselors in the 1940s. Both were progressive educators with a deep and powerful vision for the utility and power of a camp experience. By the time I got there, they had been running the camp for over thirty years, developing a robust and dynamic culture. That culture was and is, to my mind, the ultimate example of learning space. They had a clear pedagogy about what was useful to promoting growth and a long-term vision that lined up with the unfolding of development that occurs under optimal conditions for children and adolescents. This vision also included structures to provide further growth for those who came back to work as counselors.

The directors, in an unpublished essay about the camp, wrote:

Camp exists as a culture on several different levels. On the surface, there are caring counselors who can teach fascinating activities. . . . Camp is structured to develop each child's autonomy. . . . Children at this age need a slow pace and good judgment. The assumption is that each child has needs/concerns and must have the freedom in a caring environment to find ways to satisfy them in a socially acceptable way. *Plants will grow well if given enough room, fertilizer, sun, water and care. In much of a similar way, children will develop best when the counselor is a good gardener.* Beneath this layer, is another layer. This is concerned with drawing the child's concern out of himself and toward others. *Only the child that has received love can give love.* The adults in camp care. Any counselor is willing to help any child, to talk about concerns, feelings. They are important. . . . What we seek is the establishment of trust. . . . We trust the children, they trust us. They come to trust each other. . . . What we seek is the establishment of generosity. (Seeger, 2002)

The metaphor of a gardener and a garden is apt. This is another way of describing what I am calling the development of learning space. In the essay, Seeger refers to plants needing both nutrients and room. The room is the learning space, the nutrients set up the conditions to have the room to be effective. In this metaphor, the gardener is playing the parenting-like function I am referring to as creating learning space. As I will now describe, the counselors and, in my argument, the camp culture itself, especially the older campers, are the sun, water, and care.

The camp's psychological/pedagogical structure—the culture—allowed for the creation of learning space to occur. The culture itself was created by the directors, and then passed down—as from a parent to a child—to subsequent generations of counselors. They, in turn, passed this down to their campers, many of whom also returned to work as counselors, and in doing so, were put in the position to further the growth of the culture. For the great majority of us who were lucky enough to have the resources to have gone there as kids, it has shaped our lives in ways that affect every aspect of our being—work, relationships, parenting, everything.

The structure of the culture is not complicated and took several forms, all of which, as I grew older, made sense to me in terms of education and development. They were designed to provide holding and support, both of which were essential at the beginning of the experience of being a camper. As kids moved through the camp, they made use of the safety of the holding environment to use mechanisms built into the structure that, in turn, helped them to learn to make use of, and take ownership of, their time and experience. The more this happened, the more the structure fell into the background, and the more the felt experience of the children was that the structure was less essential, while still quite relevant. Said differently, the garden had been planted; now the work was allowing it the space to grow. The culture was designed to have all members of the community take on more of the gardening function as they progressed through their time at camp—from being a youngest camper to being a senior counselor.

Going to camp for the first time seemed like a great idea to me until the buses rolled into camp and everyone who already knew each other—including my only friend—went to greet each other; I suddenly found myself sad and lost. The next morning, after we had signed up for some activities, I found myself walking alone toward the cabin, wondering exactly what I had just gotten myself into, when a hulking counselor named Lars stopped me: "Ben, right? You're in my activity. I'll see you in an hour." It stopped me from my momentary dive into homesickness. He found me.

It's a simple intervention, and years later after a few weeks on the staff, I realized that counselors were actually reminded to do things like this. We were meant to take a look around and help "find" the kids who looked a little lost. I fit the bill, and it really made a difference. At that moment, my own parents were nowhere near, and my efforts to evoke them in this new and stressful situation were no match for the experience of being a new kid, away from home for the first time.

I soon was quite taken with the degree to which the older children seemed to look out for the younger ones. In addition to the counselors like Lars, older campers, some of whom I knew a little, went out of their way to greet me. In practice, this meant that rather than the adults holding all of the responsibility for tending to the culture, the older children were active participants to a large extent. It modeled a way of looking out for others that permeated the experience. The older children were essential.

The best example of the camp culture in action was the softball league. Some kids are terrific athletes, but no one goes to this camp primarily for the sports. Others never touch athletics in a competitive manner during the rest of the year. But, with very few exceptions, all hundred campers take part in the camp-wide softball league. Each team has about ten players of widely varying ages and abilities, and each team is captained by two or three of the oldest campers. The league has been running since the 1960s, and by the time I arrived in the early 1980s, its culture, which is a reflection of the larger camp culture, had been well established.

Expecting something akin to the little league team I had played on, I was surprised to find that the talents of my captains varied. One captain, Sarah, was a fantastic athlete and a great softball player. The other captain, Mike, was not. He struck out more than he hit the ball, and his fielding was even worse. He also never seemed to care about this. What he cared about was making sure everyone on that team had a good time. Thus, when the nine-year-old catcher threw the ball back to the pitcher with what could only be described as an inaccurate shot-putting motion, the whole team cheered him on. When the twelve-year-old shortstop overthrew first base by thirty feet, she was met by a chorus of kids shouting "great arm!"

As the summer went on, I became included in the culture of the softball league, which I quickly realized was the culture of the camp as a whole. Later on, as an oldest camper and then as a softball counselor, I learned that captains were told to value kids feeling included and seen over winning, and the degree to which this happened was nearly uniform. But for me as a beginning camper, I just knew that I felt seen again. I was a decent player, but watching my captains, particularly the one who struggled athletically, take care of the whole team in this way was incredibly containing.

The captains were essential to the team and to the experience of being at camp. They allowed us room to grow, space to make mistakes, and the safety to try. Mixed-age softball is a lot of fun; it is also an adventure in fielding. Mistakes are the norm, and often the shame and anxiety that can accompany them can be devastating to a child. Mike and Sarah's constant demonstration to the younger campers that mistakes were tolerated was crucial. We were all homesick, insecure, and anxious, while at the same time invested in this project of becoming independent. Mike and Sarah, both as individual oldest campers (gods in our eyes) and as representatives of the culture, held us in a way that allowed us continuity; they allowed us to go on being, first setting the tone, then backing off and letting the entire team do so. This was a powerful experience for all of the players in the larger dyad (captains/team). For Mike and Sarah, it was an opportunity for growth, to be able to lead, teach, and hold. For the younger campers, it was a chance to feel safe.

Later that summer, I signed up for a three-day canoe trip. Much to my initial chagrin and surprise, I was the youngest on the trip, and I was very anxious about being on this trip with all of these big kids I didn't know. But Mike was on this trip, and I was put in a canoe with him. This was not an accident; the directors did this purposefully. It was not a complex intervention, but a thoughtful one, one that allowed me to feel held in mind. Thus my anxiety was contained by Mike through the culture of the camp. I am reminded in this context of Winnicott's evocative quotation: "it is a joy to be hidden, but a disaster not to be found" (1963, p. 186). Though I couldn't articulate it then, on the team, and at camp, I felt seen, noticed, taken care of. It was a joy to be hidden—to strike out on my own; it would have been a disaster had I not been found. Because the organization has already been set up to create multiple interactions where I would have had the experience of being seen by Mike, I was never in danger of not being found. Regardless of whether he was pulled aside and asked to help me out, he was in the best position to do so, because he had been my captain. I trusted him. He felt essential to my development at that point.

As I moved through my years as a camper, I realized just how much this gardening was infused in the culture. Many of the activities were mixed ages and groups; all meals were eaten in mixed age groups. So, bit by bit, the younger kids internalized both the older kids and counselors who embodied these expectations, in addition to internalizing the culture itself. In turn, the older kids, from whom we had internalized the culture, had themselves internalized it from their counselors, many of whom were former campers. People took care of each other. While the felt experience of the essentialness of the oldest campers and staff was reduced as we moved through camp into our own roles as oldest kids, it remained quite relevant.

Before I knew it, I was an oldest camper. Now I was in the position of joining the caregiving in an active and official way. As this was happening, Lars approached me to see whether I wanted to try something challenging. There was a nine-year-old boy in his cabin named Chris who needed some special attention. Would I be interested in doing things like helping Lars put his cabin to bed on certain nights and being generally available to help Chris? I had gotten to know the youngest boys early in the summer when I accompanied them on a hike, and Chris and I had hit it off. This intervention was my entrée into providing this caregiving.

So for the rest of that summer, my last as a camper, but my first as an explicit caregiver, I spent several hours a week with Chris, taking him on walks and talking to him about being homesick, helping him organize his activities and making sure to notice him when he needed to be found, just as Lars had noticed me. I was giving him room to grow. In retrospect, this was my first foray into being a psychologist, as well as my first experience of feeling essential in this way. I was also chosen to be a softball captain, doing my best impersonation of Mike and Sarah and finding immense gratification in taking care of my players the way they had taken care of me.

So when I returned to camp as a counselor in my young adulthood, I was anxious to continue the work. I had the fourteen-year-old boys. These were the oldest campers in the camp, and so I was the last one to return to the staff room after putting them to bed the first night. When I got there, I was struck by this group of eighteen- to twenty-two-year-old counselors (I was twenty) referring to their cabins as "my kids." Later, when I began teaching elementary school, I found that again teachers referred to their classes as "my kids." At the time, I attributed a natural caretaking aspect to both camp counseling and teaching that appealed to me—after all, we were taking care of someone's kids, but were they really ours? And if they were our kids, weren't we their parents? We certainly were in fantasy. But when I was twenty, with no children of my own, the kids in my cabin were my kids. Over the six years that I was a counselor, I had kids between the ages of ten and fourteen. They were all my kids, though none of them was as much my kid as Charlie.

Charlie, by his own reckoning at ten years old when I met him at an open house for potential campers, was a child in distress. He had a lot in common with Chris. He was anxious in the context of having ADHD, a difficult combination for a fifth grader in a regular education classroom, and a bit reluctant to go to camp. But he was interested in music (I was one of the music counselors), and the idea of camp appealed to him, so he signed up.

When he got there he immediately came up in the first staff meeting as one who would need to be found. So I went and found him and made some comment about meeting him at the Open House, unconsciously parroting Lars. Over the next two summers, Charlie spent a lot of time with the counselors and oldest campers. He was also quite good, in the way many kids are, of getting adults to see him. As I had with Chris, Charlie and I took walks and talked; he came to my activities often, and he made use of the adults and oldest campers. The more he made use of us, the more comfortable he became with being on his own. At this point in his camp career, the other counselors and I were essential to him.

Because I had been taken care of by Lars in this way, and then in turn pushed by Lars to take care of Chris, being with Charlie felt like a natural extension of my work with Chris. Lars had shown me how to garden, first with me, and then with Chris; I was now showing Charlie.

My relationship with Charlie was a particularly strong one. Part of its strength had to do with a bit of serendipity. After Charlie's third summer, I was fortunate to end up as a student teacher at his school. I never taught him, but I saw him all the time. Charlie was generally miserable at school, and the fact that I saw this became part of our shared relationship. Over the course of that year, I put in my request to be the counselor of his cabin that following summer. He had been seen, and camp had provided a good-enough holding environment for him to be launched.

The next two summers, his last two as a camper, and my final two as a counselor, I was the counselor in Charlie's cabin. As an oldest boy, he took on the role of being a softball captain like no other I had ever seen. He had a team full of kids like Chris, and as I watched like a proud parent (while he basked in the admiration and appreciation of the younger kids as he took care of his team, creating space for them to move into independence), it felt as though life at camp had come full circle. Charlie was the one who scooped up the kids who needed to be found. And I was relevant to him, but certainly not essential.

Sure enough, Charlie returned to work at camp, which he loved; he was a spectacular counselor. One morning when I was visiting, I ran across now-counselor Charlie talking with a homesick ten-year-old girl who had woken up before the rising bell. Officially, he was showing her how to peel carrots; less obviously, he was creating a holding environment in which she could talk about feeling homesick. He was creating the room in which she would be able to make use of camp. He was as essential to the camp as anyone had ever been.

Charlie's arc from homesick, anxious kid to softball captain extraordinaire to counselor matched that of a lot of us. To varying degrees, we had all needed and made use of the camp elders, whether they were counselors or older campers. This type of generative parenting outside of the parent/child dyad happens in many different cultures, well beyond that of a summer camp. But I think the arc from essential to relevant does a good job of describing the role a camp or classroom environment can play in someone's development. Initially, the garden needs to be planted and tended in an essential fashion. As time goes on, the job of the gardener is to make sure that there is sufficient space for the seedlings to grow, relevantly pruning if need be.

After working at camp, I taught elementary school for five years. As I progressed in my teaching, I learned that I was less interested in the curriculum, and much more interested in the children and their experiences, and I decided to reevaluate my career. A few years later, I found myself beginning graduate school, this time in clinical psychology. All of a sudden, I felt as if I was a kid all over again.

During graduate school, if things go as they should, one finds a mentor. I was fortunate to find mentors and make use of them throughout the process. Though being an adult student is different than being a child, the normative anxiety that comes with being a graduate student in clinical psychology can be overwhelming, and the search and wish for a parental figure can be powerful. It certainly was for me. As had been the case with camp, I found that teachers and more advanced students were essential, or at least my felt experience was that they were essential in my development.

While I was aware of this feeling, I was unaware at the time of the degree to which being in graduate school reminded me of being at summer camp. There were many moments where I was "seen" and "found" by my teachers, as well as by more advanced students. In the same way as the adults at camp had done, they gave me enormous space to grow. My experience of graduate school was that it was an imperfect but good-enough holding environment. However, I had little awareness of the degree to which the structure of the program held me in this essential way.

There was an informal culture in the graduate program where advanced students mentored beginning students. Like the oldest kids at camp, the most senior students were gods to us. Older students were teaching assistants in the initial clinical classes, but no other student mentoring structures were formalized. There was an implicit expectation that in a jam, one could go to an advanced student, but the onus was on the beginner, and many of us were too anxious to seek out this support.

A few more years passed, and the opportunity came to help run the outpatient clinic at my old graduate program. All of a sudden, I was in the role of the teacher again. I soon focused on how to amend this culture to make it far more accessible to a culture of easier access to mutual mentoring.

The outpatient clinic was designed in such a way that student therapists were in residence for four or five years (coincidentally, the same period of time one can spend at my camp as a camper). Over time, as students advance, they take on more difficult cases and, in some instances, serve as teaching assistants. When I came back to work there, the clinic culture of mutual mentoring was still by and large an informal one that could easily be avoided if so desired. It was possible not to be found.

After some time, it dawned on me that perhaps there was a way to put an explicit structure like that of the softball league into place in the clinic, with the hope being that the structure would nudge the culture in a particular direction and, in doing so, open up some more learning space. We also hoped to be able to shift some of the essential nature of the faculty and supervisors to some of the more advanced students, thus changing the culture of the clinic itself, and doing so in an explicit fashion.

During my internship (a short-term, year-long experience), I found I really enjoyed the clinical rounds meetings. The meeting had several staff members, but many more trainees, most of whom (this writer included) were quite anxious about working with a hospital population. While the internship had a great deal of supervision, and lots of mentoring and parenting that happened in that modality, the culture of the meeting was explicit and lived by the staff and transmitted to the trainees.

The first thing said in the first meeting was that this was a place where when you needed help—which you would—you were to knock on doors. That image, and the image of the psychologist who said it, became a talisman for all of us. Whether we actually did so or not, we knew we could knock on doors. The explicit message was that at this clinic, there is always a parenting figure available. This was a necessary and essential factor for our development in this final, intensely anxiety-provoking piece of our training. The effect was to open up more learning space. We knew we could push ourselves to take risks—not clinical risks, as the door knocking was in place for that, but internal risks. It allowed us to be on our own with the knowledge that someone had our backs.

When I returned to my clinical program, now as an administrator, my sense was that this feeling was missing in our outpatient clinic. So we set out to create our version of the softball league. At the time, the clinic had roughly fifty therapists, ranging from those in their first through sixth year in the program. We split them into four groups—or teams, each of which was made up of a cross section of students from each class. We wanted to also capture some of the benefits of their having a long-term experience, so we designed it so that the student would remain on the same team for the entirety of his or her time in residence. The idea was that this structure would allow for peer mentoring to develop organically: the kind of peer mentoring that I had informally experienced as a graduate student, but now formally built into the structure of the culture. The peers, particularly the more advanced ones, could participate in the creation and maintenance of learning spaces.

One student, Laura, was treating a very complicated woman with an impossibly complex clinical presentation. As a second-year student, she was understandably overwhelmed and overmatched. I encouraged her to present the case in her team meeting to get input from the group. That day, I was struck by the degree to which the more advanced students took on the task of offering her suggestions and supervision, helping to teach her how to manage treating a difficult case like this. Over time, her presentations made it clear that, alongside her formal education, supervision, and didactic instruction, something else had contributed to her becoming able to manage this case. She had taken the words of the advanced students to heart. Over several years of meetings, she had taken in other students' discussions of their mistakes, confusions, and foibles. She had done the equivalent of watching my old captain Mike swing, miss, and live to tell the tale.

Recently, Laura graduated, and her treatment of this woman ended. What had begun as a nearly impossible case to treat ended up as a successful four-year treatment. The buy-in of the older students to the culture, and their contributions to the creation of the learning space, allowed Laura to make optimal use of their supervision. They were essential to the success of the case.

Over time, the teams have largely accomplished what we have set out to achieve: they have created holding environments that have allowed for the creation and maintenance of learning spaces. When new students arrive in those first tense weeks of graduate school, they are thrust into a culture of holding that is modeled and lived by the current students. While the faculty and supervisors remain essential (and, like parents, imperfect) in certain respects, the advanced students are just as essential. They take on caregiving in myriad ways, and, over and over again, the felt experience of the beginning students is that the "captains" are essential. Their buy-in to the culture allows the entire program to function more cohesively.

More recently, advanced students have begun formally supervising beginning students. This is the newest explicit piece of the culture, the newest form of gardening. In supervising, they are necessarily creating their own holding environments while learning how to create a learning space for their supervisees to bring themselves—faults and all—to peer supervision. Just as they have reached the status of master student, they are able to draw upon their own struggles in the holding of the struggles of their new charges. In so doing, they have broadened what is essential to include the very culture of the clinic.

In order to oversee both the supervision and the cases, I now supervise the advanced students. I imagine this experience finds its companion in grandparenting. I am a step removed from the beginning students; in this version of the dyad, the advanced student is the teacher, having "grown up" and taken on the new role. This has been made possible on both ends by the culture of the clinic, which, like the softball league, explicitly and implicitly draws upon the advanced students to play this crucial caregiving function.

Laura was among the first group of peer supervisors, charged with supervising a first-year student who was normatively struggling with many of the same things Laura had struggled with when she was at that point in her training. To no one's surprise, she is an outstanding supervisor.

Bonovitz (2009) writes eloquently that allowing one's mind to welcome in the totality of countertransference can have the effect of not only evoking memories of one's childhood but actually allowing the analyst to come to new understandings of his or her own past. As I sat in these team meetings, week after week, year after year, I was continually reminded of my softball captain Mike, and of being a kid again. And then I was reminded of what it had been like to be a graduate student. Seeing the function this culture provided (specifically, the degree to which it helped to shift essential caregiving functions to other students) took me back to being a camper again.

In imagining this chapter, I had no idea that I would end up writing about camp. In fact, I had intended to write solely about being on both sides of the teacher/student dyad in clinical psychology. But as I wrote, I realized that it had to be about camp as well. What teaching has really allowed me to do is locate the genesis of my own parenting and teaching style in the culture of camp.

The camp directors lived well into their eighties and nineties. Memorial services were held for each of them at the end of the summers when they passed away. Each memorial was attended by a few hundred people, all of whom were raised at camp. The directors were practicing Quakers, so each memorial was structured in the style of a Quaker meeting. There was no set program. Rather, people who felt so inclined could stand up and speak. Person after person spoke about how essential camp had been and continued to be in their adult lives. Nearly everyone mentioned the space camp had given them to grow.

These camp directors hadn't been involved in the day-to-day running of the camp for decades; yet, summer after summer, children, adolescents, and adults come home from camp with renewed insight into themselves, more confidence, having taken more risks, and feeling as though something generative has happened. We entered camp at a point where the directors were relevant, never quite essential, but always relevant. But the culture—trial and error, partnership, risk taking, standing up for what you believe in—started with its two parents. They were visionary and dynamic, imperfect and flawed, more than good enough. But they created something that had its own texture, drive, mission, and force. They planted the seeds and then worked to keep the nutrients flowing.

At times, it can be much easier to see someone else's child than it is to see your own. If children are lucky enough to have teachers and other caregiving figures (a camp counselor, a coach) who can see them with the clarity that is sometimes afforded to those who do not have to have such an intense, parental view, they can make use of them in this manner.

The camp today continues to function as it does because everyone who is raised there ends up taking part in the parenting. There are generations tending this garden. As they gracefully aged, the directors passed the camp down to their actual and figurative children. Kids who came to camp after this transition knew them to be relevant but not essential. But the genesis of the camp and all of the culture that came with it would not have happened without them. They were essential in the birth and growth of the institution, relevant to those who came after it was established.

Recently, I found what I had written to say at Ellie's memorial that took place three years into my own clinical training.

> As I thought about what to say about Ellie, it occurred to me that she was a shining example of someone who practiced one of the real truisms about working with children: she had the required stores of patience. Working with kids takes time—lots and lots of it. There is little, if any, immediate gratification. *You have to take it on faith that your work with children will bear fruit, even if that fruit does not ripen for several years, and even if you are not there to see it.* Spending an entire summer, school year, or several years working with a child only to lose track of that child after he or she graduates or moves on from camp is bittersweet. Only rarely are you ever in a position to see how it turns out. Ellie took it on faith that the countless hours she put in paid off. She was quick to impart this point of view upon me and her example has carried me in my work as a counselor, then a teacher, and now as a psychologist. Ellie always said that camp was a culture. Looking around the campfire last night and today I see people who taught and helped me, and people whom I taught and helped who now teach and help others. It's a tremendously powerful feeling; this continual cycle of people who have the required faith and patience that what they do makes a difference in other people's lives is what makes camp unique. Like many of us here, I feel indescribably fortunate to have grown up here in this culture and had Ellie's guidance in beginning the lifelong process of figuring out who I am. It takes a long time and it is not an easy thing to do. Ellie remained genuinely interested in this through the end of her magnificent life.

They created something that perpetuates caregiving. How can one be more essential than that?

So, at the end of this chapter, I find myself looking back upon myself as an eleven-year-old, wanting to strike out on my own, and thinking about the ways in which this decision set the course of my life. The process of writing this has brought clarity to the way in which I bring the lessons I learned and lived to my present life as a teacher. Perhaps some of us teach in part to stretch out the period of our lives when we are essential. For me, the pleasure is more fully in watching the next generations pick up the tools and tend to the garden.

REFERENCES

Bonovitz, C. (2009). Countertransference in child psychoanalytic psychotherapy: The emergence of the analyst's childhood. *Psychoanalytic Psychology, 26,* 235–45.
McCallum, J. (2013). Pop art. *Sports Illustrated,* April 29, p. 36. http://www.si.com/vault/2013/04/29/106316155/pop-art.
Nurse, D. (2014). Why the Spurs won. *Hoopshype.com,* June 16. http://hoopshype.com/2014/06/16/why-the-spurs-won/.
Seeger, J. (2002). Killooleet: Why we try to do it this way. Unpublished manuscript.
Winnicott, D. W. (1960). The theory of the parent-infant relationship. In *Maturational processes and the facilitating environment* (1965), 37–55. New York: International Universities Press.
Winnicott, D. W. (1963). Communicating and not communicating leading to a study of certain opposites. In *Maturational processes and the facilitating environment* (1965), 179–92. New York: International Universities Press.
Winnicott, D. W. (1971). *Playing and reality.* New York: Routledge.

Index

abandonment: anger of, 162; relational stories and repetition of, 161–164; for therapist-parent, 161–162

abuse: in marriage, 159; parental, 160–161, 163

acceptance, 135–136

acculturation, 48–49, 55

achievement/accomplishment: effort over, 70; of immigrant children, 43, 46

acting, 165

adolescents: adoption and, 148; disappointment with, 14; essentialness shift with, 15–16; fiscal responsibility of, 122–124; hatred with, 139–140, 141–142, 146–148, 149; "negative identity" in, 141–142; peer group for, 15; reparative efforts by, 135

adoptive family system: adolescents and, 148; hatred in, 142, 146–148, 150

adult children, 149; connecting with, 94–95; essentialness loss with, 16–17; essentialness with grandparenting and, 21–22; relevance from essentialness for, 17–20, 56–57

adulthood stages, 30, 32, 33, 186

The Adventures of Beekle, the Unimaginary Friend (Santat), 169, 171, 181–182

affection, 134–135

age: child's view of, 6; grandparents' awareness of, 185–186, 187–188; relevance with, 20–21; therapist-parent and, 98–100; women's experience of, 33–34

aggression: caretaker's role in, development, 117; in children,

86–89, 156–157; strategies for handling, 156, 157–159

aloneness, 24, 181

ambition and aspirations: of children, 125–126; gender differences in, 32

anger: of abandonment, 162; expressions of, 64, 116–117, 126–128; forgiveness for, 129, 131; futurizing as trigger for, 124–126; generational expressions of, 118–119; guilt with, at child, 116, 119–120, 128–129, 131; modeling of, 132; parenting strategies for, 118, 130–131, 136; reparative moments after, 134–135; at self-involvement and entitlement, 120–122, 123–124; triggers for child's, 132–133; triggers for parental, 116, 124–126, 128. *See also* hatred; rage

appreciation, lack of, 120–122, 124

approval, 65

Aron, L., 208

artistic expression: in clinical work with children, 201–202; human nature understanding with, 181; therapeutic impact of, 159, 164–165

aspirations. *See* ambition and aspirations

attachment: emotion with activation of, systems, 108–109; hatred connection to, 141, 142; in mother-infant relationship, 31–32; outside of children, 23; role of, status, 13

attachment relationships, 31–32, 91

attunement: essential object and time-bound, 37–38; illusion of absolute, 38–39; of infants, 31, 36; parental, 9, 23, 31

authority, 118–119

List of Contributors

Kenneth Barish, PhD, is clinical associate professor of psychology at Weill Medical College, Cornell University. He is the author of *Emotions in Child Psychotherapy: An Integrative Framework* and *Pride and Joy: A Guide to Understanding Your Child's Emotions and Solving Family Problems* (winner of the 2013 International Book Award [Parenting and Family]).

Monique S. Bowen, PhD, is a clinical instructor in the Department of Psychiatry, SUNY Downstate Medical Center. She completed postdoctoral training in forensic psychiatry at Kings County Hospital. Her professional interests include clinical interviewing and assessment, coping and resilience across childhood and adolescence, and the application of psychoanalytic ideas to social problems.

Paul Donahue, PhD, is the founder and director of Child Development Associates in Scarsdale, New York. He is the author of *Parenting Without Fear: Letting Go of Worry and Focusing on What Really Matters* (2007) and coauthor of *Mental Health Consultation in Early Childhood* (2000). Dr. Donahue has also published a number of articles on integrating mental health services in community-based settings for children.

Leslie Gibson, PhD, is visiting faculty member in the Child and Adolescent Psychotherapy Program and a graduate of the Couples Psychotherapy Program at the Westchester Center for the Study of Psychoanalysis and Psychotherapy. She maintains a private practice in Dobbs Ferry, New York, working with children, adolescents, adults, couples, and families.

Benjamin Harris, PhD, is associate director of the Psychological Center, the Doctoral Training Clinic at CCNY, since 2009, where he is a clinical professor in the Department of Psychology. He is also an instructor in clinical psychology in the Department of Psychiatry at Columbia University Medical Center, where he has supervised predoctoral interns and externs since 2007.

Lauren Levine, PhD, is part of the faculty of the Stephen A. Mitchell Center for Relational Studies and an assistant editor for psychoanalytic dialogues. She is a supervisor in the clinical psychology doctoral program at City University of New York and visiting faculty at the Tampa Bay Psychoanalytic Society. Dr. Levine is a psychoanalyst in private practice in New York City.

Marsha Levy-Warren, PhD, is a clinical psychologist and psychoanalyst. She is also the author of *The Adolescent Journey* (2004) and numerous articles on clinical and developmental theory, adolescence, and various aspects of culture. She is currently president of the Contemporary Freudian Society and an adjunct clinical associate professor of psychology in New York University's Postdoctoral Program in Psychotherapy and Psychoanalysis.

Kevin B. Meehan, PhD, is associate professor in the PhD program in clinical psychology at Long Island University, Brooklyn. He is also adjunct clinical assistant professor of psychology in the Department of Psychiatry at Weill Cornell Medical College and an associate editor of psychoanalytic psychology. He maintains a private practice in downtown Brooklyn.

Jerry Meyer, MD, has always been curious about what is hidden beneath the surface, whether as a young child taking his toys apart, as an adolescent fascinated by subways, as a practicing and teaching psychiatrist and psychoanalyst, and as a full-time visual artist whose aesthetic and sense of irony is informed by his awareness of unconscious wishes and conflicts.

Diana Puñales Morejon, PhD, is assistant professor of clinical psychiatry at Columbia University Medical Center/NY Presbyterian Hospital, where she directs a mental health clinic for Spanish-speaking patients. She also directs the training clinic for the Clinical Psychology PhD Program at the City College of New York. Her areas of interest include multicultural psychology and immigrant health.

Lisa Samstag, PhD, is professor in the Department of Psychology at Long Island University, Brooklyn; director of psychotherapy research and supervising psychologist at the Psychological Services Center, Long Island University, Brooklyn; associate editor/book review editor of *PSYCHOTHERAPY*; psychoanalyst at William Alanson White Institute; and a wife and mother. She has conducted research on psychotherapy process and outcome, attachment, and the psychological experience of infertility.

Nick Samstag, PhD, is a training and supervising analyst at William Alanson White Institute; president of the William Alanson White Psychoanalytic Society; and a husband and father. He has published work on the paradoxes inherent in psychoanalytic training.

Banu Seckin-Erkal, PhD, is a senior psychologist at North Central Bronx Hospital's day treatment program working primarily with mood and psychotic spectrum disorders. She is also an advanced candidate at the Institute for Psychoanalytic Training and Research, and she maintains a private practice in New York City. She is interested in applied psychoanalysis and writing about the use of psychoanalytic ideas in exploring a variety of topics.

Steven Tuber, PhD, ABPP, is professor of psychology and director of clinical training in the doctoral program in clinical psychology of the City College of New York, where he has taught for thirty years. He is the author of four critically acclaimed books—two on child therapy, one on the work of Donald Winnicott, and one on projective testing.

Elizabeth Zick, PhD, is coordinator of psychology, JCCA Brooklyn Foster Home Services. She also maintains a private practice in downtown Brooklyn.